WINNING THE

Un-War

A NEW STRATEGY FOR
THE WAR ON TERRORISM

Charles Peña

Potomac Books, Inc.
Washington, D.C.

First Paperback Edition 2007

Library of Congress Cataloging-in-Publication Data

Peña, Charles V.
Winning the un-war : a new strategy for the war on terrorism / Charles Peña. — 1st ed.
p. cm.
Includes bibliographical references and index.
ISBN 978-1-59797-006-8 (paperback: alk. paper)
1. War on Terrorism, 2001–2. 2. Terrorism — Government policy — United States. I. Title.
HV6432.P46 2006
363.320973 — dc22

                              2005029408

Printed in the United States of America on acid-free paper that meets the American National Standards Institute Z39-48 Standard.

Potomac Books, Inc.
22841 Quicksilver Drive
Dulles, Virginia 20166

First Edition

10 9 8 7 6 5 4 3 2 1

For my daughter, Marin Elizabeth, and my nephews and nieces, Nick, Lauren, Cullen, and Charlotte, with the hope that their generation will not inherit the un-war.

For my wife, Karen, who helps the Pentagon survivors of 9/11 and thus does something far more noble and worthy than me.

And in memory of my good friend, PJW 50, and my father, Max Manuel Peña, May 5, 1913–April 21, 2005.

Contents

List of Figures   ix

Foreword   xi

Preface   xv

Acknowledgments   xix

Introduction: The Un-War   xxiii

1. Enemy at the Gates   1

2. A Dangerous Distraction   25

3. Clearing the Decks for War   49

4. A War Not Won by the Military   73

5. Yin and Yang of al Qaeda   97

6. Tao of Strategy   119

7. The Last Line of Defense   149

Afterword   171

Appendix 1   175

Appendix 2   187

Notes   189

Suggested Reading   227

Index   233

About the Author   241

Figures

Figure 4.1   Defense Expenditures Compared, 2003   75

Figure 4.2   Defense Expenditure Growth Rates Compared   76

Figure 4.3   U.S. Defense Spending, 1945–2005   77

Figure 4.4   U.S. Defense Budget and Overseas Troop
             Deployment, 1945–2005   80

Figure 4.5   Manpower Density on the Battlefield   82

Table 4.1   Comparison of V-22 to Helicopters   85

Figure 4.6   Balancer of Last Resort Defense Budget   86

Figure 5.1   Top-Down Centralized Hierarchy   102

Figure 5.2   Centralized Network   103

Figure 5.3   Decentralized Network   104

Figure 5.4   Distributed Network   105

Figure 5.5   Network Adaptability to Change   106

Figure 5.6   Al Qaeda as a Network of Networks   108

Figure 5.7   Al Qaeda Operational Links   109

Figure 5.8   Al Qaeda Personal Links   110

Table 7.1   MANPADS Attacks on Civil Aircraft   151

Table 7.2   Reported Non-state Use of MANPADS, 1996–2001   152–153

Foreword

In *Winning the Un-War: A New Strategy for the War on Terrorism*, Charles Peña presents a precise, well-wrought, and thought-provoking gift to his fellow citizens. He describes the world clear-eyed and challenges Americans to avoid diversions and focus seriously on the mortal threat posed by Osama bin Laden and al Qaeda. This book is no small compliment to the intelligence of Americans. In an era when the political elite of both parties deliver oracular policy pronouncements, to which no criticism is brooked, and which, when implemented, seem invariably to make the United States less secure and poorer in lives and treasure, Peña's well-documented book helps Americans to see that their interests are being neither protected nor furthered. No book could be more timely or important.

Mr. Peña's analysis benefits from his use of a rapier, not a broadsword. The war in Iraq, he argues, was a monumental strategic mistake not only because it lacked proper planning, adequate forces, and attainable war aims, but because it distracted America's attention and resources from the growing Islamist threat led and personified by bin Laden. Avoiding polemics, the author uses generous quotations from President George W. Bush, Secretary of Defense Donald Rumsfeld, and other administration officials to show how clearly, repeatedly, and definitively wrong they were when describing the invasion of Iraq as an essential component in the war on terrorism.

Instead of pushing the terror war closer to victory, the invasion and occupation of Iraq created a twenty-first-century version of the Soviet experience in Afghanistan smack in the heart of the Middle East, and in the country that was the center of Islamic civilization for more than eight centuries. In short, U.S. actions have made Iraq a magnet for al Qaeda and its allies. Still more dangerous, the invasion has given al Qaeda contiguous territory in which to base and from which to project its forces into Turkey, Jordan, Syria, Egypt, Lebanon, Israel, and the states of the Arabian Peninsula. This section of *Winning the Un-War* will leave the reader wondering if any U.S. administration has ever made a major strategic decision that was underpinned with fewer contact points with reality.

With steady evenhandedness, Mr. Peña also shows that fault on Iraq is widespread and bipartisan — indeed, it extends across the spectrum of our political, academic, military, and media elites. No Democratic leader and few in the media or the academy, for example, seriously challenged the administration's decision for war in Iraq. Congress, as usual, unconstitutionally delegated its war-making power to the president, and it and the others — mesmerized by the acronym "WMD" — followed the administration's counterintuitive decision to parlay what they "knew" would be the quick and easy defeat of al Qaeda into a chance to smash Saddam — the "real enemy." Mr. Peña shows that few noted three obvious failings in the decision to start a war with Iraq: (1) al Qaeda was and is infinitely more dangerous and elusive than Iraq, an annoying but dilapidated fourth-rate military power; (2) even if Iraq had WMD, it had no way of delivering such weapons to the continental United States, and so was no immediate threat; and (3) there was no plausible evidence that Saddam intended to share WMD know-how with terrorists. Admirably, Mr. Peña does not call attention to himself in this book, but it should be noted that he published articles warning of the salience of these three ignored factors well *before* the invasion of Iraq.

Having described how America got into its current fix, Mr. Peña proceeds to offer a precise definition of the most serious national security threat facing the United States and provides a set of recommendations about how we can begin to climb out of the deep pit we have dug for ourselves. Quite simply, al Qaeda, its networks, and the independent Islamist networks that have proliferated since September 2001 are the most — and, today, the only — dire threat to America's survival. Peña usefully discredits the nonsensical assertion that America must wage war against all terrorist groups, a view that equates groups that have never attacked the United States — the Spanish Basque terrorists and Hamas, for example — with al Qaeda and its allies. Like the Iraq war, this definition of the foe is distracting, and it disperses available resources in a way that weakens our offensive against al Qaeda. Peña argues that the first step toward wisdom — and security for Americans — is to accurately identify the enemy and then focus all war-making efforts on him.

The second and equally important step toward wisdom, Peña cogently argues, is to recognize that the United States is at war with Islamist militants—or Islamic terrorists, if you prefer—because of U.S. foreign policy choices in the Islamic world over the past thirty years and more. Our elections, gender equity, and liberties are clearly not admired by our Islamist enemies, but as Peña notes, their opposition to these factors would not yield the type of stubborn and spreading warfare we are encountering. The enemies' motivation, instead, is a religious one, based on the prevalent perception in the Islamic world that U.S. foreign policy amounts to an attack on Muslims and their faith. Unqualified support for Israel, the U.S. military presence in multiple Muslim countries, and Washington's staunch support for tyrannical Muslim governments from the Atlantic to the Indian Ocean— these are the motivations driving al Qaeda and its supporters. Peña warns that attributing the Islamists' motivation to such ephemera as early primaries in New Hampshire and women in the work place not only is incorrect but ensures America will not take the measure of its enemy and could be defeated without ever focusing the will and resources needed to prevail.

Finally, readers of *Winning the Un-War* will encounter Mr. Peña's precise prescriptions for moving ahead toward victory. Once we have squared away that al Qaeda and its networks are the top-priority threat to America and that we cannot defeat the enemy with the present set of U.S. policies toward the Islamic world, we can begin to restructure our military so it can be, at once, more effective and less expensive. Mr. Peña correctly points out that in the post–Cold War world America is vastly overcommitted abroad, that our military garrisons in Europe and East Asia can be pared to almost zero, and that these savings can be applied to efforts to make our military more capable against the Islamist enemy, with more focus on building larger special forces, for example. To root out Islamic terrorists, our need for soldiers who speak the languages of the Islamic world and for better human intelligence are vastly more important than our need for the F-22 Raptor fighter plane, new aircraft carriers, and Virginia-class nuclear submarines— all weapons systems that, today, have no plausible nation-state opponent. Peña's suggestions would yield a less expensive, more flexible, and more lethal military.

On homeland security, Mr. Peña rightly points out that we cannot defend everything and initiates a commonsense groundwork for prioritizing defensive measures, focusing first on protecting nuclear power plants, the dam system in the western states, and civilian aircraft from attack by shoulder-fired missiles. Readers will naturally have their own ideas regarding appropriate weapon systems and homeland security priorities, but Mr. Peña takes a long step toward setting the terms of a rational debate on these issues.

In sum, Charles Peña has written a book that outlines where we are as a nation and how we got into the current mess, and suggests ways we can emerge triumphant. Peña's book is an optimistic one because he sees — accurately, I believe — that America's destiny in the war against al Qaeda and its allies is in its own hands. With a clear understanding of the enemy's motivation, policy changes aimed at terminating the Islamists' growing strength, a more thoughtful and better focused homeland security scheme, and the aggressive application of a more effectively structured and appropriately armed military, America can certainly prevail.

Mr. Peña's brave book clearly depicts the hard realities of our war against militant Islam, breaks new ground, and precisely sets the terms for a much-needed national debate on amending U.S. foreign and defense policies to ensure they do the only job they need to do — protect American interests and citizens. Well done, Sir.

Michael Scheuer

Preface

If blood will flow when flesh and steel are one
Drying in the color of the evening sun
Tomorrow's rain will wash the stains away
But something in our minds will always stay
Perhaps this final act was meant
To clinch a lifetime's argument
That nothing comes from violence and nothing ever could
For all those born beneath an angry star
Lest we forget how fragile we are

—Sting, "Fragile"

For someone like my brother Rich, who came of age in the 1960s, a defining question is: "Where were you and what were you doing when President Kennedy was shot?" I was only four years old at the time, so I don't really remember. But I do remember watching on television the long lines of people paying their respects in the rotunda of the Capitol and the horse-drawn caisson going from the Capitol to Arlington Cemetery. The image of John F. Kennedy Jr. as a young boy (we were born exactly five months apart) saluting is an indelible one.

For my daughter, and the generation who will inherit the rest of the twenty-first century, the defining question will be: "Where were you and what were you doing on 9/11?"

I was in my office on the third floor at the Cato Institute. I remember getting a phone call (but can't remember from whom) telling me that a plane had crashed into the World Trade Center in New York City. My immediate reaction was, "This is a joke, right?" and I waited for the punch line. But there wasn't one. This was real. I went upstairs to the fifth floor to watch a television in front of which a small crowd had already gathered. Sure enough, smoke billowed out of tower one. I remember thinking, "How does a jet airliner manage to crash into the side of a skyscraper?" There's a whole lot of open sky to fly around in. In the back of my mind, I thought it could be a terrorist attack. After all, the World Trade Center had been the object of an attack in 1993. But I didn't want to jump to conclusions and was willing to give the incident the benefit of the doubt—that it was somehow possible that what I was looking at on TV was some sort of bizarre aviation accident. And then I remember seeing a speck in the distance on the small television screen. I knew in that instant that it was an airplane and immediately there was a sinking feeling in my stomach. Right there, live on television, I saw the second plane hit tower two. Any previous doubts were instantly erased. These were deliberate acts of suicide terrorism.

Less than an hour later, my wife, Karen, called me to tell me a plane had crashed into the Pentagon. At the time, she was working for a computer consulting firm with employees who worked in the Pentagon. Fortunately, they were able to get out of the building uninjured. Just as fortunately, one of my best friends, Jim Truesdell—whose office was on the same side of the Pentagon that American Airlines flight 77 hit—also escaped injury. But he saw firsthand the carnage and the chaos.

I remember walking home on the afternoon of September 11, 2001, a brilliant fall day that would otherwise have been considered beautiful were it not for the morning's tragic events. I had to walk because there really was no other way to get home. The metro wasn't running, and there wasn't a taxi in sight. Fortunately, at the time, we were living in Arlington, Virginia, in Rosslyn just over the river from Georgetown via Key Bridge. Ordinarily, Washington, D.C., would have been engulfed in the hustle and bustle of rush-hour traffic. Instead, K Street was devoid of cars and people and looked like a ghost town. It was a chilling vision that brought back childhood memories of watching the science fiction B-movie classic, *The Day the Earth Stood Still*.

I don't remember exactly what I did that night with my wife and daughter, Marin, but I remember the eerie silence that had fallen on the city. We lived in a high-rise condominium that was directly in the flight path of Reagan National Airport. For the first time in nearly fifteen years, we couldn't hear the rumble of jets flying in and out of the airport. While I listened to the silence, unbeknownst to me, thousands of miles away in Italy, one of my favorite musicians, Sting, was playing a concert for a few hundred friends and fans at his villa in Tuscany. I found out about it when my wife and I watched a special on the A&E cable television channel two months later that documented the making of and the actual concert.[*] Upon learning of the 9/11 attacks, Sting and the musicians he assembled for the concert debated whether they could or should play that evening as scheduled. As Sting said, "What was supposed to be a joyous occasion now simply can't be." In the end, the band decided to go ahead with the concert and opened, appropriately enough, with "Fragile," which was dedicated to all those who lost their lives that day.

I subsequently purchased the DVD, *All This Time*, and have watched it regularly. It is a way for me to connect back to and reflect on 9/11 without having to watch the images of the Twin Towers and the Pentagon. It is a therapy of sorts. Some say laughter is the best medicine, but for me, it is probably music. I can thank my brother for that. He is a jazz musician, and his playing and listening to music influenced me and made me appreciate music — all music, not just jazz — as more than just songs on the radio. Music is about painting pictures of life and capturing moments in time.

Two songs on *All This Time* stand out for me. The first is "Fragile" because it is a reminder to me that our situation vis-à-vis the Islamic world is fragile and that there is a tipping point at which the war on terrorism could become a larger war against more than a billion Muslims that could last a generation or longer and cost countless lives. The second is "Desert Rose," a duet with Cheb Mami, a French-Algerian recording artist, that brings together Western and Islamic cultures (according to Sting, "the first duet between a Western singer and an Arab singer").[**] Ironically, "Desert Rose" is a song about longing, but it is not melancholy — rather, it is uplifting and

---

[*] "A&E in Concert: Sting in Tuscany . . . All This Time" first aired on November 24, 2001, and encored on December 16, 2001. It won an Emmy for Outstanding Individual Performance in a Variety or Music Program in 2002.

[**] The dress rehearsal performance on September 10, 2001, is on the DVD but not on the CD *All This Time*, which is just the concert itself. The studio version of the song is on the CD *Brand New Day*.

thus gives me hope that we can avoid a clash of civilizations between America and the Muslim world.

These are the two currents that have propelled me to write and that flow through *Winning the Un-War*.

Acknowledgments

I never really intended to write a book—any book, let alone this one. This is probably one of the reasons I never got my Ph.D.: writing a dissertation is the same as writing a book. So the fact that I was willing and able to put fingers to keyboard and words and sentences together is something of a minor miracle. As the author, I take responsibility for all the words that follow, but this book would not have been possible completely on my own. As such, I owe much thanks to many people.

Amy Mitchell was the first person to say I should write a book, and her cajoling was relentless. She constantly assured me that if I put on paper what I say on television and radio about the war on terrorism, people would want to read it. Hopefully, she's right.

Chris Preble was also an instigator in getting me to write a book. He insisted that I had something to say and that it was important. As he was completing his own book when the idea for my book first bubbled up, it became something of a dare and challenge to me to write my book. As the author of six and editor of ten books, Ted Galen Carpenter was also a great source of inspiration and motivation to me. He was also the best boss I ever had. Both Chris and Ted were sounding boards for my ideas and arguments, unafraid to tell me when they thought I wasn't quite hitting the mark. Both are great colleagues and even greater friends.

My oldest friend in Washington, D.C., Ivan Eland, must be credited with being one of the first defense policy scholars (if not *the* first) to make an empirical analytic argument that what the United States does in the world—not who we are—matters tremendously when it comes to motivating terrorist attacks against U.S. targets. Indeed, Ivan's work several years before 9/11 is eerily prescient, and his thesis is central to my analysis.

I spent many a morning having coffee at the Java Shack in Arlington, Virginia, discussing the ideas for this book with my friend Michael Vlahos. He was one of the first American scholars to understand the war on terrorism as a struggle within Islam. His perspective was critical to my own thinking. I've also had many conversations with Michael Scheuer at the Java Shack, and I'm especially grateful that he — as someone who knows more about and has had real hands-on experience dealing with bin Laden and al Qaeda — agreed to write the foreword to *Winning the Un-War*.

The actual idea for the theme of this book is the result of an interview about the war on terrorism on MSNBC's *Buchanan and Press*. Pat Buchanan asked me: "Can we say this war is ever over as long as we don't address the fundamental causes of why they [the terrorists] hate us?" I replied that I thought we could win the war but that it would likely take a decade or longer. Also, winning and losing such a war might not be defined in traditional military terms of defeating an enemy on the battlefield. Then I said: "Two things have to happen at the same time. First, we have to continue to try and dismantle the al Qaeda network — operative by operative, cell by cell — working with countries all around the world." And: "Simultaneously with that, we have to address the problem you've mentioned here, Pat, which is to get at the root causes of why it is these people are willing to engage in suicidal terrorism against the United States. I think that starts, fundamentally, with U.S. foreign policy around the world, which plays a big role in inflaming anti-American sentiment." Although I had made these two points in previous interviews, that was the first time I'd linked them together. Bill Press kidded me during that interview, saying: "I want you to always remember, your television career [as an MSNBC analyst] started with Pat Buchanan and Bill Press, OK?" Well, my book started with them too. Thanks, guys.

Bill Press is also the first link in the chain of getting this book published. Bill connected me to Ron Goldfarb, who is his book agent and subsequently became my agent and, more importantly, a friend. Ron then negotiated my book deal with Potomac Books, where I've been in good hands. I have to thank Don McKeon for deciding to take on this book project, but we are connected by more than just a contractual relationship — it turns out that we're both motorcycling enthusiasts. And I've had the great fortune of working with an editor par excellence, Lisa Camner, who did more than just find all the errors in my book manuscript. She made the process of producing a manuscript easy and painless. But more importantly, her feedback, comments, and suggestions made the manuscript better.

While the wonder of the World Wide Web allowed me to do a lot of my own research, I have to thank several of my interns—Anna Maria Barcikowska, Jasna Dzudzelija, Peter Eyre, Karly Foland, Covadonga Iglesias, Julie Kesselman, Michael Podguski, and Mercedes Stephenson—for their tireless efforts. The truth is that I couldn't have written this book without their unflagging and invaluable assistance. No matter the size of the task, the obscurity of the research question asked, or the deadline imposed, they always delivered and with a smile.

And I have to thank my research assistant, Justin Logan, for his time and effort helping me take Lisa's comments on the first draft and turning the manuscript into a finished and polished product. Justin is a gifted writer with sharp wit and an even sharper mind.

I would be the first to admit that I do not consider myself an Islamic expert, an al Qaeda expert, or even a terrorism expert per se. I am a defense analyst by training and experience. That means I look at national security problems, try to break them down, try to understand them as best as possible, and then try to solve them in some sensible way. *Winning the Un-War* is my analysis and prescription. But the actual expertise that my analysis is based on is resident with many others (some of whom I am fortunate to be able to call friends) who have done more in-depth study about terrorism and al Qaeda. They have already made and continue to make contributions to the growing body of work that has emerged since 9/11. Although I don't agree with everything they write, I certainly respect the work of Peter Bergen, Rohan Gunaratna, Maria Ressa, Marc Sageman, and Michael Scheuer. They and others certainly know more about the nitty-gritty details of al Qaeda and terrorism than I do, and I am in their debt for their work, as well as their occasional counsel.

"All work and no play makes Chuck a dull boy," not to mention that it dulls the brain. Thinking about the problem of national security and writing this book would not have been possible without being able to clear my head every now and again. To do that, I would don my Alpinestars racing leathers and climb aboard my Honda CBR600RR. There's nothing like the rush of scenery passing you at extralegal speeds on twisty back roads, extreme lean angle, and a knee skimming the pavement to sharpen one's focus and thinking. Even more so in the company of my moto crew: Chris, George, Gerald, Rich, Judy, Lisa, and Sally. Not only are they great riding pals, but they are part of my circle of friends who help keep me grounded in reality. Ditto for Jimbo, Sharon, and Barry.

Finally, thank you to my wife, Karen, for her support and understanding—especially when writing cut into family time at night and on weekends. And to my daughter, Marin, for making me smile and laugh and being my biggest fan. I will always remember the first time she saw me interviewed on television and screamed "Daddy!" She is my constant reminder of what is truly important in life.

Introduction: The Un-War

The first, the supreme, the most far-reaching act of judgment that the statesman and commander have to make is to
establish by that test the kind of war on which they are
embarking; neither mistaking it for, nor trying to turn it into,
something that is alien to its nature.

—Carl Von Clausewitz, *On War*

In a thirty-two minute speech at the Oak Ridge National Laboratory in Tennessee in July 2004, President George W. Bush declared no less than six times
that "the American people are safer" as a result of invading Iraq[1] — although
polls at that time showed that more than half of Americans thought the war
in Iraq was not worth fighting[2] and less than half thought that the United
States was winning the war on terrorism.[3] When the 9/11 Commission issued its report later that month, it concluded that Iraq could not be linked to
al Qaeda and the 9/11 attacks: "To date we have seen no evidence that these
or the earlier contacts [between al Qaeda and Iraq] ever developed into a
collaborative operational relationship. Nor have we seen evidence that Iraq
cooperated with al Qaeda in developing or carrying out any attacks against
the United States"[4] — this calls into question whether attacking Iraq had anything to do with the terrorist threat to America. Adding further confusion
was then–Department of Homeland Security Secretary Tom Ridge's warning of "credible reporting" that al Qaeda was planning "a large-scale attack
in the United States in an effort to disrupt our democratic process"[5] — hardly
a message that America was safe from another terrorist attack.

These mixed — even contradictory — messages indicate that the United

States still lacks a clear focus for waging the war on terrorism. It is as if America is the little Dutch boy trying to plug all the holes in the dike with his fingers. There is no widescreen, big picture view of the terrorist threat and no top-to-bottom plan to combat it. That we cannot see the forest for the trees is evident in an April 2004 prime-time address to the nation by President Bush:

> The violence we are seeing in Iraq is familiar. The terrorist who takes hostages or plants a roadside bomb near Baghdad is serving the same ideology of murder that kills innocent people on trains in Madrid, and murders children on buses in Jerusalem, and blows up a nightclub in Bali, and cuts the throat of a young reporter for being a Jew.
>
> We've seen the same ideology of murder in the killing of 241 Marines in Beirut, the first attack on the World Trade Center, in the destruction of two embassies in Africa, in the attack on the USS *Cole*, and in the merciless horror inflicted upon thousands of innocent men and women and children on September the 11th, 2001.[6]

The only thing all these events have in common is the killing of innocent people, but the people responsible and their motivations weren't the same in every case—although that is clearly what the president meant to imply. In December 2004, after a deadly attack that killed twenty-two people, including eighteen Americans, at a base in Mosul, Iraq, then-chairman of the Joint Chiefs of Staff, U.S. Air Force Gen. Richard Myers, said much the same thing: "This attack, of course, is the responsibility of insurgents, the same insurgents who attacked on 9/11, the same type of insurgents who attacked in Beirut, the same insurgents who—type of insurgents who attacked the Cole, Khobar Towers, and the list goes on."[7] But the insurgents in Iraq are not the same terrorists who attacked the United States on 9/11. Further confirmation that the war on terrorism has been expanded to include targets that are completely unconnected to al Qaeda is the addition of the Basque separatist movement Euskadi Ta Askatasuna (ETA) to the list of organizations that the Bush administration is taking financial action against as part of the war on terrorism. Even the U.S. war on drugs in Colombia has been combined with the war on terrorism.

Expanding the threat beyond al Qaeda, however, not only means losing focus but also risks making enemies out of terrorist groups who do not attack the United States. Because all acts of terrorism are unjustifiable acts that kill innocent people, lumping all terrorist groups (especially those that are Muslim-affiliated or in the Arab world) in with al Qaeda is all too easy — and would be a grave error. The State Department lists thirty-six designated foreign terrorist organizations and thirty-eight other terrorist groups. But other than al Qaeda, none have attacked America and few — if any — attack U.S. targets in other regions of the world. Those terrorist groups that attack other countries (e.g., Hamas in Israel, ETA in Spain) are not direct threats to America, and the United States cannot realistically target everyone else's terrorist enemies — more than seventy groups. Moreover, including terrorist groups that do not currently attack the United States gives them an incentive to make America their target, which would only compound an already difficult problem.

Worse yet is the notion that Iraq is the central front in the war on terrorism, an assertion first made by President Bush in September 2003. His assertion is more self-fulfilling prophecy than anything else. When then–Secretary of State Colin Powell went to the United Nations Security Council to make the case for war, he claimed, "Iraq today harbors a deadly terrorist network headed by Abu Musab al-Zarqawi, an associate and collaborator of Osama bin Laden and his al Qaeda lieutenants."[8] It would have been more correct to say that Zarqawi was operating in Iraq (largely Kurdish northern Iraq, which was under the protection of the U.S.-led no-fly zone), but was not harbored by Saddam Hussein's regime in the same way al Qaeda was given sanctuary in Afghanistan by the Taliban regime. And many analysts in the intelligence community saw Zarqawi as independent of — even a competitor to — al Qaeda. But in October 2004, six months after the U.S. invasion, Zarqawi declared his allegiance to bin Laden, and in a December 2004 audiotape, bin Laden suggests that he accepted Zarqawi's offer, making a previously nonexistent al Qaeda threat in Iraq impossible to ignore. Now, with so much public and political attention focused on Iraq — and Iraq is likely to remain a center of attention for many years — are we inadvertently making the same mistake we made before 9/11 of not paying enough attention to the real threat?

And are we unwittingly creating new enemies as a consequence? For example, prior to the January 2005 Iraqi elections, the insurgency was di-

rected against the U.S. military occupation and those Iraqis seen as collabo-
rating with the Americans. In other words, the insurgents were not terrorists who would fly thousands of miles to kill innocent Americans. But on
January 3 the insurgency took on a new dimension when the Islamic Army
in Iraq threatened attacks against the United States. According to a statement posted on a website, the group claimed that the year would "bring
woes on America. The mujahideen (holy warriors) have prepared big sur-
prises for your sons outside America and a big surprise for you inside
America" and that the mujahideen "will take the battle from inside our country (Iraq) to yours."[9] Such statements could simply be boastful rhetoric backed
with no real capability to carry them out, but the mere threat creates yet
another complexity in the terrorist threat matrix.

Because we use the shorthand phrase "war on terrorism" to describe
the U.S. response to the September 11, 2001, terrorist attacks, it is easy to
believe that this war—like all previous wars—can be won by killing the enemy. Given that suicide terrorists are, by definition, undeterrable, it seems
that we have no choice except to kill them before they kill us.

But the struggle the United States is engaged in is not war in the traditional sense, i.e., armed conflict between two or more nations.[10] Ironically,
we must take Clausewitz's admonition to know "the kind of war on which
[we] are embarking; neither mistaking it for, nor trying to turn it into, something that is alien to its nature" to heart,[11] but at the same time we must
realize that Clausewitz's seminal manual for war is not a suitable guide because he wrote about war between political leaders of nation-states. The
war on terrorism is not against another nation-state and thus not "an act of
force to compel our enemy to do our will."[12] Indeed, the war on terrorism is
not "merely the continuation of policy by other means."[13]

The war on terrorism is the "un-war" because it is unlike any previous war we have fought—this was acknowledged by President Bush in the
immediate aftermath of 9/11[14] but seems to have been forgotten because of
Iraq. Our enemies do not wear uniforms or command military forces. They
do not operate in or emanate from a specific geographic region. So U.S. forces
with overwhelming military superiority and advanced technology will not
be the appropriate instruments to wage this war. Precision-guided smart
bombs and cruise missiles are not smart enough to know who the enemy is
and where they are.

This is a different kind of war that requires a different paradigm. We must shed conventional Western thinking conditioned by the European wars of the eighteenth and nineteenth centuries, two world wars, Korea, Vietnam, the Gulf War, and more recently, Iraq. Instead of Clausewitz's *On War*, the Chinese philosopher Sun Tzu's twenty-three-hundred-year-old *The Art of War* is more applicable. "War" for Sun Tzu meant the conflict that occurs throughout all aspects of life. And the "art of war" is how to conquer without aggression: "Subduing the other's military without battle is the most skillful."[15] The lesson for the war on terrorism is not that aggression is unnecessary or should be avoided. In war, aggression is inevitable, and this conflict is no different. But the weapons and skills for the un-war will be different. Special forces rather than armor or infantry divisions will be the norm. Unmanned aerial vehicles patrolling expanses of desert or inaccessible mountain regions will often replace fighter pilots and foot soldiers. Arabic and Islam will be part of the syllabus for un-warriors.

More importantly, our enemy—the al Qaeda terrorist network—is more than just an organizational entity. So although it is counterintuitive, the un-war cannot be won by simply destroying the organization. Al Qaeda has grown from a relatively small group of radical Muslim extremists to a larger ideological movement in the Muslim world. The threat now goes beyond the al Qaeda that existed on September 11, 2001, to include a growing number of radical Muslim groups who share at least some of al Qaeda's ideology, many of which are not directly connected to or formally affiliated with al Qaeda. The core issue is the question Secretary of Defense Donald Rumsfeld raised in his now famous October 2003 leaked memo: "Are we capturing, killing, or deterring and dissuading more terrorists every day than the madrassas and radical clerics are recruiting, training, and deploying against us?"[16] With over a billion Muslims in the world, a strategy that focuses only on the former without addressing the latter is a losing strategy.

So what is a winning strategy?

The day after the terrorist attacks against the World Trade Center and the Pentagon, President Bush said: "This will be a monumental struggle of good versus evil."[17] And three days later in a radio address he said: "We are planning a broad and sustained campaign to secure our country and eradicate the evil of terrorism."[18] The notion that evil is at the root of terrorism and that the U.S. course of action should be to eradicate evil is echoed by

David Frum (former special assistant to President Bush and the person credited with coining the phrase "axis of evil," used by Bush in his 2002 State of the Union address) and Richard Perle (former chairman of the Defense Policy Board under Bush): "Terrorism remains the great evil of our time, and the war against this evil, our generation's great cause. We do not believe that Americans are fighting this evil to minimize it or to manage it. We believe they are fighting to win — to end this evil before it kills again and on a genocidal scale. There is no middle way for Americans: It is victory or holocaust."[19]

But terrorism is simply a tactic, not an enemy. As Eliot Cohen, a member of the Defense Policy Board in the current Bush administration, said, a war on terrorism "makes as much sense as if Americans had responded to Pearl Harbor by declaring a global war on dive bombers."[20] Moreover, terrorism can trace its roots back at least two thousand years. Trying to eradicate it is a quixotic quest that does not focus on the actual group responsible for the 9/11 attacks. It is exactly this kind of logic that led the Bush administration to wage a war against Iraq, even though the White House has conceded that Saddam Hussein had nothing to do with 9/11 and its allegations of linkages between the former regime in Baghdad and al Qaeda remain unproven.[21]

Fighting the un-war requires discarding the state-sponsored terrorism paradigm, which is traditionally defined as nations using "terrorism as a means of political expression."[22] This is exactly the wrong approach because al Qaeda's terrorism is not state-sponsored; it is privatized terrorism, independent of any one nation-state. To be sure, U.S. military action deprived al Qaeda of the sanctuary granted by the Taliban regime in Afghanistan. While — thankfully — the United States has not been attacked again, the bombings of the Marriott in Bali, the HSBC bank headquarters in Istanbul, the train network in Madrid, and the London tube system have all been attributed to al Qaeda; this indicates that the terrorist network is not dependent on state-sponsorship to be active.

The popular belief is that al Qaeda attacked America for "who we are" and because they hate us. But such thinking demonstrates an unwillingness to recognize the importance of "what we do" in motivating acts of terrorism. This is not to say that 9/11 was America's fault or that the United States deserved to be attacked. Nothing could be further from the truth. All acts of terrorism perpetuated against innocent victims are deplorable, unconscionable, and inexcusable. But we cannot afford to be blind to the effects of U.S. actions and policies. If we misdiagnose the motivations for al Qaeda's terrorism against the United States, then we cannot craft a proper solution to the problem.

We also tend to think of al Qaeda in organizational terms as a centralized hierarchy, much like an organized crime family. The popular belief is that if we can decapitate the leadership, e.g., capture or kill bin Laden and his top lieutenants, then we can collapse the organization. This may have been true for regime change in Iraq, but it is the wrong conceptual approach for al Qaeda, which is a distributed and cellular network. As such, while bin Laden and al Qaeda's senior leadership remain important targets, the organization itself must be painstakingly dismantled piece by piece until it is no longer operationally effective. This will not happen overnight, so we must be prepared for a long conflict.

But al Qaeda is more than just an organization. It is an ideology that has taken on a life of its own. The extent to which al Qaeda's radicalism has taken hold throughout the Muslim world is unknown, but certainly the U.S. preoccupation with Iraq for more than four years after 9/11 (starting with President Bush's "axis of evil" State of the Union address in January 2002) has given time for the radical Islamic message to spread and has provided a rallying cry to recruit more Muslims to al Qaeda's radical cause.

Finally, we too easily assume that al Qaeda attacked the United States because they want to destroy America. While there is certainly some element of truth to this, it misses the fundamental fact that al Qaeda's struggle is first and foremost a battle for the soul of Islam. Thus, it is an internal struggle in which the United States is, by and large, an external player. As such, the United States may not be able to win the war on terrorism in the conventional sense, but its actions and policies could lose the war if they incline the Muslim world to sympathize and take sides with the radicals.

Instead of embarking on another Iraq (Frum and Perle specifically name North Korea, Iran, and Syria as targets—as do retired generals and Fox News analysts Thomas McInerney and Paul Vallely in their book, *Endgame: The Blueprint for Victory in the War on Terror*, Washington, D.C.: Regnery, 2004), a strategy for the war on terrorism must focus on the real threat to the United States: al Qaeda. Such a strategy would consist of three central elements: (1) dismantling and degrading the al Qaeda terrorist network, (2) establishing a new U.S. foreign policy that does not needlessly create new al Qaeda terrorists, and (3) bolstering homeland security against future terrorist attacks.

1

ENEMY AT THE GATES

You've got to be careful if you don't know where you're going, because you might not get there.

— Yogi Berra

President Bush claims that even before 9/11 the al Qaeda threat was "obvious." While the intelligence community recognized al Qaeda as a known threat responsible for the 1998 U.S. embassy bombings in Kenya and Tanzania as well as the attack against the USS *Cole* in 2000, the preponderance of evidence shows that the president was not at all focused on al Qaeda. In fact, the president did not mention al Qaeda once in any public statements before the 9/11 attacks; his national security focus was on missile defense, weapons of mass destruction (WMD), and rogue states. This preoccupation is evident in his many public statements.

On January 26, 2001, at the swearing-in ceremony for Secretary of Defense Donald Rumsfeld: "We will work to defend our people and our allies against growing threats: the threats of missiles; information warfare; the threats of biological, chemical, and nuclear weapons."[1]

At Norfolk Naval Air Station on February 13, 2001:

We must prepare our nations against the dangers of a new era. The grave threat from nuclear, biological and chemical weapons has not gone away with the Cold War. It has evolved into many separate threats, some of them harder to see and harder to answer. And the adversaries seeking these tools of terror are less predictable, more diverse. With advance technology [*sic*], we must confront the threats that come on a missile. With shared intelligence and enforcement, we must confront the threats that come in a shipping container or in a suitcase. . . . We have no higher priority than the defense of our people against terrorist attack.[2]

Although President Bush acknowledged the threat of terrorism, it was tied to the WMD threat and he did not specifically cite al Qaeda as the terrorist threat to the United States.

At a joint press conference with British prime minister Tony Blair on February 23, 2001:

We had a long discussion about missile defense. I will, obviously, let the Prime Minister speak for himself. I made the case, like I will do to all the leaders with whom I meet, that we need to think differently about the post–Cold War era, that there are new threats that face people who love freedom.

There is the threat of an accidental launch of a missile; there are threats of potential blackmail when one of these nations develops weapons of mass destruction and be willing to point at America, Britain, our allies, our friends, people with whom we've got commitments. And we've got to deal with those in a realistic way.[3]

A March 7, 2001, joint statement between the United States and South Korea: "President Bush and President Kim agreed that the global security environment is fundamentally different than during the Cold War. New types of threats, including from weapons of mass destruction and missiles as a means of delivery, have emerged that require new approaches to deterrence and defense. The two leaders shared the view that countering these threats requires a broad strategy involving a variety of measures, including active non-proliferation diplomacy, defensive systems, and other pertinent measures."[4] It is not obvious what the president meant when he referred to WMD and missiles as new threats. Soviet nuclear weapons delivered by long-range missiles defined the security paradigm during the Cold War. So President Bush's preoccupation with rogue states and WMD reflected a continuation of Cold War–era thinking, not a departure from it. And still, the WMD litany continued at the National Defense University on May 1, 2001:

More nations have nuclear weapons and still more have nuclear aspirations. Many have chemical and biological weapons. Some already have developed the ballistic missile technology that would allow them to deliver weapons of mass destruction at long distances and at incredible speeds. And a number of these countries are spreading these technologies around the world.

Most troubling of all, the list of these countries includes some of the world's least-responsible states. Unlike the Cold War, today's most urgent threat stems not from thousands of ballistic missiles in the Soviet hands, but from a small number of missiles in the hands of these states, states for whom terror and blackmail are a way of life. They seek weapons of mass destruction to intimidate their neighbors, and to keep the United States and other responsible nations from helping allies and friends in strategic parts of the world.[5]

At a roundtable with members of the foreign press on June 17, 2001, President Bush acknowledged the threat of terrorism and even fundamentalist extremism, but as an argument for building a missile defense:

The threats that the ABM Treaty addressed no longer exist. . . . There are new threats, new forms of terror: cyberterrorism, fundamentalist extremists, extremism that certainly threatens us, threatens Israel, who is our strong ally and friend, threatens Russia. We've got to deal with it. The threat in Europe at sometime, perhaps. We must deal with that issue. And one way to do that is coordinate security arrangements, is to talk about how to—as to how to deal with the new threats, but also is to be able to have the capacity to rid the world of blackmail, terrorist blackmail.

And so we have to have the capacity to shoot somebody's missile down if they threatened us.[6]

Speaking at the American Legion's annual convention on August 29, 2001: "We are committed to defending America and our allies against ballistic missile attacks, against weapons of mass destruction held by rogue leaders in rogue nations that hate America, hate our values and hate what we stand for."[7]

And on the day before the 9/11 attacks, from a joint statement between the United States and Australia: "President Bush and Prime Minister Howard expressed shared concern about the threat to global stability posed by ballistic missile proliferation and weapons of mass destruction and increasingly capable ballistic missiles as a means of delivery. They agreed on the need for a comprehensive approach to counter these threats, including enhanced non-proliferation and counter-proliferation measures as well as continued nuclear arms reductions. They also agreed that missile defense could play a role in strengthening deterrence and stability as part of this comprehensive approach."[8]

This is not to say that 9/11 was President Bush's fault, but simply to point out that if the al Qaeda threat was as obvious as the president claims, it is curious that he did not talk about it when discussing U.S. national security prior to the 9/11 attacks.

Of course, some would point out that President Bill Clinton was not exactly focused on the al Qaeda terrorist threat either; this is a fair and valid criticism. According to former Clinton adviser Dick Morris:

> For all of his [Clinton's] willingness to act courageously and decisively—against the advice of his liberal staff—on issues like deficit reduction and welfare reform, he was passive and almost inert on terrorism in his first term . . .
>
> Everything was more important than fighting terrorism. Political correctness, civil liberties, fear of offending the administration's supporters, Janet Reno's objections, considerations of cost, worries about racial profiling and, in the second term, surviving impeachment, all came before fighting terrorism.[9]

Not surprisingly, some conservative commentators, such as Bill Gertz, go so far as to place all the blame for 9/11 on the doorstep of the Clinton administration without any criticism of the Bush administration.[10] But such biased analysis ignores the fact that Clinton did attempt (however ineffectively) to go after al Qaeda in retaliation for the August 1998 bombings of the U.S. embassies in Kenya and Tanzania.[11] And making the case that the Clinton administration did not pay enough attention to al Qaeda—which is true enough—does not inherently mean that the Bush administration was doing a better (or worse) job. The bottom line is that neither the Bush nor the Clinton administration had made al Qaeda the highest priority threat to U.S. national security.

So if the Bush administration wasn't focused on the al Qaeda threat before 9/11, what about after? President Bush says that he "did contemplate a larger strategy as to how to deal with al Qaeda."[12] However, except for U.S. military action against al Qaeda and the Taliban in Afghanistan, U.S. actions and attention have been almost singularly focused on Iraq, which is representative of the administration's pre-9/11 threat and national security paradigm—rogue states and WMD.

It seems blindingly obvious—indeed almost silly—but we must remind ourselves who attacked the United States on September 11, 2001: al Qaeda led by Osama bin Laden. Therefore, the focus of what we have come to call the war on terrorism must be the al Qaeda terrorist network, thought to be operating in sixty or more countries around the world.

But even calling the U.S. effort to dismantle the al Qaeda terrorist network a war on terrorism has allowed the threat to become inflated and unbounded. As a visiting research professor at the Strategic Studies Institute at the Army War College, Jeffrey Record, wrote:

> The administration has thus postulated a broad, international terrorist threat to U.S. national security interests that encompasses (1) three geographic levels of terrorist organizations—national, regional, and global, as well as (2) rogue states—specifically Saddam Hussein's Iraq, Iran, and North Korea. Also on the threat list are (3) any individuals or entities that proliferate WMD to terrorist organizations or rogue states, and (4) like the Taliban's Afghanistan, that may not sponsor terrorism overseas but that willingly or unwillingly provide safe haven and assistance to organizations that do. . . . [13]
>
> Unfortunately, stapling together rogue states and terrorist organizations with different agendas and threat levels to the United States as an undifferentiated threat obscures critical differences among rogues states, among terrorist organizations, and between rogue states and terrorists organizations.[14]

The danger of this evolution is that unnecessary actions of choice against non-al Qaeda related threats distract attention and divert resources. While we should expect a superpower to be able to multitask, it is not possible to devote 100 percent attention to more than one thing at a time. If the al Qaeda threat demands nearly all of our focus, the United States can ill afford nonessential dalliances that do not contribute to the goal of destroying al Qaeda. More importantly, America cannot afford to take actions that actually contribute to making the threat worse by increasing anti-American sentiment in the Muslim world, which is the basis for al Qaeda to gain sympathy and support and for Muslims to become terrorists.

Yet, despite acknowledging the threat posed by al Qaeda after 9/11, the administration was quick to change course and focus its efforts on Iraq rather than al Qaeda — seemingly intent on going back to the future and the already conceived pre-9/11 paradigm of rogue states and WMD. Indeed, in the immediate aftermath of 9/11, Iraq was already being discussed as an eventual target. According to Bob Woodward in *Bush at War*, at a National Security Council meeting on the afternoon of September 12, 2001, "Rumsfeld raised the question of Iraq. Why shouldn't we go against Iraq, not just al Qaeda? he asked. Rumsfeld was speaking not only for himself when he raised the question. His deputy, Paul D. Wolfowitz, was committed to a policy that would make Iraq a principal target of the first round in the war on terrorism."[15] In fact, Wolfowitz argued that Iraq would be easier than Afghanistan.[16] And five days later: "As for Saddam Hussein, the president ended the debate. 'I believe Iraq was involved, but I'm not going to strike them now. I don't have the evidence at this point.'"[17]

Although military action against Iraq was put on hold to focus on Afghanistan, the wheels had been put in motion. In fact, former Secretary of the Treasury Paul O'Neill claims that the Bush administration began planning to invade Iraq almost from the time it took office in January 2001.[18] Former White House counterterrorism official Richard Clarke in his book *Against All Enemies: Inside America's War on Terror* supports O'Neill's allegation:

> Former Treasury Secretary Paul O'Neill has written that the Administration planned early on to eliminate Saddam Hussein. From everything I saw and heard, he is right. . . .
>
> The administration of the second George Bush did begin with Iraq on its agenda. So many of those who had made the decision in the

first Iraq War were back: Cheney, Powell, Wolfowitz. Some of them had made clear in writings and speeches while out of office that they believed the United States should unseat Saddam, finish what they failed to do the first time. In the new administration's discussions of terrorism, Paul Wolfowitz urged a focus on Iraqi-sponsored terrorism against the U.S. even though there was no such thing.[19]

To illustrate Clarke's point, these are just two examples from Paul Wolfowitz (considered by many as the architect of the Bush administration's Iraq policy):

- In testimony before the House National Security Committee in September 1998: "The United States is unable or unwilling to pursue a serious policy in Iraq, one that would aim at liberating the Iraqi people from Saddam's tyrannical grasp and free Iraq's neighbors from Saddam's murderous threats."[20]
- In the March/April 1999 issue of *Foreign Affairs*: "On balance, however, containment entails much greater long-term risks than using force to help the Iraqi people rid themselves and us of this tyrannical menace."[21]

And Wolfowitz was one of eighteen signatories (along with Donald Rumsfeld) to a January 26, 1998, letter to President Clinton advocating regime change in Iraq:

> We are writing you because we are convinced that current American policy toward Iraq is not succeeding, and that we soon face a threat in the Middle East more serious than any we have known since the end of the Cold War. In your upcoming State of the Union Address, you have an opportunity to chart a clear and determined course for meeting this threat. We urge you to seize that opportunity, and to enunciate a new strategy that would secure the interests of the U.S. and our friends and allies around the world. That strategy should aim, above all, at the removal of Saddam Hussein's regime from power.[22]

A subsequent letter on May 29, 1998, to Representative Newt Gingrich and Senator Trent Lott (with Wolfowitz and Rumsfeld as two of the seventeen signatories) encouraged Congress to "take what steps it can to correct

U.S. policy toward Iraq" and further said that "U.S. policy should have as its explicit goal removing Saddam Hussein's regime from power and establishing a peaceful and democratic Iraq in its place."[23]

Although the administration did focus on al Qaeda in the immediate aftermath of the 9/11 attacks, that focus returned over time to the pre-9/11 policy paradigm. It is impossible to know exactly why, but the evidence suggests a stubbornness to fit a square peg in a round hole — the square peg being rogue states with WMD and the round hole being non-state actors. Instead of recognizing that the threat posed by al Qaeda required changing how the administration thought about the problem, it changed the problem to fit its thinking.

On September 20, 2001, before a joint session of Congress, President Bush addressed the American people and named Osama bin Laden and the al Qaeda terrorist network responsible for the 9/11 attacks on the World Trade Center and the Pentagon. He also condemned the Taliban regime in Afghanistan for aiding and abetting al Qaeda. Bush said: "Our enemy is a radical network of terrorists, and every government that supports them" and the war on terrorism "will not end until every terrorist group of global reach has been found, stopped, and defeated."[24] Ostensibly, the only terrorist group with demonstrated global reach was (and still is) al Qaeda.

In an October 2001 radio address to the nation, the rhetoric began to shift slightly and subtly when the president stated that "America is determined to oppose the state sponsors of terror" and that the "enemy is the terrorists themselves, and the regimes that shelter and sustain them." And instead of a war against terrorist groups with global reach, Bush spoke of a "global campaign against terror."[25]

In a November 2001 Rose Garden ceremony welcoming back aid workers Heather Mercer and Dayna Curry, who were rescued from Afghanistan, President Bush remarked: "If anybody harbors a terrorist, they're a terrorist. If they fund a terrorist, they're a terrorist. If they house terrorists, they're terrorists. . . . If they develop weapons of mass destruction that will be used to terrorize nations, they will be held accountable."[26] Thus, the president linked the war on terrorism to WMD, claiming that countries that develop WMD were always part of his definition of terrorists.[27] And he specifically cited Iraq and North Korea as needing to allow inspectors into their respective countries. In response to a question about the consequences for Saddam

Hussein if he did not allow inspectors into Iraq, Bush said: "He'll find out."[28] This statement had a tone similar to that of his statements against the Taliban on September 20 and fueled speculation that the administration was planning military action against Iraq.

The rhetoric about rogue states and WMD was used again when President Bush addressed cadets at the Citadel in December 2001: "Rogue states are clearly the most likely sources of chemical and biological and nuclear weapons for terrorists." And Bush was explicit about expanding the war on terrorism: "America's next priority to prevent mass terror is to protect against the proliferation of weapons of mass destruction and the means to deliver them."[29]

In his State of the Union address on January 29, 2002, President Bush did not make a single direct reference either to al Qaeda or Osama bin Laden. Instead, he stated that the United States would be "steadfast and patient and persistent in the pursuit of two great objectives. First, we will shut down terrorist camps, disrupt terrorist plans, and bring terrorists to justice. And second, we must prevent the terrorists and regimes who seek chemical, biological or nuclear weapons from threatening the United States and the world." The president specifically named North Korea, Iran, and Iraq as regimes that "constitute an axis of evil, arming to threaten the peace of the world" and said that "by seeking weapons of mass destruction, these regimes pose a grave and growing danger."[30]

Yet little over a week after the president named the axis of evil, then–Director of Central Intelligence George Tenet testified before the Senate Select Committee on Intelligence and said that "al Qaeda leaders still at large are working to reconstitute the organization and to resume its terrorist operations" and that the al Qaeda terrorist network was still "the most immediate and serious threat" to the United States.[31] Subsequently, the *New York Times* reported that Abu Zubaydah, a thirty-year-old Palestinian, was believed to be organizing remnants of a terrorist network. According to the *New York Times*, American investigators "were convinced that Mr. Zubaydah was now trying to activate al Qaeda sleeper cells for new strikes on the United States and its allies."[32] According to the director of the Federal Bureau of Investigation, Robert Mueller, "we believe that we are still targeted, that there are al Qaeda associates or individuals around the world and some in the United States that are intent on committing terrorist acts within the country."[33]

And in early March 2002 U.S. forces were engaged in what was described as the fiercest fighting to date against al Qaeda and Taliban forces in the Gardez mountain region in the Paktia province of Afghanistan. As one senior Defense Department official said, "The war isn't over, we've got a lot of work to do."[34]

But if al Qaeda still represented the most immediate and serious threat—and possibly had cells in the United States—and the war against al Qaeda in Afghanistan was not yet over, why then did President Bush expand the war on terrorism to include the axis of evil? According to Bush, "North Korea is a regime arming with missiles and weapons of mass destruction, while starving its citizens." He asserted that "Iran aggressively pursues these weapons [of mass destruction] and exports terror, while an unelected few repress the Iranian people's hope for freedom." And the president contended that "Iraq continues to flaunt its hostility toward America and to support terror. The Iraqi regime has plotted to develop anthrax, and nerve gas, and nuclear weapons for over a decade."[35]

Just as tends to happen with military operations, the rhetoric surrounding the war on terrorism has been subject to "mission creep." And the escalating rhetoric has allowed the Bush administration to expand the war with virtually no question or opposition—despite the fact that the joint resolution by Congress was more limited and specific, authorizing the president "to use all necessary and appropriate force against those nations, organizations, or persons he determines planned, authorized, committed, or aided the terrorist attacks that occurred on September 11, 2001, or harbored such organizations or persons."[36]

The question is: Did the axis of evil (or any other so-called rogue states) and WMD represent a terrorist threat to the United States or even a direct military threat that could not be contained or deterred? The evidence in January 2002 suggested otherwise.

Most obviously, neither Iran, Iraq, nor North Korea perpetrated the 9/11 attacks. And even characterizing those countries as an axis of evil was misleading—clearly intended to conjure up an image of the threat posed by the Axis powers of Germany, Italy, and Japan during World War II. Although White House spokesperson Ari Fleischer stated that the president did not mean such a comparison and that the expression was "more rhetorical than historical,"[37] the term "axis" means partnership or alliance[38] and the truth is that North Korea, Iran, and Iraq were neither an axis nor direct threats to the United States.

Although both Iran and Iraq had animosity toward the United States, there was no evidence that they had worked together to advance mutual interests and policies. To begin, Iraq was a secular Muslim state while Iran is governed by a religious Islamic regime. More significantly, the two countries had a long-standing hatred toward each other and fought a bloody war from 1980 to 1988. Concerned that Iran's new Islamic revolutionary leadership was a threat, Iraq invaded Iran in late 1980. What was supposed to be a quick victory became a protracted war of attrition that saw the use of chemical weapons by Iraq and claimed an estimated 375,000 Iraqi casualties and at least 300,000 Iranian lives.[39] Iraq was deemed to have won the war (which ended when Iran accepted a cease-fire under United Nations Security Council Resolution 598), but the two countries remained at odds with each other and both governments supported opposition groups in the other country.

There is no doubt that a military assistance relationship exists between North Korea and Iran. During the 1980–88 war, Iran received much of its weaponry from North Korea (in fact, it is estimated that Iran accounted for as much as 90 percent of North Korea's arms exports in the early 1980s).[40] In return for such military aid, Iran has shipped hundreds of thousands of barrels of oil to North Korea. Much of Iran's current ballistic missile technology is directly from North Korea—the Iranian Shabab-3 medium-range (800–900 miles) missile is considered a version of the North Korean No Dong missile. But arms sales in and of themselves do not necessarily constitute an alliance or partnership between two countries. For example, Russia had $500 million in military arms transfer agreements with Iran between 1993 and 2000. By comparison, "all others" (of which North Korea was just one country) sales to Iran for the same period totaled $300 million.[41] The value of arms deliveries from Russia to Iran was $2.1 billion compared to $300 million for all others.[42] Yet Russia was not considered part of the axis of evil with Iran. More likely, the deliveries are simple business transactions, with the Iranians gaining wanted weaponry and the North Koreans getting needed currency or oil.[43]

It is also important to view the military assistance relationship between North Korea and Iran in a larger perspective. For example, testimony by Vice Adm. Thomas R. Wilson, then-director of the Defense Intelligence

Agency (DIA), to the Senate Select Committee on Intelligence mentioned China more than North Korea as providing military aid to Iran.[44] And according to one administration official, "North Korea has had more exchanges of missile technology with Pakistan [now a U.S. ally in the war on terrorism] than with Iran."[45] So while a relationship between Iran and North Korea may exist, it is certainly not exclusive and it would be difficult to characterize it as a military or political partnership or alliance.

If evidence of an axis-like relationship between North Korea and Iran was thin (at best), such a relationship between North Korea and Iraq was essentially nonexistent because of sanctions imposed on Iraq after the Gulf War. The only indication that there might have been some cooperative relationship between the two countries is a report in August 2000 that Iraq was financing construction of a Scud missile production facility in Sudan and that North Korean personnel would build and run the plant.[46] That the director of central intelligence made no mention of this relationship in the December 2001 *Foreign Missile Developments and the Ballistic Missile Threat Through 2015* is probably a good indicator that either the arrangement never materialized or that the information provided for the news report was false.[47]

Just as it was difficult — if not impossible — to make the case that North Korea, Iran, and Iraq were an axis, it was equally difficult to depict those countries as military threats to the United States, the world's sole superpower. The U.S. economy eclipsed the axis of evil countries — United States gross domestic product was $9.9 trillion in 2000 compared to $15 billion for North Korea, $99 billion for Iran, and $15 billion for Iraq.[48] Put another way, the U.S. economy was seventy-six times larger than the combined economies of the axis of evil. Defense expenditures were similarly lopsided. U.S. defense spending was $295 billion in 2000. By comparison, North Korea spent $2 billion, Iran spent $7.3 billion, and Iraq spent $1.5 billion.[49] Altogether, the combined defense expenditures of the axis of evil were less than 4 percent of the U.S. total.

Not only is the U.S. military significantly larger than almost all other countries' forces,[50] it is far and away the most modern and technologically advanced in the world. For example, the U.S. Air Force's F-15 Eagle and F-16 Fighting Falcon are considered the world's premier fighter aircraft, even though their designs date back to the 1970s. Similarly, the U.S. Army's Abrams tank does not have an equal. No other country in the world has a Navy with large-deck aircraft carriers. And the U.S. military has a virtual monopoly on precision-guided or "smart" weapons, such as the Global Positioning System–guided Joint Direct Attack Munition. By comparison, countries of the axis of evil ilk tend to be equipped with older weapons purchased from either the former Soviet Union or China.

If North Korea, Iran, and Iraq were not direct military threats to the United States, what about the prospect of those countries using WMD? According to the Central Intelligence Agency's *Unclassified Report to Congress on the Acquisition of Technology Relating to Weapons of Mass Destruction and Advanced Conventional Munitions, 1 July Through 31 December 2001*:

- North Korea probably has produced enough plutonium for at least one, and possibly two, nuclear weapons. Spent fuel rods canned in accordance with the 1994 Agreed Framework contain enough plutonium for several more weapons.
- Despite Iran's status in the Treaty on the Nonproliferation of Nuclear Weapons (NPT), the United States is convinced Tehran is pursuing a nuclear weapons program.
- A sufficient source of fissile material remains Iraq's most significant obstacle to being able to produce a nuclear weapon. The Intelligence Community is concerned that Baghdad is attempting to acquire materials that could aid in reconstituting its nuclear weapons program.[51]

So, at best, North Korea had one or two nuclear weapons while Iran and Iraq were thought to be pursuing nuclear weapons programs. Given the vast U.S. strategic nuclear arsenal of thousands of warheads that could be delivered by land-based missiles, submarine-launched ballistic missiles, and long-range bombers, even rogue states with a few nuclear weapons are no more able to escape the reality of credible U.S. nuclear deterrence than the Soviet Union or Communist China could. All nation-states have a return address, and their leaders know that any attack on the United States would be met with an obliterating retaliatory attack by the massive U.S. nuclear arsenal. Also, while individual fanatics may sometimes be willing to commit suicide for a cause, prominent political leaders rarely display that characteristic.

Moreover, over the years, the United States had deterred the likes of Joseph Stalin, Nikita Khrushchev, Leonid Brezhnev, and Mao Zedong. None of those leaders seriously contemplated attacking the United States. And the reason for their restraint was quite simple: they knew that such an attack would mean certain retaliation resulting in their own annihilation. So why would erratic and unpredictable leaders such as North Korea's Kim Jong-il, Saddam Hussein before he was deposed by the United States, or the so-called mad mullahs in Tehran, not be similarly deterred? It cannot be that those leaders are more brutal than America's previous adversaries. Khrushchev and Brezhnev were thuggish, and Mao and Stalin were genocidal monsters. Likewise, a credible case cannot be made that the current crop of tyrants is more erratic and unpredictable than the tyrants the United States deterred in the past. Stalin epitomized paranoia, and Mao was the architect of China's utterly bizarre Cultural Revolution in the late 1960s and early 1970s—at the very time that China was acquiring a nuclear weapons capability.

Finally, none of the axis-of-evil countries had long-range military capability to strike the United States. In fact, the only potentially hostile countries that currently have sufficient long-range nuclear capability to threaten the United States are Russia and China. According to *Foreign Missile Developments and the Ballistic Missile Threat Through 2015*:

- The multiple-stage Taepo Dong-2—capable of reaching parts of the United States with a nuclear weapon–sized payload—may be ready for flight testing. . . . The Taepo Dong-2 in a two-stage ballistic missile configuration could deliver a several-hundred-kg payload up to 10,000 km—sufficient to strike Alaska, Hawaii, and parts of the continental United States. If the North uses a third stage similar to the one used on the Taepo Dong-1 in 1998 in a ballistic missile configuration, then the Taepo Dong-2 could deliver a several-hundred-kg payload up to 15,000 km—sufficient to strike all of North America.

- All agencies agree that Iran *could* attempt to launch an ICBM/SLV [intercontinental ballistic missile/space launch vehicle] about mid-decade, although most agencies believe Iran is *likely* to take until the last half of the decade to do so. One agency further judges that Iran is unlikely to achieve a successful test of an ICBM before 2015.

- Iraq's ballistic missile initiatives probably will focus on reconstituting its pre-Gulf war capabilities to threaten regional targets and probably will not advance beyond MRBM [medium range ballistic missile] systems. . . . Although Iraq *could* attempt before 2015 to test a rudimentary long-range missile based on its failed Al-Abid SLV, such a missile almost certainly would fail. . . . Most agencies believe that Iraq is *unlikely* to test before 2015 any ICBMs that could threaten the United States, even if UN prohibitions were eliminated or significantly reduced in the next few years. (Emphasis in original.)[52]

It is important to underscore that North Korea's Taepo Dong-2 missile is a postulated capability, has not been flight tested, and is not an operationally deployed system. Furthermore, North Korea's ability to build a ballistic missile capable of reaching the United States was based on a two-stage Taepo Dong-2 missile "believed to consist of four No Dong engines clustered together as the first stage, and a single No Dong as the second stage."[53] Not only is such a missile at least five times more likely to fail than a single-stage No Dong missile (itself far from reliable),[54] but it also sounds more like something the Wile E. Coyote cartoon character would think up in his ever-futile quest to catch the Roadrunner. And North Korea's ballistic missiles may be intended more for political and propaganda purposes rather than as usable military weapons. According to Joseph S. Bermudez, a leading expert on North Korean missile programs, the August 1998 missile test of the Taepo Dong-2 "made America wake up and pay attention to them [North Korea], which is one of the things they desperately want. They want to be perceived as a powerful nation."[55]

As previously mentioned, Iran has received ballistic missiles and technology from North Korea and China. Iran has also enlisted the aid of Russian scientists for its ballistic missile program.[56] But Iran's intentions are not clearly aimed directly at the United States. According to Gary Samore, a senior fellow at the International Institute for Strategic Studies in London, "There is a big difference between Iranians trying to cover the region, and developing a system that will allow them to attack the U.S. I don't think the Iranians have yet made a fundamental decision about developing an ICBM capability."[57] And Clyde Walker, director of the Missile and Space Intelligence Center in Huntsville, Alabama, states, "Iran went into this [ballistic missile] business because they got clobbered by Iraq [in the 1980–88 war]."[58] So Iran's concerns and aspirations appear more regional than international, and not necessarily a direct challenge or threat to the United States.

Undoubtedly, some of Iraq's motivation for seeking to acquire WMD and ballistic missiles was to deter any future potential U.S. military action similar to the Gulf War. But both the CIA and DIA concurred that regional power considerations were also a large factor. According to Admiral Wilson, "Saddam's goals remain to reassert sovereignty over all of Iraq, end Baghdad's international isolation, and, eventually, *have Iraq reemerge as the dominant regional power*" (emphasis added).[59] And according to the National Intelligence Council, "*Baghdad's goal of becoming the predominant regional power and its hostile relations with many of its neighbors are the key drivers behind Iraq's ballistic missile program*" (emphasis added).[60]

In the final analysis, the direct threat of WMD against the United States by North Korea, Iran, or Iraq was in January 2002 and remains minimal. Any real WMD—especially nuclear weapons—capability was close to nonexistent and none had the long-range delivery capability to attack the United States. And if WMD capability was the basis for membership in the axis of evil, then why was it limited to only these three countries when—according to the Department of Defense—the extant and emerging threats to the United States, friends, and allies encompasses twelve nations with nuclear weapons programs, thirteen nations with biological weapons, sixteen nations with chemical weapons, and twenty-eight nations with ballistic missiles?[61]

If North Korea, Iran, and Iraq did not represent a direct WMD threat to the United States, what about the possibility that they were terrorist threats—especially in their support for al Qaeda—when President Bush named those countries an axis of evil and a target in the war on terrorism in January 2002? The State Department's *Patterns of Global Terrorism* published in April 2001 is revealing.

To begin, North Korea was no longer an active sponsor of terrorism. Although at the time it was still on the State Department's list of "state sponsors of terrorism," the only direct linkage to terrorism cited is that North Korea "continued to provide safehaven to the Japanese Communist League–Red Army Faction members who participated in the hijacking of a Japanese Airlines flight to North Korea in 1970."[62] The goal of the Red Army Faction is to overthrow the Japanese government, but with only *six* hardcore members, they can hardly be characterized as a threat to the United States. In a potential allusion to al Qaeda, the State Department also mentions that "Philippine officials publicly declared that the Moro Islamic Liberation Front had purchased weapons from North Korea with funds provided by Middle East sources,"[63] but this is an allegation and not confirmed.

According to the State Department, "Iran remained the most active state sponsor of terrorism in 2000."[64] But the groups supported by Iran—Hezbollah, Hamas, the Palestine Islamic Jihad, and Ahmad Jibril's Popular Front for the Liberation of Palestine—focus their terrorist attacks against Israel and do not currently target the United States. Previous attacks against U.S. targets by Hezbollah were in Lebanon in the early- and mid-1980s in retaliation for the U.S. military presence there.[65]

The State Department listed the Arab Liberation Front (ALF), the *inactive* 15 May Organization, the Palestine Liberation Front (PLF), and the Abu Nidal Organization (ANO) as having offices in Baghdad. The ALF is just one of many anti-Israel Palestinian groups. The PLF is a splinter group with pro-Palestinian Liberation Organization, pro-Syrian, and pro-Libyan factions. They attacked targets in Israel and Egypt, and the group is perhaps best known for its 1985 attack on the Italian cruise ship *Achille Lauro*, which resulted in the murder of U.S. citizen Leon Klinghoffer. The ANO is an extremist Palestinian organization but, according to the State Department, has "not attacked Western targets since the late 1980s."[66] Like the groups supported by Iran, these groups are anti-Israel and had not recently attacked U.S. targets. The other terrorist group supported by Iraq cited by the State Department was the Mujahedin-e Khalq, an Iranian terrorist group that "regularly claimed responsibility for armed incursions into Iran that targeted police and military outposts, as well as for mortar and bomb attacks on security organization headquarters in various Iranian cities."[67]

The bottom line is that the few terrorist groups that received some support from North Korea, Iran, and Iraq were not direct threats to the United States and those that had previously attacked U.S. targets had not done so for almost twenty years.

More important, it was not proven that North Korea, Iran, or Iraq had any linkages to or were providing support or safe haven to al Qaeda. And none were shown to be complicit in the planning, financing, or conduct of the 9/11 attacks. The one possible connection was that Mohammed Atta (one of the 9/11 suicide hijackers) met with an Iraqi intelligence officer (Ahmad Khalil Ibrahim Samir al Ani) in Prague, Czech Republic, in April 2001. But shortly after this meeting was reported, U.S. officials stated that it did not constitute hard proof that Iraq was involved in the 9/11 attacks;[68] North Atlantic Treaty Organization secretary general Lord Robertson told

U.S. senators that there was "not a scintilla" of evidence linking Iraq with the 9/11 attacks;[69] and Israel's chief of military intelligence stated, "I don't see a direct link between Iraq and the hijackings and terror attacks in the United States."[70] Even the Czech government distanced itself from its original stance.

> [In December 2001] Czech President Vaclav Havel was retreating from the more definitive accounts provided by his government, saying there was "a 70 percent" chance the meeting took place. Indeed, while Czech officials never officially backed away from their initial stance, officials at various agencies say that, privately, the Czechs have discredited the accuracy of the untested informant who came to them with the information. According to one report, Havel quietly informed the White House in 2002 there was no evidence to confirm the meeting.
>
> The Czechs had reviewed records using Atta's name and his seven known aliases provided by the CIA and found nothing to confirm the April 2001 trip.[71]

According to FBI director Robert Mueller: "We ran down literally hundreds of thousands of leads and checked every record we could get our hands on, from flight reservations to car rentals to bank accounts,"[72] but neither the FBI nor the CIA could find any evidence that Atta left or returned to the United States (either using his name or known aliases) at the time of the alleged meeting.[73] And the 9/11 Commission concluded, "No evidence has been found that Atta was in the Czech Republic in April 2001. . . . The available evidence does not support the original Czech report of an Atta-Ani meeting."[74]

As a result of naming an axis of evil just four months after the 9/11 attacks, rogue states and WMD became conflated with the specific terrorist threat to the United States: al Qaeda. Although President Bush did not completely ignore al Qaeda, rogue states and WMD increasingly became in integral part of his rhetoric after the January 2002 State of the Union address. And eventually, Saddam Hussein and WMD came to dominate the administration's focus. For example, at a cattle industry convention in Colorado in February 2002, President Bush said, "This nation cannot afford, and must not rest, until we have done everything in our power to rally our coalition and rid the world of terror. . . . That not only means those who are associated with the terrorist networks of global reach; it also means nations which develop weapons of mass destruction aimed at destroying America and attacking our friends and our allies."[75]

At the George C. Marshall ROTC Award Seminar on National Security at the Virginia Military Institute in April 2002, the president told the cadets:

> The civilized world faces a grave threat from weapons of mass destruction. A small number of outlaw regimes today possess and are developing chemical and biological and nuclear weapons. They're building missiles to deliver them, and at the same time cultivating ties to terrorist groups. In their threat to peace, in their mad ambitions, in their destructive potential, and in the repression of their own people, these regimes constitute an axis of evil and the world must confront them.[76]

In his commencement address to graduating cadets at West Point in June 2002, Bush asserted:

> The gravest danger to freedom lies at the perilous crossroads of radicalism and technology. When the spread of chemical and biological and nuclear weapons, along with ballistic missile technology — when that occurs, even weak states and small groups could attain a catastrophic power to strike great nations. Our enemies have declared this very intention, and have been caught seeking these terrible weapons. They want the capability to blackmail us, or to harm us, or to harm our friends — and we will oppose them with all our power. . . .
>
> Containment is not possible when unbalanced dictators with weapons of mass destruction can deliver those weapons on missiles or secretly provide them to terrorist allies.[77]

Speaking to the troops of the Tenth Mountain Division — many of whom had recently returned from serving in Operation Enduring Freedom in Afghanistan — in July 2002, the president said, "We fight against a shadowy network that hides in many nations, and has revealed its intention to gain, and use, weapons of mass destruction. We're threatened by regimes that have sought these ultimate weapons, and hide their weapons programs from the eyes of the world."[78]

In September 2002, a little over a year after 9/11, President Bush said, "My job is to make sure the world's worst leader [Saddam Hussein] is not able to blackmail or hurt America or our friends and allies with the world's worst weapons. We've got to make sure that these dictators aren't able to team up with terrorist groups, use their weapons of mass destruction as a way to intimidate those of us who love freedom."[79] In this speech, al Qaeda is only mentioned once and the president's remarks are more about Saddam Hussein and WMD.

Even after the Iraq war, the administration has remained focused on rogue states and WMD. In April 2003, just a few days after Baghdad fell and Saddam Hussein's statue was toppled, when asked whether the success of the U.S. military had sent a message to the Syrians, President Bush responded: "I think that people have got to know that we are serious about stopping the spread of weapons of mass destruction and that each situation requires a different response." When asked if he thought the Syrians had WMD: "I think that we believe there are chemical weapons in Syria."[80] And in the ensuing months, when WMD could not be found in Iraq, Syria became more of a target. Testifying before a House International Relations Subcommittee in September 2003, then–Undersecretary of State for Arms Control John Bolton said: "In Syria, we see expanding WMD capabilities and continued state sponsorship of terrorism" and "we cannot allow the world's most dangerous weapons to fall into the hands of the world's most dangerous regimes, and will work tirelessly to ensure this is not the case for Syria."[81] On December 12, 2003, President Bush signed into law HR 1828, the *Syria Accountability and Lebanese Sovereignty Restoration Act of 2003*, which calls on the government of Syria to "halt the development and deployment of medium- and long-range surface-to-surface missiles and cease the development and production of biological and chemical weapons."[82] And finally, in May 2004 the United States imposed sanctions on Syria, including:

- Prohibition on the export to Syria of any items that appear on the United States Munitions List (arms and defense weapons, ammunition, etc.) or Commerce Control List (dual-use items such as chemicals, nuclear technology, propulsion equipment, lasers, etc.).

- Prohibition on the export to Syria of products of the United States, other than food and medicine.
- Prohibition on aircraft of any air carrier owned or controlled by the Syrian government to take off from or land in the United States.
- Under Section 311 of the USA PATRIOT Act, the Secretary of the Treasury is to issue a notice of proposed rulemaking with respect to a measure to require U.S. financial institutions to sever correspondent accounts with the Commercial Bank of Syria based on money laundering concerns.
- Pursuant to the International Emergency Economic Powers Act (IEEPA), the President has authorized the Secretary of the Treasury, in consultation with the Secretary of State, to freeze, within the jurisdiction of the United States, assets that belong to certain Syrian individuals and government entities.[83]

Libya was also a target and the country in which the administration can claim some measure of success. In August 2003, after Libya stated that it "accepts responsibility for the actions of its officials" in the bombing on Pan Am 103 on December 21, 1988,[84] the United States notified the UN Security Council that it would not oppose the lifting of UN sanctions against Libya. However, because of concerns about the Libyan regime's behavior — "including its poor human rights record and lack of democratic institutions, its destructive role in perpetuating regional conflicts in Africa, and its continued and worrisome pursuit of weapons of mass destruction and their related delivery systems"[85] — the White House elected to maintain U.S. bilateral sanctions on Libya. Four months later Libya pledged to dismantle its WMD programs.

But even this purported victory cannot necessarily be hailed as a decisive result of the Bush administration's policies. To be sure, Libyan leader Moammar Gadhafi could hardly ignore the U.S. decision to depose Saddam Hussein. Former chief UN weapons inspector in Iraq Hans Blix has surmised that Gadhafi's decision might have been spurred by "what he saw happen in Iraq."[86] Nonetheless, as British foreign secretary Jack Straw pointed out, the decision was the result of "painstaking diplomacy . . . going back for six or seven years where we had sought to re-establish a diplomatic relationship."[87] Thus, Libya's decision was a natural evolution of a process that had been ongoing even before the Bush administration came to power and declared a policy of preemptive regime change.

Perhaps more important, it appeared that Libya may not have given up all that much in terms of its weapons program. On the one hand, Libya was reportedly much further advanced than previously thought—including, according to a senior Bush administration official, "nuclear fuel-cycle projects that were intended to support a nuclear weapons program, weapons development, including uranium enrichment."[88] Yet within ten days of Libya's pledge to dismantle its WMD programs, the International Atomic Energy Agency's Mohamed El Baradei declared that Libya's nuclear program was "very much at an early stage of development, where it is right now . . . quite dismantled in fact. It's all in boxes. They were far away from having an industrial-scale enrichment capability."[89] So Libya's nuclear program was about as real and threatening as Iraq's—which is to say not very much.

The Bush administration has also maintained a hard-line tone toward Iran. For example, in response to a possible Iran–al Qaeda link suggested by the 9/11 Commission citing strong evidence that Iran facilitated the transit of several al Qaeda members before 9/11, including perhaps eight or more of the hijackers, President Bush said:

> They're harboring al Qaeda leadership there [Iran]. And we've asked that they be turned over to their respective countries. Secondly, they've got a nuclear weapons program that they need to dismantle. We're working with other countries to encourage them to do so. Thirdly, they've got to stop funding terrorist organizations such as Hezbollah that creates great dangers in parts of the world. . . . As to direct connections with September the 11th, we're digging into the facts to determine if there was one.[90]

This could just as easily have been one of the president's prewar statements about Iraq.

And in a possible case of déjà vu all over again, the administration has not ruled out the use of force against Iran. In December 2005 then–Undersecretary of Defense for Policy Douglas Feith (considered one of the architects of the administration's Iraq policy) told the *Jerusalem Post*: "I don't think that anybody should be ruling in or ruling out anything while we are conducting diplomacy"[91] — referring to the possibility of military action if the diplomatic path with Iran failed. And after Iran rejected an EU proposal and resumed uranium conversion in August 2005, President Bush said, "All options are on the table. The use of force is the last option for any president and you know, we've used force in the recent past to secure our country."[92]

Ultimately, all the rhetoric and attention on rogue states and WMD misses the mark. As Jeffrey Record reminds us, "It was, after all, al Qaeda, not a rogue state, that conducted the 9/11 attacks, and it is al Qaeda, not a rogue state, that continues to conduct terrorist attacks against U.S. and Western interests worldwide."[93] Seemingly forgotten are President Bush's previous comments about wanting bin Laden "dead or alive."[94] Yet audiotapes and videotapes from bin Laden are a constant reminder that the man responsible for 9/11 is still alive and that our efforts have not been focused on al Qaeda the way our precision-guided weapons zero in on their targets.

Computer security expert (and former U.S. Army officer) Lance Spitzner, founder of the Honeynet Project (an information security research organization), advises, "My commander used to tell me that to secure yourself against the enemy, you have to first know who your enemy is: their methods of attack, tools and tactics, and objectives. This military doctrine readily applies to network security just as it did in the Army."[95] We would do well to remember this advice in prosecuting the war on terrorism. The first and most important thing to remember is who the enemy is: al Qaeda is the enemy at the gates.

2

A DANGEROUS DISTRACTION

Pay attention to your enemies, for they are the
first to discover your mistakes.

—Antisthenes of Athens (c. 444–365 BC)

This is no time to make new enemies.
—Voltaire

Standing aboard the USS *Abraham Lincoln* on May 1, 2003, President Bush declared an end to major combat operations in Operation Iraqi Freedom and told U.S. servicemen and women: "Because of you, our nation is more secure."[1] On September 7, 2003, Bush addressed the nation and declared, "Iraq is now the central front"[2] in the war on terrorism. And on November 3, 2003, in Birmingham, Alabama, he said: "We are aggressively striking the terrorists in Iraq, defeating them there so we will not have to face them in our own country"[3]—a claim the president reiterated in his January 2005 State of the Union address.[4] These assertions are central in determining whether Iraq was a legitimate target in the war on terrorism or an unnecessary war.

According to President Bush, Saddam Hussein's material breach of UN Security Council Resolution 1441 was casus belli.[5] But Resolution 1441 never really set forth grounds for military action nor did it make clear that military action would be an explicit consequence of noncompliance.[*] Even if Iraq was in violation of UN resolutions, the U.S. military exists to defend the United States: its territorial integrity and national sovereignty, its population, and the liberties that underlie the American way of life. So the real question is: Did Iraq represent a direct and imminent threat to the United States that could not otherwise have been deterred? If that was the case, then preemptive self-defense — such as Israel's military action against Egypt, Syria, Jordan, and Iraq in the 1967 Six Day War — would have been warranted. And if Iraq was not a threat — especially in terms of being a direct terrorist threat to America by aiding and abetting al Qaeda — then the United States fought a needless war against a phantom menace.

The potential threat Iraq posed to the United States could be assessed in several ways. First, Iraq could have developed and deployed WMD against the United States, up to and including nuclear-armed ballistic missiles. Second, the Saddam Hussein regime could have developed WMD and handed them off to a terrorist group that would then use them to attack the United States. Third, the regime could have developed a collaborative relationship with al Qaeda, harboring and/or assisting its operatives in plotting against the United States. On each of these fronts, a thorough threat assessment would have revealed that Iraq did not represent a clear and present danger to the United States.

Bush administration officials made repeated dire warnings about the threat of Iraqi WMD in the months before the war. Speaking in Nashville, Tennessee, in August 2002, Vice President Dick Cheney said that "Saddam Hussein will acquire nuclear weapons fairly soon" and that "there is no doubt that Saddam Hussein now has weapons of mass destruction; there is no doubt that he is amassing them to use against our friends, against our allies, and against us."[6] In Cincinnati, Ohio, in October 2002, the president said:

---

* Resolution 1441 states that "Iraq has been and remains in material breach of its obligations under relevant resolutions" and that the resolution is "a final opportunity to comply with its disarmament obligations under relevant resolutions of the Council." Furthermore, " failure by Iraq at any time to comply with, and cooperate fully in the implementation of, this resolution shall constitute a further material breach of Iraq's obligations" and Iraq is warned " that it will face serious consequences as a result of its continued violations of its obligations." Military action is never explicitly directed. At best it is implied by the term "serious consequences" and the statement that " resolution 678 (1990) authorized Member States to use all necessary means to uphold and implement its resolution 660 (1990) of 2 August 1990 and all relevant resolutions subsequent to resolution 660 (1990) and to restore international peace and security in the area." United Nations Security Council Resolution 1441 (2002), November 8, 2002, http://ods-dds-ny.un.org/doc/UNDOC/GEN/N02/682/26/PDF/N0268226.pdf?OpenElement. To be sure, these statements could be interpreted to authorize the use of force (and may even be generally accepted to mean such), but they are not an explicit verbatim authorization.

Iraq's weapons of mass destruction are controlled by a murderous tyrant, who has already used chemical weapons to kill thousands of people. This same tyrant . . . holds an unrelenting hostility towards the United States. . . .

As a former chief weapons inspector for the U.N. has said, "The fundamental problem with Iraq remains the nature of the regime itself: Saddam Hussein is a homicidal dictator who is addicted to weapons of mass destruction."

In 1995 . . . the regime was forced to admit that it had produced more than 30,000 liters of anthrax and other deadly biological agents. The inspectors, however, concluded that Iraq had likely produced two to four times that amount. This is a massive stockpile of biological weapons that has never been accounted for, and is capable of killing millions.

We know that the regime has produced thousands of tons of chemical agents, including mustard gas, sarin nerve gas, and VX nerve gas. Saddam Hussein also has experience in using chemical weapons. He has ordered chemical attacks on Iran, and on more than forty villages in his own country. These actions killed or injured at least 20,000 people, more than six times the number of people who died in the attacks of September 11.

And surveillance photos reveal that the regime is rebuilding facilities that it has used to produce chemical and biological weapons.[7]

And just three days before the war began, Cheney reiterated: "We know he's [Saddam Hussein] absolutely devoted to trying to acquire nuclear weapons, and we believe he has, in fact, reconstituted nuclear weapons."[8]

To be sure, from December 1998 until November 2002, Iraq had refused to allow UN weapons inspectors into the country despite the requirements of Security Council Resolution 687. Many analysts understandably surmised that Iraq had used that period to reconstitute its prohibited WMD programs. According to a 2002 CIA report: "Since inspections ended in 1998, Iraq has maintained its chemical weapons effort, energized its missile program, and invested more heavily in biological weapons."[9] But an important part of the CIA's assessment about Iraq's chemical weapons program was that "Baghdad continues to rebuild and expand dual-use infrastructure that it could divert quickly to CW [chemical weapons] production."[10] The CIA cited the chlorine and phenol plants in Fallujah as an example of dual-use infrastructure but also noted that "both chemicals have legitimate civilian uses."[11] Iraq's biological weapons program was considered similar to its chemical weapons program: "Iraq has the capability to convert quickly legitimate vaccine and biopesticide plants to biological warfare (BW) production."[12]

It is also important to note that the CIA estimates about Iraq's chemical and biological weapons that were used as the basis for the Bush administration's decision to go to war against Iraq were not significantly different from the CIA's pre-9/11 assessment that Iraq "has attempted to purchase numerous dual-use items for, or under the guise of, legitimate civilian use. This equipment—in principle subject to U.N. scrutiny—also could be diverted for WMD purposes."[13] So there was really nothing significantly new about Iraq's chemical and biological weapons capabilities or programs that constituted an imminent threat. Iraq's potential WMD programs posed a threat that was equivalent to that the United States had endured at a relatively low cost during the 1990s.

Despite ominous claims by administration officials (most notably Vice President Cheney) about a seemingly imminent nuclear threat from Iraq, the 2002 CIA report was more equivocal. According to the CIA:

> Although Saddam probably does not yet have nuclear weapons or sufficient material to make any, he remains intent on acquiring them. . . . How quickly Iraq will obtain its first nuclear weapons depends on when it acquires sufficient weapons-grade fissile material. . . .[14]
>
> More than ten years of sanctions and the loss of much of Iraq's physical nuclear infrastructure under IAEA [International Atomic Energy Agency] oversight have not diminished Saddam's interest in acquiring or developing nuclear weapons. . . . The acquisition of sufficient fissile material is Iraq's principal hurdle in developing a nuclear weapon.[15]

Significantly, the CIA concluded that "Iraq is unlikely to produce indigenously enough weapons-grade material for a deliverable nuclear weapon until the last half of this decade. Baghdad could produce a nuclear weapon within a year if it were able to procure weapons-grade fissile material abroad."[16] But even this possibility was not a foregone conclusion. The International Institute for Strategic Studies (IISS) agreed with the CIA's assessment, but with an important caveat: "If Iraq were somehow able to acquire nuclear weapons–usable nuclear material from a foreign source, however, it could probably produce nuclear weapons in a relatively short time, assuming that Iraq's nuclear weapons design team has completed their work."[17]

It is clear now that the administration's statements about Iraq's WMD were overblown. Before and during the Iraq war, administration officials implied that the United States was relatively certain where WMD were located.* But in the aftermath of the war, the WMD rationale has unraveled. Six months after the fall of Baghdad, David Kay—who initially headed the U.S.-led, fourteen-hundred-person inspection team in Iraq (the Iraq Survey Group [ISG]) and had supported the administration's case for war—testified before Congress in October 2003 that the United States had "not yet found stocks of weapons" and only discovered "WMD-related program activities."[18] According to Kay: "It clearly does not look like a massive, resurgent program, based on what we discovered."[19] More pointedly, Kay admitted that "information found to date suggests that Iraq's large-scale capability to develop, produce, and fill new CW munitions was reduced—if not entirely destroyed—during Operations Desert Storm and Desert Fox, 13 years of U.N. sanctions, and U.N. inspections."[20] In January 2004, after again coming up empty handed with WMD, Kay conceded, "It turns out that we were all wrong."[21]

The ISG, under the direction of Charles Duelfer, in September 2004 concluded that "the problem of discerning WMD in Iraq is highlighted by

---

* In his presentation to the UN on February 5, 2003, making the case for military action against Iraq, Secretary of State Colin Powell stated: "We also have satellite photos that indicate that banned materials have recently been moved from a number of weapons of mass destruction facilities. . . . This one is about a weapons munitions facility, a facility that holds ammunition at a place called Taji. This is one of about 65 such facilities in Iraq. We know that this one has housed chemical munitions." Colin L. Powell, "Remarks to the United Nations Security Council," February 5, 2003, New York, http://www.state.gov/secretary/former/powell/remarks/2003/17300.htm. During the war, on March 30, 2003, Secretary of Defense Donald Rumsfeld said: "We know where they [WMD] are. They're in the area around Tikrit and Baghdad and east, west, south and north somewhat." He has since backtracked: "I should have said, 'I believe they're in that area; our intelligence tells us they're in that area.'"Quoted in Vernon Loeb, " Rumsfeld Backs U.N. Resolution on Iraq," Washington Post, September 11, 2003, A17.

the prewar misapprehensions of weapons, *which were not there*" (emphasis added).[22] According to the ISG, "Iraq unilaterally destroyed its undeclared chemical weapons stockpile in 1991"[23] and "in 1991 and 1992, Iraq appears to have destroyed its undeclared stocks of BW weapons and probably destroyed the remaining holdings of bulk BW agent."[24]

Iraq's alleged nuclear weapons program has also been debunked. The claim by President Bush in his 2003 State of the Union address (and three other Bush administration statements that month) that Saddam Hussein was seeking "significant quantities of uranium from Africa"[25] is now discredited.[26] According to the Senate Select Committee on Intelligence, "the language in the October 2002 National Intelligence Estimate [the basis for the Bush administration's WMD claims] that 'Iraq also began vigorously trying to procure uranium ore and yellowcake' overstated what the Intelligence Community knew about Iraq's possible procurement attempts."[27] Similarly, the committee concluded that the aluminum tubes purchased by Iraq—which the administration claimed were for building centrifuges for uranium enrichment[28]—"were intended to be used for an Iraqi conventional rocket program and not a nuclear program."[29] Australian Brig. Gen. Stephen Meekin, who commanded the Joint Captured Enemy Material Exploitation Center in Iraq, claimed, "The tubes were used for rockets."[30] Even Kay acknowledged that the aluminum tubes were not for nuclear centrifuges: "Finally, with regard to the aluminum tubes, as I said in my unclassified statement in October, the tubes were certainly being used for rockets."[31]

Postwar inspections have revealed that while Saddam Hussein certainly had nuclear ambitions, Iraq did not have an active nuclear weapons program. Before stepping down as head of the ISG, Kay conceded, "Despite evidence of Saddam's continued ambition to acquire nuclear weapons, to date we have not uncovered evidence that Iraq undertook significant post-1998 steps to actually build nuclear weapons or produce fissile material."[32] And the ISG concluded that "Iraq ended the nuclear program in 1991 following the Gulf war" and "found no evidence to suggest concerted efforts to restart the program."[33]

The final nail in the WMD coffin: after nearly two years searching military installations, factories, and laboratories in Iraq, the Bush administration gave up its search for WMD at the end of 2004.[34] But, even as the president had to admit that there were no WMD in Iraq, he amazingly enough defended his decision to invade Iraq as "worth it" on the basis of such weapons in a January 2005 *ABC 20/20* interview with Barbara Walters:

> Barbara Walters (off camera): Mr. President, it was announced this week that we're no longer going to be looking for weapons of mass destruction. Which, of course, was the basic argument used when we were invading. Now, yes, we toppled Saddam Hussein, and yes, he was a bad man. But this was our main reason for going in. So, now when we read, "okay, the search is over," what do you feel?
>
> President George W. Bush: Well, like you, I felt like we would find weapons of mass destruction, or like many, many here in the United States, many around the world. The United Nations thought he had weapons of mass destruction. And so, therefore, one, we need to find out what went wrong in the intelligence gathering. Saddam Hussein had the capability and the desire to reconstitute weapons programs when the world looked the other way. And the world is safer without him in power.
>
> Barbara Walters (off camera): But was it worth it if there were not weapons of mass destruction? Now we know that that was wrong. Was it worth it?
>
> President George W. Bush: Oh, absolutely. . . . And he [Saddam Hussein] no longer has the capacity to reconstitute a weapons program. Yes, it's worth it.[35]

But even if Iraq possessed chemical or biological weapons (which was a fair assumption) or even a nuclear weapon (which was a stretch of the imagination), it did not have the long-range military capability to strike the United States and thus pose a direct threat. According to the IISS in a 2002 report:

> Iraq's current ballistic missile capabilities are very modest, compared to its robust missile force and substantial missile development and production infrastructure in 1991. The Gulf War and subsequent UN efforts cost Iraq its large missile force and destroyed most of its infrastructure for indigenous development and production of Scud-based missiles. . . .
>
> Since the end of inspections in 1998, it is unlikely that Iraq has

been able to reconstitute its previous missile production capabilities for long range missiles, which would have required significant
foreign assistance.[36]

None of the Iraqi ballistic missiles cited by the CIA had the range to
reach the United States: al-Husayn variants of Soviet Scud B missiles with
an extended range of 650 kilometers, the al-Abbas with a range of 900 kilometers, and the Badr-2000 with an estimated range of 750 to 1,000 kilometers.[37] The latter two missiles were considered to be in development but were
not operationally deployed. The CIA's 2001 assessment of the ballistic missile threat had previously concluded that Iraq may be able to try to develop
a longer-range missile but that the prospect of success before 2015 was very
low.[38] The CIA assessment went so far as to argue that even if UN restric-
tions were lifted, Iraq was very unlikely to successfully test an interconti-
nental ballistic missile that could threaten the United States before 2015.[39]

Finally, the idea that Iraq had unmanned aerial vehicles (UAVs) that
posed a WMD threat to the United States was hyperbole. According to the
Senate Select Committee on Intelligence:

> The Intelligence Community assessment in the key judgements sec-
> tion of the National Intelligence Estimate that Iraq was developing
> an unmanned aerial vehicle (UAV) "[p]robably intended to deliver
> biological warfare agents" overstated both what was known about
> the mission of Iraq's small UAVs and what intelligence analysts
> judged about the likely mission of Iraq's small UAVs. The Air Force
> footnote which indicated that biological weapons (BW) delivery
> was a possible, though unlikely, mission more accurately reflected
> the body of intelligence reporting. . . .
>
> Other than the Air Force's dissenting footnote, the Intelligence
> Community failed to discuss possible conventional missions for
> Iraq's unmanned aerial vehicles (UAV) which were clearly noted
> in the intelligence reporting and which most analysts believed were
> the UAV's primary missions. . . .
>
> The Intelligence Community's assessment that Iraq's procurement
> of United States[-]specific mapping software for its unmanned aerial
> vehicles (UAV) "strongly suggests that Iraq is investigating the use

of these UAVs for missions targeting the United States" was not supported by the intelligence provided to the Committee.[40]

Furthermore, even if Saddam Hussein had possessed WMD, historical precedent suggests that he could have been deterred from using such weapons against the United States. During the Gulf War, Iraq was believed to possess chemical and biological weapons but did not use those weapons against coalition forces—presumably because of the possibility of U.S. nuclear retaliation. In August 1990 then–Defense Secretary Cheney stated that "it should be clear to Saddam Hussein that we have a wide range of military capabilities that will let us respond with overwhelming force and extract a very high price should he be foolish enough to use chemical weapons on United States forces."[41] And the American government reportedly used third-party channels to privately warn Iraq that "in the event of a first use of a weapon of mass destruction by Iraq, the United States reserved the right to use any form of retaliation (presumably up to and including nuclear weapons)."[42] According to Keith Payne, a former deputy assistant secretary of defense in the first term of the Bush administration:

> Senior Iraqi wartime leaders have explained that while U.S. conventional threats were insufficient to deter, implicit U.S. nuclear threats did deter Saddam Hussein's use of chemical and biological weapons. As the then-head of Iraqi military intelligence, Gen. Waffic al Sammarai, has stated, Saddam Hussein did not use chemical or biological weapons during the war, "because the warning was quite severe, and quite effective. The allied troops were certain to use nuclear arms and the price will be too dear and too high."[43]

That Iraq could be deterred was reinforced by an October 7, 2002, letter from CIA director George Tenet to Senator Bob Graham (D-FL), then-chairman of the Select Committee on Intelligence. According to Tenet, the Hussein regime was unlikely to use terrorism to attack the United States. The most likely scenario in which that could happen, Tenet argued, was if the United States prepared an attack: "Should Saddam conclude that a U.S.-led attack could no longer be deterred, he probably would become much less constrained in adopting terrorist actions. . . . Saddam might decide that the extreme step of assisting Islamist terrorists in conducting a WMD attack against the United States would be his last chance to exact vengeance by taking a large number of victims with him."[44]

The October 7 letter also declassified the following dialogue at a closed hearing:

> Senator Levin: If [Saddam] didn't feel threatened, did not feel threatened, is it likely that he would initiate an attack using a weapon of mass destruction?
> Senior Intelligence Witness: My judgment would be that the probability of him initiating an attack—let me put a time frame on it—in the foreseeable future, given the conditions we understand now, the likelihood I think would be low.[45]

So even the mere existence of WMD in Iraq would not qualify as an imminent threat that absolutely required preemptive military action.

To make the threat of WMD seem even direr in the case of Iraq, President Bush argued either explicitly or implicitly on several occasions that Saddam Hussein could (the implication being that he would) give WMD to terrorists. This tied the debate over Iraq to the pressing issue of terrorism. In his State of the Union address on January 29, 2002, Bush claimed, "By seeking weapons of mass destruction, these regimes pose a grave and growing danger. They could provide these arms to terrorists, giving them the means to match their hatred."[46] At the UN on September 12, 2002, the president said, "With every step the Iraqi regime takes toward gaining and deploying the most terrible weapons, our own options to confront that regime will narrow. And if an emboldened regime were to supply these weapons to terrorist allies, then the attacks of September the 11th would be a prelude to far greater horrors."[47] In the Rose Garden on September 26, 2002, President Bush asserted that "[t]he [Hussein] regime has long-standing and continuing ties to terrorist organizations. And there are al Qaeda terrorists inside Iraq."[48]

At the Cincinnati Museum Center on October 7, 2002, President Bush discussed the Iraqi threat:

> Iraq could decide on any given day to provide a biological or chemical weapon to a terrorist group or individual terrorists. Alliances

with terrorists could allow the Iraqi regime to attack America without leaving any fingerprints.

If the Iraqi regime is able to produce, buy, or steal an amount of highly-enriched uranium a little larger than a single softball, it could have a nuclear weapon in less than a year. . . . And Saddam Hussein would be in a position to pass nuclear technology to terrorists.[49]

In a speech calling for Iraq to disarm on November 3, 2002, in Sioux Falls, South Dakota, Bush said that Hussein "would like nothing better than to hook-up with one of these shadowy terrorist networks like al Qaeda, provide some weapons and training to them, let them come and do his dirty work, and we wouldn't be able to see his fingerprints on his action."[50]

And a year after naming Iraq as a member of the axis of evil, President Bush declared in his State of the Union address on January 28, 2003:

With nuclear arms or a full arsenal of chemical and biological weapons, Saddam Hussein could resume his ambitions of conquest in the Middle East and create deadly havoc in that region. And this Congress and the America people must recognize another threat. Evidence from intelligence sources, secret communications, and statements by people now in custody reveal that Saddam Hussein aids and protects terrorists, including members of al Qaeda. Secretly, and without fingerprints, he could provide one of his hidden weapons to terrorists, or help them develop their own.[51]

But these "doom-and-gloom" statements have to be contrasted with the fact that Saddam Hussein never gave chemical and biological weapons to the anti-Israeli Palestinian terrorist groups that he supported. And after being briefed by David Kay in Iraq, Center for Strategic and International Studies military expert Anthony Cordesman concluded that there was "no evidence of any Iraqi effort to transfer weapons of mass destruction or weapons to terrorists."[52]

To further blend fears of Iraq's alleged WMD with the threat of terrorism, the president and other senior administration officials often created the impression — without explicitly making the charge — that Iraq was involved with the 9/11 terrorist attacks. On countless occasions, the president discussed Hussein and 9/11 in the same context. For example, in his 2003 State of the Union address, the president warned:

> Before September the 11th, many in the world believed that Saddam Hussein could be contained. But chemical agents, lethal viruses and shadowy terrorist networks are not easily contained. Imagine those 19 hijackers with other weapons and other plans — this time armed by Saddam Hussein. It would take one vial, one canister, one crate slipped into this country to bring a day of horror like none we have ever known. We will do everything in our power to make sure that that day never comes.[53]

And at a press conference just prior to invading Iraq, President Bush said:

> If the world fails to confront the threat posed by the Iraqi regime, refusing to use force, even as a last resort, free nations would assume immense and unacceptable risks. The attacks of September the 11th, 2001 showed what the enemies of America did with four airplanes. We will not wait to see what terrorists or terrorist states could do with weapons of mass destruction. . . ."[54]

The president continued to imply a connection between 9/11 and Iraq after the war. Announcing that major combat operations in Iraq had ended, President Bush declared, "The battle of Iraq is one victory in a war on terror that began on September the 11th, 2001."[55] And addressing the nation some two years after the 9/11 attacks, he said:

> For America, there will be no going back to the era before September the 11th, 2001 — to false comfort in a dangerous world. We have learned that terrorist attacks are not caused by the use of strength; they are invited by the perception of weakness. And the surest way to avoid attacks on our own people is to engage the enemy where he lives and plans. We are fighting that enemy in Iraq.[56]

On *Good Morning America* on September 8, 2003, National Security Adviser Condoleezza Rice responded to a question about Iraq being the central front on the war on terrorism by saying, "The president told the American people shortly after September 11th that we were going to fight this war on the offense. We were going to fight it on the territory of the terrorists."[57] Clearly, the implication was that Iraq was the territory of the terrorists responsible for 9/11. Vice President Cheney was even more explicit on *Meet the Press* less than a week later:

> If we're successful in Iraq, if we can stand up a good representative government in Iraq, that secures the region so that it never again becomes a threat to its neighbors or to the United States, so it's not pursuing weapons of mass destruction, so that it's not a safe haven for terrorists, now we will have struck a major blow right at the heart of the base, if you will, the geographic base of the terrorists who have had us under assault now for many years, but most especially on 9/11.[58]

It should come as no surprise, then, that according to an August 2003 *Washington Post* poll, 69 percent of Americans believed that it was likely that Saddam Hussein was involved in the 9/11 terrorist attacks.[59] But the following month, President Bush was forced to concede that "there is no evidence that Saddam Hussein was involved with September the 11th."[60] Amazingly however, a Harris poll conducted a year later found that 41 percent of Americans still believed "that Saddam Hussein helped plan and support the hijackers who attacked the U.S. on September 11th, 2001."[61]

If the evidence linking Hussein to 9/11 amounts to nothing, then the evidence of any active cooperation between Hussein and al Qaeda is next to nothing. The alleged link between Saddam Hussein's regime and al Qaeda was largely based on the presence of the Ansar al-Islam terrorist group in northern Iraq. This was the evidence Secretary of State Colin Powell brought to the UN Security Council in February 2003:

> But what I want to bring to your attention today is the potentially much more sinister nexus between Iraq and the al Qaeda terrorist network, a nexus that combines classic terrorist organizations and modern methods of murder. Iraq today harbors a deadly terrorist network headed by Abu Mus'ab al-Zarqawi, an associate and col-

laborator of Osama bin Laden and his al Qaeda lieutenants. . . .

Those helping to run [an Iraqi terrorist] camp are Zarqawi lieutenants operating in northern Kurdish areas outside Saddam Hussein's controlled Iraq. But Baghdad has an agent in the most senior levels of the radical organization, Ansar al-Islam, that controls this corner of Iraq. In 2000 this agent offered al Qaeda safe haven in the region. After we swept al Qaeda from Afghanistan, some of its members accepted this safe haven. They remain there today.[62]

While it is true that in October 2004 Zarqawi pledged his loyalty to al Qaeda and that bin Laden apparently accepted Zarqawi's oath, such an alliance is more likely the result of the U.S. invasion of Iraq rather than a reason for the invasion. According to British investigative journalist Jason Burke:

Al-Zarqawi had operated independently of bin Laden, running his own training camp near Herat. It was a small operation and al-Zarqawi was not considered a significant player in Afghanistan at the time. It is likely he had some contact with bin Laden but never took the bayat [sworn oath of loyalty to bin Laden] and never made any formal alliance with the Saudi or his close associates. He was just one of the thousands of activists committed to jihad living and working in Afghanistan during the 1990s.[63]

And Zarqawi and bin Laden have disagreed on one important point. According to the Jamestown Foundation, "[h]istorically, whilst bin Laden in the last decade focused on the far enemy in the United States, Zarqawi has focused on enemies near at hand like the Jordanian regime."[64]

As Secretary Powell himself acknowledged, Zarqawi and Ansar al-Islam were based "in northern Kurdish areas outside Saddam Hussein's controlled Iraq"; this is hardly a strong case for close ties between Hussein and al Qaeda (and raises the question: Why didn't the U.S. military take previous action against an alleged al Qaeda target inside the coalition-controlled no-fly zone?). Moreover, the State Department described Ansar al-Islam as "a radical Islamist group of Iraqi Kurds and Arabs who have vowed to establish an independent Islamic state in northern Iraq."[65] This represented a divergence—not a convergence—of ideology and goals between Ansar al-

Islam and the former regime in Baghdad — again, not convincing evidence that Hussein and al Qaeda were in league with each other.

In fact, the evidence suggests the opposite. Rohan Gunaratna, director of terrorism research at Singapore's Institute of Defense and Strategic Studies and author of *Inside al Qaeda*, is considered one of the world's foremost experts on al Qaeda and was afforded the opportunity to examine several thousand al Qaeda documents and videos after Operation Enduring Freedom in Afghanistan. Gunaratna "could not find any evidence of al Qaeda links to Saddam Hussein or the Baghdad administration," and the videos he watched "speak of [Saddam] as a real monster and not a real Muslim."[66] And a senior U.S. official acknowledged, "We could find no provable connection between Saddam and al Qaeda."[67]

Even more telling is the administration's failure to unearth any new and compelling evidence in Iraq in the war's aftermath to support its claim that Saddam Hussein had ties to al Qaeda in the same way that the Taliban regime in Afghanistan did — which would have been a clear justification for war. One would think that with all of Hussein's documents in the hands of U.S. military and intelligence and with so many high-ranking members of the regime in custody that more than two years after the fall of Baghdad such evidence would have surfaced. Instead, the president and other senior administration officials simply keep repeating the mantra that Saddam and al Qaeda were linked without providing any real proof.[*]

To be sure, there was a previous history of contacts between al Qaeda and Iraq. But according to the 9/11 Commission, "The reports describe friendly contacts and indicate some common themes in both sides' hatred of the United States. But to date we have seen no evidence that these or the earlier contacts ever developed into a collaborative operational relationship. Nor have we seen any evidence indicating that Iraq cooperated with al Qaeda

---

[*] For example, within days of each other in June 2004 both President Bush and Vice Predent Cheney claimed Iraq-al Qaeda links without providing any proof. According to Cheney, "He [Hussein] had long established ties with al Qaeda," Richard B. Cheney, " Vice President's Remarks at a Reception for the James Madison Institute," June 14, 2004, http://www.whitehouse.gov/news/releases/2004/06/20040614-20.html. And according to Bush, "The reason I keep insisting that there was a relationship between Iraq and Saddam and al Qaeda is because there was a relationship between Iraq and al Qaeda," George W. Bush, " President Discusses Economy, Iraq in Cabinet Meeting," June 17, 2004, http://www.whitehouse.gov/news/releases/2004/06/20040617-3.html.

in developing or carrying out any attacks against the United States."[68]

Despite President Bush's assertion that "there's no question that Saddam Hussein had al Qaeda ties,"[69] at most both shared a common hatred of the United States. This was hardly enough to make them allies or to warrant the conclusion that Hussein would give WMD to al Qaeda. Hussein was a Muslim secular ruler while bin Laden is a radical Muslim fundamentalist—hardly compatible ideological views. Indeed, Saddam Hussein's regime was exactly the kind of government that bin Laden claims is illegitimate and would actually be a target for al Qaeda. Any sympathy bin Laden expressed toward Iraq was for the Iraqi people, not the regime in Baghdad. For example, an audiotape attributed to bin Laden released a month before the Iraq war describes Iraq as a "former capital of Islam" and said that Muslim resistance of American aggression "should not be for championing ethnic groups, or for championing the non-Islamic regimes in all Arab countries, including Iraq."[70] Intelligence analysts inside and outside the government pointed out that bin Laden went out of his way in the recording to show his disdain for Hussein and the Baath Party by referring to them as "infidels" and as an "infidel regime."[71]

That does not mean that the former Iraqi regime did not have links to terrorism. According to the State Department's 2002 *Patterns of Global Terrorism* report, Hussein supported two types of terrorist groups: "Iranian dissidents devoted to toppling the Iranian Government and a variety of Palestinian groups opposed to peace with Israel. The groups include the Iranian Mujahedin-e Khalq, the Abu Nidal Organization (although Iraq reportedly killed its leader), the Palestine Liberation Front (PLF), and the Arab Liberation Front (ALF)."[72] But the few terrorist groups that previously received some support from Iraq were not direct threats to the United States, and those that had previously attacked U.S. targets had not done so for almost twenty years.[73]

In the final analysis, Iraq was the wrong war. Not because the United States used preemptive military force—preemptive self-defense would have been justified in the face of a truly imminent threat. Not because the United States acted without the consent of the UN—no country should surrender its defense to a vote of other nations. And not because, so far, WMD have not been discovered—even if those weapons existed, they were not a threat.

Iraq was the wrong war because the enemy at the gates was—and continues to be—the al Qaeda terrorist network operating in sixty or more countries around the world. Although it seems obvious, it is important to remember that the 9/11 attacks were not carried out with any assistance from Saddam Hussein. None of the nineteen hijackers were Iraqis. Iraq has not been proved to be linked to the planning, financing, or execution of those attacks. And the former regime was not known to support or provide safe harbor to al Qaeda, as the Taliban regime did in Afghanistan. Therefore, President Bush's three postwar declarations do not ring true.

#1 "Our nation is more secure."

This statement presumes that Iraq—like the Taliban regime in Afghanistan—was a correct target in the war on terrorism to dismantle the al Qaeda terrorist network. But Iraq was more a case of "back to the future" than real progress against al Qaeda. In the rush to war against Iraq, we seem to have forgotten that prior to 9/11, much of the national security focus of the Bush administration was on WMD and so-called rogue states, including Iraq—largely in the form of missile defense. In other words, Iraq was already a target even before—and unrelated to—9/11.

Moreover, the paradigm used by the administration then (and now) was that of state-sponsored terrorism, which has traditionally been defined as nations using "terrorism as a means of political expression."[74] But this is exactly the wrong approach because al Qaeda's terrorism is not state-sponsored; it is privatized terrorism, independent of any one nation-state.[75] To be sure, al Qaeda will take advantage of a willing host as it did in Afghanistan. However, al Qaeda's ideology and agenda are internally driven, not a political extension of a government. And their capabilities are largely self-financed and self-acquired, not bestowed upon them by a nation-state benefactor. So removing an unfriendly regime and admittedly brutal dictatorship in Iraq, however beneficial that might be for the people of Iraq and however noble the intention of bringing democracy to that country and region, did not diminish—and may have increased—the al Qaeda terrorist threat, which is the real threat to U.S. security.

#2 "Iraq is now the central front [in the war on terrorism]."

If Iraq has become the central front in the war on terrorism, it is so only because of the U.S. decision to invade that country. Iraq was not a hotbed for al Qaeda under Saddam Hussein's brutal rule, but al Qaeda has skillfully used the Iraq war to rally more to its cause. In February 2003 an audiotape of what was believed to be the voice of Osama bin Laden called for Muslim resistance against an American attack on Iraq:

We stress the importance of the martyrdom operations against the enemy — operations that inflicted harm on the United States and Israel that have been unprecedented in their history, thanks to Almighty God. . . .

We also stress to honest Muslims that they should move, incite, and mobilize the [Islamic] nation, amid such grave events and hot atmosphere so as to liberate themselves from those unjust and renegade ruling regimes, which are enslaved by the United States. . . .

Regardless of the removal or the survival of the socialist party or Saddam, Muslims in general and the Iraqis in particular must brace themselves for jihad against this unjust campaign and acquire ammunition and weapons.[76]

A May 2003 audiotape of what was believed to be the voice of bin Laden's top lieutenant, Ayman al-Zawahiri, condemned Arab countries that supported the U.S.-led war against Iraq and urged Muslims to carry out more suicide attacks.[77] A videotape aired on the second anniversary of 9/11 showed bin Laden and al-Zawahiri and included audio of al-Zawahiri calling on Iraqi guerillas to "bury" U.S. troops.[78] An October 2003 audiotape broadcast on Al Jazeera and attributed to bin Laden called on young Muslims to take up holy war against the United States: "O young people of Islam everywhere, especially in the neighboring countries [of Iraq] and in Yemen, you should pursue jihad and roll your sleeves up."[79]

A January 2004 audiotape attributed to bin Laden urged Muslims to fight the U.S. occupation of Iraq: "There can be no dialogue with occupiers except through arms. This is what we need today, and what we should seek. Islamic countries in the past century were not liberated from the crusaders' military occupation except through jihad in the cause of God."[80] In May 2004 an audiotape that offered a reward to anyone who killed Paul Bremer, the head of the U.S. Coalition Provisional Authority (CPA) in Iraq, used the occupation to exhort Muslims: "The American campaign has nothing to do with weapons of mass destruction or lifting the suffering of the Iraqi people. . . . It is a blatant occupation. . . . You should know that defending Muslim land . . . begins by fighting on the front lines in Iraq."[81]

The Iraq war has made the anti-U.S. terrorist problem worse. Although the administration claims that the war on terrorism is not a crusade against

Islam—Gen. William Boykin's remarks to the contrary[*]—the U.S. occupation makes the case for the radical Islamists that the West is invading Islam itself;[82] this only encourages the Muslim world to unite against the United States. The U.S. military presence in Iraq serves as a target (much as it was in Lebanon in the 1980s) and is a magnet and recruiting poster for Isalmic jihadists, al Qaeda or otherwise, because the U.S. military is seen as a foreign occupier not a liberator—this is borne out consistently by polling data.

For example, shortly after the fall of Baghdad, one Iraqi proclaimed, "We thank the Americans for getting rid of Saddam's regime, but now Iraq must be run by Iraqis."[83] A *USA Today*/CNN/Gallup poll a year later showed that such gratitude had turned to resentment with 71 percent of Iraqis viewing U.S. forces "mostly as occupiers." Fifty-seven percent wanted U.S. forces to "leave immediately."[84] A poll conducted for the CPA before the Abu Ghraib prison scandal came to light showed that 82 percent of Iraqis disapproved of the U.S. military presence.[85] And just before the January 31, 2005, elections in Iraq, a Zogby International poll of Iraqis for Abu Dhabi television found that 82 percent of Sunni Arabs and 69 percent of Shiites wanted U.S. forces to withdraw immediately or after a new elected government was in place.[86] Indeed, such may have been the motivation for many Iraqis to go to the polls—according to one Iraqi, "The elections will go ahead regardless and we have to vote in spite of all those sacrifices. The people have to seize this opportunity because voting is the only viable way of ending the occupation."[87]

And the occupation clearly is fuel for violence against Americans—military and civilian—in Iraq. A Gallup poll conducted in August and September 2003 showed that "those who believed such attacks [against U.S. troops] were somewhat or completely justified—11 percent and 8 percent, respectively—would translate to 440,000 adults 18 or older among Baghdad's adult population of 2.3 million."[88] Subsequently, according to the April 2004 *USA Today*/CNN/Gallup poll, 39 percent of Iraqis thought attacks against

---

[*] At the time, Lt. Gen. William Boykin was the deputy undersecretary of defense for intelligence and war-fighting support. He is an evangelical Christian who has made several controversial statements about Islam while wearing his military uniform at private gatherings. Some of his remarks include: "I knew that my God was a real God, and his [a Muslim fighter in Somalia] was an idol" and "The enemy [Islamic extremists] is a spiritual enemy. He's called the principality of darkness. The enemy is a guy called Satan." Quoted in Reuters, "Rumsfeld Praises Army General Who Ridicules Islam as 'Satan,'" New York Times, October 17, 2003, A7.

U.S. forces in Iraq could be "justified" and another 22 percent thought they could be "somewhat justified"[89] — the equivalent of about 15 million Iraqis. The Zogby International poll taken just before the January 2005 elections found that 53 percent of Sunni Arabs (which would translate to more than 2.5 million) believed "ongoing attacks in Iraq are a legitimate form of resistance."[90]

These Iraqis are not just potential insurgents against the U.S. military occupation in Iraq; they form the basis of a recruiting pool for al Qaeda. Indeed, according to a May 2005 classified CIA report, Iraq has become the kind of training ground for Islamic extremists that Afghanistan was in the 1980s and 1990s, when al Qaeda was formed. Moreover, Iraq may be more effective and dangerous than Afghanistan was because it is a real-world laboratory for urban combat and terrorism.[91]

#3 "We are aggressively striking the terrorists in Iraq, defeating them there so we will not have to face them in our own country."

To be sure, al Qaeda is taking advantage of the U.S. situation in Iraq and is linked to some of the terrorist attacks there. Certainly that is the case since Abu Musab al-Zarqawi pledged his loyalty to Osama bin Laden in October 2004 and renamed his terrorist group Al Qaeda in the Land of Two Rivers[*] (Iraq is commonly known as the land of two rivers, the Tigris and Euphrates). Al Qaeda may have also had a hand in the bombing of the UN headquarters in Baghdad in August 2003[92] and the bombing of the Red Cross in Baghdad in October 2003.[93]

But the opposition to U.S. occupation in Iraq is not exclusively from al Qaeda or al Qaeda sympathizers (especially if al Qaeda and foreign fighters are considered the same). First and foremost, the Sunni Baathists who formerly held the reins of power under Saddam Hussein are resisting the change brought about by U.S. military action[94] — but these are not terrorists who would otherwise attack the United States. Also, the insurgency is not exclusively Sunni Arab–based. The spring 2004 uprising in Fallujah and fall 2004 violent resistance in Najaf were both orchestrated by Shiite cleric Moqtada al-Sadr. Second — as is evident from all the polling data — the majority of Iraqis view the U.S. military as an occupying force and want them to leave their country. This does not make all these Iraqis insurgents, but the insurgency can play to their sympathies and draw from their ranks. More important, many of the

---

[*] Previously, Zarqawi's terrorist network in Iraq was called Jama'at al Tawhid wal Jihad.

insurgents in Iraq are not people who would otherwise flock to al Qaeda's cause and kill innocent Americans — but the longer the U.S. military occupation drags on the more likely it is that they could be recruited by al Qaeda.

Those al Qaeda operatives who are in Iraq are more than likely there simply because the U.S. military presence is a convenient target in their own neighborhood. Al Qaeda can more easily filter over the relatively porous and largely unguarded Iraqi borders (essentially the equivalent length of the U.S.-Mexican border, which hundreds of thousands of illegal immigrants sneak across every year), than it can fly thousands of miles to the United States. But that does not make the threat to America less because, as the CIA concluded, the likely result is that fighters trained in Iraq (Iraqis and foreigners alike) are likely to disperse to other countries.

And if al Qaeda's presence in Iraq is measured by the estimated number of foreign fighters in the insurgency, then their numbers are relatively small. For example, according to *The Economist*, "General George W. Casey, Jr., the commander-in-chief of coalition forces in Iraq, credits foreigners with a minimal role in the insurgency. Of over 2,000 men detained during the fighting in Fallujah during the late fall of 2004, fewer than 30 turned out to be non-Iraqi."[95] In September 2002 deputy commander of coalition forces in Iraq, British Maj. Gen. Andrew Graham, estimated that there were 40,000 to 50,000 active insurgent fighters.[96] That same month, Gen. John Abizaid, head of U.S. Central Command, estimated that there were fewer than 1,000 foreign fighters in Iraq.[97] More recently, a senior U.S. military official pegged the number of insurgents in Iraq at between 13,000 and 17,000 with "about 500 other fighters . . . from other countries" and another group of "fewer than 1,000 . . . believed to be followers of Jordanian-born Islamic terrorist Abu Musab al-Zarqawi."[98]

The cruel irony is that Zarqawi may not have previously been an al Qaeda threat, but now he cannot be ignored. In October 2004 Zarqawi's group in Iraq declared its loyalty to Osama bin Laden and al Qaeda: "We announce that Tawhid and Jihad, its prince and its soldiers, have pledged allegiance to the leader of the mujahideen, Osama bin Laden."[99] In a December 2004 audiotape bin Laden urged Iraqis to boycott the upcoming elections and showed his support for Zarqawi:

I believe that the mujahid emir, dignified brother Abu Musab al-

Zarqawi, and the groups affiliated with him are good and from the group that fights according to the orders of God. . . . We are pleased with their daring operations against the Americans and Allawi's renegade government. . . . We in the al Qaeda organization warmly welcome their union with us. . . . It should be known that mujahid brother Abu Musab al-Zarqawi is the emir of the al Qaeda organization in the Land of the Two Rivers.[100]

President Bush's statement also assumes that just because the U.S. military is engaged in Iraq and al Qaeda is behind some of the terrorist attacks in Iraq, al Qaeda is precluded from attacking elsewhere. The evidence suggests otherwise. Car bombings in Riyadh on May 12, 2003, and November 9, 2003; in Casablanca on May 16, 2003; and in Istanbul on November 15, 2003, have all been linked to al Qaeda, as have been the March 11, 2004, railway bombings in Madrid and the July 7, 2005, London subway bombings. If al Qaeda does not presently have the resources and capabilities to mount an attack against the United States (especially a massive attack on the scale of 9/11), Operation Enduring Freedom in Afghanistan—not U.S. military operations in Iraq—is responsible for degrading al Qaeda. According to IISS:

U.S.-led military action in Afghanistan in response to the 11 September 2001 attacks and the continued allied military presence there released the Taliban's stranglehold on the country and deprived bin Laden, his inner circle, and hundreds of rank-and-file al Qaeda members of a friendly host, a recruiting 'magnet,' and a comfortable physical base for training and operations.[101]

And since al Qaeda did not subsequently take up residence in Iraq, U.S. military operations in Iraq are—by definition—not directed against bin Laden and the al Qaeda threat.

But engaging the U.S. military in Iraq is worse than not directing our attention against the al Qaeda terrorist threat. U.S. military actions in Iraq actually make the problem worse because of the inevitable unintended consequences of those actions that create anti-American sentiment, the first step toward becoming a terrorist. For example, in the so-called Sunni Triangle— which is viewed as the hotbed of the Iraqi resistance and where most of the coalition deaths have occurred—the United States picked up the intensity of its operations in mid-November 2003.[102] According to one U.S. officer: "Part of warfare is coercion and affecting the hearts and minds of the enemy and certainly a show of force is a tool that can be used by a commander."[103] One such "show of force" was U.S. F-16 fighter jets dropping several five-hundred-pound bombs in Fallujah, but this may have had more of an effect on Iraqis previously sympathetic to the United States rather than the enemy. According to one resident in the area where the bombs exploded, "We used to have hopes of the Americans after they removed Saddam. We had liked them until this weekend. Why did they drop bombs near us and hurt and terrify my children like this?"[104]

Similarly, in January 2005 after an alleged raid on his house, an Iraqi who had previously supported the U.S. occupation denounced Americans as "the devil." The Iraqi man, Imaad, claims he was humiliated in front of his mother by soldiers who found magazines featuring pictures of girls in swimsuits and erotic poses in his bedroom and then placed them on his bed with the Koran. According to Imaad, "I used to have a good opinion of the Americans. But they are the enemy. They are bad."[105] This does not automatically mean that these Iraqis will become al Qaeda terrorists, but we must recognize that the continued U.S. military presence in Iraq expands the pool of people willing to listen to, and follow, terrorist demagogues.

The outcome for the United States may be a cycle very similar to what the Israelis experience in the West Bank, where military action—however well-justified—creates spillover effects that result in creating terrorists. For example, the suicide bomber responsible for killing nineteen Israelis in Haifa at the beginning of October 2003 was a twenty-seven-year old apprentice lawyer, Hanadi Jaradat. According to John Burns of the *New York Times*, Ms. Jaradat's parents "had no indication that their daughter had any contacts with Islamic militants—no sense, they said, that she had any ambition but to establish her career as a lawyer, marry, and have children."[106] But she had motivation: an Israeli crackdown that resulted in the shooting death of her brother, Fadi, twenty-three, and her cousin, Saleh, thirty-one. Aggressive U.S. military tactics may, in fact, be necessary to deal with Iraqi insurgents and terrorists. But such tactics may do more to create terrorists. If the Israeli experience is any indication, such a cycle may only play into the hands of Osama bin Laden and al Qaeda.

Finally, we know that the presence of five thousand U.S. troops in Saudi Arabia after the Gulf War was a basis for Osama bin Laden's hatred of the United States and one of his stated reasons for engaging in terrorism, including the devastating 9/11 attacks that killed more than three thousand innocent people.[107] Even Deputy Defense Secretary Paul Wolfowitz — one of the principal architects of the administration's Iraq policy — admits that U.S. forces in Saudi Arabia were "a huge recruiting device for al Qaeda. In fact if you look at bin Laden, one of his principle grievances was the presence of so-called crusader forces on the holy land, Mecca and Medina."[108] Although virtually all U.S. troops have now been removed from Saudi Arabia,[109] President Bush has talked about making a "generational commitment to the advance of freedom, especially in the Middle East"[110] that "must be a focus of American policy for decades to come."[111] President Bush asserts that "We will stay there [in Iraq] until the job is done and then we will leave,"[112] but the question of when "the job is done" remains unanswered.[113] Secretary of Defense Donald Rumsfeld once thought that U.S. forces could be drawn down to forty thousand to sixty thousand troops relatively quickly — i.e., within months — after toppling the regime in Baghdad.[114] Instead, the "catastrophic success" of Operation Iraqi Freedom has required a steady state deployment of more than one hundred thousand U.S. soldiers in Iraq for more than three years. In January 2005 the Army's top operations officer acknowledged that the U.S. Army was expecting to keep about 120,000 troops in Iraq through 2006.[115] And in August 2005 the chief of staff of the U.S. Army, Gen. Peter Schoomaker, announced that the Army was preparing for the possibility of keeping the current number of soldiers in Iraq for four more years.[116] With no timetable for an eventual U.S. military withdrawal,[117] one can only imagine how such a large U.S. military presence in the heart of the Middle East over a protracted period might fuel al Qaeda's rhetoric, recruiting, and future actions.

Ironically, President Bush provided his own indictment of the Iraq war when he addressed the UN General Assembly in September 2003: "No government should ignore the threat of terror, because to look the other way gives terrorists the chance to regroup and recruit and prepare."[118] But that is exactly what the Iraq war has been — a dangerous distraction in the war on terrorism against the real threat: al Qaeda.

3

CLEARING THE DECKS FOR WAR

Cry "Havoc," and let slip the dogs of war.

—Shakespeare, *The Life and Death of Julius Caesar*

When a family suffers an unexpected hardship or tragedy—such as unemployment or the death of the primary income earner—it does not continue with business as usual, leaving its priorities and spending patterns unchanged. Instead, a family must make tough decisions to ensure that the mortgage and other bills are paid and that the basic necessities—such as food—are provided for. Luxuries such as exotic vacations, expensive designer clothes, and dining out at five-star restaurants are foregone.

After the Japanese attacked Pearl Harbor, the United States engaged in an all-out effort to defeat Japan and Germany in World War II. This meant transitioning the peacetime economy to produce military equipment. Women who were previously homemakers became a vital part of the workforce. Food and gasoline were rationed. The survival of the country was at stake and any commitments that did not contribute to the war were secondary, at best.

Although the war on terrorism is a different kind of war and will not require the kind of military and civilian effort the United States mustered to win World War II, knowing that al Qaeda represents *the* clear and present danger to U.S. national security means the United States must clear the decks for war by reducing or eliminating unnecessary commitments. The United States can retain a preponderant capacity for defending the homeland and deterring great powers from challenging it while casting off the obsolete requirements that have endured past their expiration date at the end of the Cold War.

The U.S. Constitution makes clear that one of the paramount responsibilities of the federal government is to "provide for the common defense." In the past, the primary threats to the United States and U.S. interests were hostile nation-states. During the Cold War, that meant the Soviet Union. But the United States is no longer faced with a serious military challenger or a global hegemonic threat. In fact, the United States is in a unique geostrategic position. Two great oceans act as vast moats to protect America's western and eastern flanks. And America is blessed with two friendly and stable neighbors to the north and south. Thus, the American homeland is safe from a traditional conventional military invasion, and the U.S. strategic nuclear arsenal acts as an effective and credible deterrent against possible nuclear attack — even against rogue states that might eventually acquire nuclear weapons.

Russia is not the threat that the former Soviet Union was. Indeed, Russia now has observer status with the North Atlantic Treaty Organization (NATO) — a dramatic change given that the NATO alliance was created to contain the former Soviet Union. And in May 2002 Russia and the United States signed the Strategic Offensive Reductions Treaty to reduce their strategic nuclear arsenals to between seventeen hundred and twenty-two hundred warheads by December 2012. According to the International Institute for Strategic Studies, "despite disagreement over the U.S.-led action in Iraq, the bilateral relationship between Washington and Moscow remains firm."[1]

Even if Russia backslides on democratic and economic reform, it is not in a position to challenge the United States — either economically or militarily. In 2003 Russia's GDP was a little more than a tenth of U.S. GDP ($1.3 trillion versus $10.9 trillion).[2] And although a larger share of Russia's GDP was for defense expenditures (4.9 percent versus 3.7 percent),[3] in absolute terms the United States outspent Russia by more than six-to-one. So Russia would have to devote more than 20 percent of its GDP to defense — which would exceed what the Soviet Union spent during the height of the Cold War in the 1980s[4] — to equal the United States.

Many see China as a threat,[5] but it is by no means certain that China will become an aggressive great power that challenges the United States. According to a Council on Foreign Relations task force chaired by former Secretary of Defense Harold Brown:

> [T]he People's Republic of China is pursuing a deliberate and focused course of military modernization but . . . it is at least two

decades behind the United States in terms of military technology and capability. Moreover, if the United States continues to dedicate significant resources to improving its military forces, as expected, the balance between the United States and China, both globally and in Asia, is likely to remain decisively in America's favor beyond the next twenty years.[6]

Certainly, Chinese military developments bear watching. But even if China modernizes and expands its strategic nuclear force (as many military experts predict), the United States will retain an overwhelming advantage in warheads, launchers, and a variety of delivery vehicles that provide a credible deterrent capability. So the United States need not be alarmist about the potential for China to become a threat.

And like Russia, China may not have the wherewithal to compete with and challenge the United States. In 2003 U.S. GDP was almost eight times more than China's ($10.9 trillion versus $1.4 trillion).[7] China spent fractionally more of its GDP than the United States spent on defense (3.9 percent versus 3.7 percent),[8] but in absolute terms the U.S. defense expenditures were seven times China's ($404.9 billion versus $55.9 billion).[9] So China would have to devote one-quarter of its GDP defense to equal U.S. spending.

If the Russian and Chinese militaries are not serious threats to the United States,[10] so-called rogue states—such as North Korea, Iran, Syria, and Cuba—are even less of a threat. Admittedly, these countries are unfriendly to the United States but none have any real military capability to threaten or challenge vital American security interests. North Korea is a concern because of its ongoing nuclear weapons and ballistic missile programs.[11] But even if the North Koreans eventually acquire a long-range nuclear capability that could reach the United States, the U.S. strategic nuclear arsenal would continue to act as a powerful deterrent. Iran is also pursuing a ballistic missile program and may be attempting to develop nuclear weapons, but their programs are less advanced than North Korea's.[12] And both North Korea's and Iran's conventional military capabilities pale in comparison to the U.S. military.

The resulting bottom line is that a conventional military threat to the U.S. homeland is, for all intents and purposes, nonexistent.[*] This is a wel-

---

[*] Only Russia and China possess long-range nuclear capability to attack the United States, but that capability is offset by the U.S. strategic nuclear arsenal.

come situation for America. It does not call for isolationism but does demand a judicious, realistic, and prudent deployment of the power bestowed by such good fortune, so as not to squander America's strength.

This is not to say that threats to America do not exist. As 9/11 so devastatingly demonstrated, the real threat to the U.S. homeland is not a foreign military power but terrorist groups.[13] According to Ted Galen Carpenter at the Cato Institute, "The terrorist attacks on America have given added urgency to the need to adjust Washington's security policy.... [W]e cannot afford the distraction of maintaining increasingly obsolete and irrelevant security commitments around the globe."[14]

Yet in the aftermath of 9/11, U.S. national security policy has become more sprawling rather than focused on protecting the American homeland and public against the threat of terrorism. The new *National Security Strategy of the United States* promulgated by President Bush in September 2002 includes a laundry list of priorities alongside considerations of protecting the U.S. homeland. Some of the central planks of the national security strategy include a desire to:

- "champion aspirations for human dignity";
- "work with others to defuse regional conflicts";
- "ignite a new era of global economic growth through free markets and free trade";
- "expand the circle of development by opening societies and building the infrastructure of democracy";
- "develop agendas for cooperative action with other main centers of global power";[15]

Indeed, the Bush administration's national security strategy describes itself as being "based on distinctly American internationalism," which is "the union of our values and our national interests." The outcome is a strategy with the aim of helping to "make the world not just safer but better."[16]

That the Bush administration chose such a posture is surprising for a president who as a candidate in 2000 said, "If we're an arrogant nation, they'll resent us.... And that's why we've got to be humble" and "I don't think our troops ought to be used for what's called nation building."[17] But in a reversal of his campaign rhetoric, the Bush national security strategy draws on Woodrow Wilson's belief that America's mission is to spread democracy and that it is possible to teach people how "to elect good men."[18] It also reproduces a rather Clinton-esque foreign policy vision of promoting democracy. After all, President Clinton declared in a speech at the UN in 1993: "Our overriding purpose must be to expand and strengthen the world's community of market-based democracies. During the Cold War, we fought to contain a threat to the survival of free institutions. Now we seek to enlarge the circle of nations that live under those free institutions."[19]

Of course, neoconservatives would challenge liberal internationalists' preference for working with the UN and cultivating the support of the international community. But both arrive at the same end point. The result is an alliance of strange bedfellows brought together by the belief that American security is best served by using military power to spread democracy throughout the world. Evidence of this convergence is a January 2005 letter from the Project for the New American Century to the leadership of the U.S. Congress calling for increasing the size of the Army and Marine Corps by "at least 25,000 troops each year over the next several years" because "our national security, global peace and stability, and the defense and promotion of freedom in the post-9/11 world require a larger military force than we have today."[20] The signatories included many of the "usual suspects" on the hawkish political right—e.g., Max Boot, Thomas Donnelly, Frank Gaffney, William Kristol, and Danielle Pletka—as well as many left-leaning luminaries—e.g., Ivo Daalder, Michele Flournoy, Michael O'Hanlon, and James Steinberg (all except O'Hanlon having served in the Clinton administration).

But what the Bush administration calls a national security strategy is really a *global* security strategy to "defend liberty and justice because these principles are right and true for all people everywhere"[21] based on the false belief that the best and only way to achieve U.S. security is by forcibly creating a better and safer world in America's image. Although the administration's original argument for military action against Iraq was the purported threat of Iraqi WMD, at the eleventh hour the larger and more ambitious goal of spreading democracy was added as a rationale:

> The world has a clear interest in the spread of democratic values, because stable and free nations do not breed the ideologies of murder. They encourage the peaceful pursuit of a better life. . . .
>
> It is presumptuous and insulting to suggest that a whole region of the world—or the one-fifth of humanity that is Muslim—is some-

how untouched by the most basic aspirations of life. Human cultures can be vastly different. Yet the human heart desires the same good things, everywhere on Earth. In our desire to be safe from brutal and bullying oppression, human beings are the same. In our desire to care for our children and give them a better life, we are the same. For these fundamental reasons, freedom and democracy will always and everywhere have greater appeal than the slogans of hatred and the tactics of terror.[22]

And it is clear now that the Bush administration's national security strategy was not tailor-made simply as part of justification to invade Iraq. In his second term inaugural address, President Bush asserted, "The survival of liberty in our land increasingly depends on the success of liberty in other lands. The best hope for peace in our world is the expansion of freedom in all the world." The president declared, "[Freedom] is the urgent requirement of our nation's security, and the calling of our time. So it is the policy of the United States to seek and support the growth of democratic movements and institutions in every nation and culture, with the ultimate goal of ending tyranny in our world."[23] He reiterated these goals in his February 2005 State of the Union address.[24]

No one would dispute that democracy is a worthy goal. And certainly the United States should encourage the formation of liberal democracies throughout the world. But at least twenty countries in the world can be categorized as undemocratic[25] by the dictionary definition of democracy: "government by the people, exercised either directly or through elected representatives."[26] And some governments that claim to be democratic are democratic in name only. For example, since 1981 Egypt (considered a democratic republic) has had presidential elections, but no opposition candidates were allowed to run against President Hosni Mubarak until February 2005.[27] Zimbabwe is nominally a parliamentary democracy, but according to the CIA, "Robert Mugabe, the nation's first prime minister, has been the country's only ruler (as president since 1987) and has dominated the country's political system since independence" and "Mugabe rigged the 2002 presidential election to ensure his reelection."[28] Venezuela has a democratically elected government, but according to the State Department, in December 2004 "the legislature passed laws that erode freedom of the media, freedom of speech, and which in effect make criticism of the government a criminal offense."[29]

Whether any of these countries is a threat to the United States, however, is not a function of whether they are democracies. It is true that almost all democratic governments in the world are friendly to the United States. But the fact that a military government rules Burma does not make that country a threat to America. Threats are defined by hostile intentions and military capability. And U.S. national security is based on being able to counter (either by deterring or defeating) direct threats. Thus, the litmus test is not whether a country meets U.S.-imposed criteria of democratic government, but whether it has hostile intentions and real military capability to threaten the United States directly.

The Bush administration's national security strategy correctly recognizes the threat posed by al Qaeda: "Our priority will be first to disrupt and destroy terrorist organizations of global reach and attack their leadership; command, control, and communications; material support; and finances"[30] (al Qaeda is the only such group to demonstrate global reach). But in many ways, the guiding principle seems to be "to stop rogue states and their terrorist clients [which are not the same as 'terrorist organizations of global reach'] before they are able to threaten or use weapons of mass destruction against the United States and our allies and friends."[31] Clearly, this was the administration's rationale for its war against Iraq. In his January 2003 State of the Union address President Bush said:

> With nuclear arms or a full arsenal of chemical and biological weapons, Saddam Hussein could resume his ambitions of conquest in the Middle East and create deadly havoc in the region. And this Congress and the American people must recognize another threat. Evidence from intelligence sources, secret communications, and statements by people now in custody reveal that Saddam Hussein aids and protects terrorists, including members of al Qaeda. Secretly, and without fingerprints, he could provide one of his hidden weapons to terrorists, or help them develop their own.[32]

Thinking in terms of "terrorist clients" implies state-sponsored terrorism, but since al Qaeda is not a client of a rogue state, focusing U.S. national security strategy on rogue states will not address the terrorist threat posed by al Qaeda. Moreover, no evidence suggests that rogue states with (or seeking to acquire) WMD will provide them to terrorists. Thus, the administration's national security focus on rogue states passing WMD to terrorists is based on speculation rather than any historical precedent.

So what is described in the *National Security Strategy of the United States* as preemptive action against rogue states to prevent hostile acts by terrorists is not an appropriate action for dealing with the terrorist threat. And "preemption" is not even an accurate description because the term implies the threat of impending attack. A classic example of preemptive self-defense is Israel's military action against Egypt, Syria, Jordan, and Iraq in the 1967 Six Day War.[33] Instead, what the Bush administration endorses is preventive war, and its logic — to "act against such emerging threats before they are fully formed"[34] — is a prescription for a state of perpetual war. By the standards set forth in the *National Security Strategy of the United States*, the simple existence of conditions in which one of many outcomes might be the emergence of a threat (the likelihood of the threat notwithstanding) is sufficient. Thus, the casus belli is the plausible allegation of a potential threat but not the convincing proof of the existence of such a threat. Speculation about unknown future intentions and capabilities of potential enemies become sufficient reason for military action — thus, the claim that Saddam "could provide one of his hidden weapons to terrorists"[35] is adequate without a reason to believe that he *would* take such action.

Ultimately, the Bush administration's national security strategy seems increasingly like the Cold War paradigm run amok — with rogue states and WMD replacing the Soviet Union — but without a superpower enemy to confront. Indeed, the lack of a powerful enemy is what seems to make the strategy alluring and the implementation of it possible — the United States is unopposed and the dominant military power in the world. But the U.S. Cold War strategy was based on a zero-sum mentality that assumed any gain by one side resulted in a commensurate loss by the other. Thus, the United States sought to keep the Soviet Union in check — a strategy of containment — to ensure that it did not make inroads in key strategic areas. However, as Richard K. Betts at Columbia University recognized long before 9/11:

> [I]t is no longer prudent to assume that important security interests complement each other as they did during the Cold War. The interest at the very core — protecting the American homeland from attack — may now often be in conflict with security more broadly conceived

and with the interests that mandate promoting American political values, economic independence, social Westernization, and stability in regions beyond Western Europe and the Americas.[36]

In the post–Cold War environment the United States no longer needs to check the advances of a superpower enemy. Instead it is faced with an unconventional foe in a war that has no distinct battle lines. Indeed, the many layers of the extended U.S. defense perimeter designed to defend against the Soviet threat during the Cold War were not able to prevent al Qaeda from carrying out the attacks on 9/11. Nonetheless, U.S. national security thinking continues to be guided by the belief that a global U.S. military presence is fundamental to making the United States more secure. Most striking is that such thinking permeates the administration's approach to homeland security. According to the *National Strategy for Homeland Security* issued by the White House in July 2002:

> For more than six decades, America has sought to protect its own sovereignty and independence through a strategy of global presence and engagement. In so doing, America has helped many other countries and peoples advance along the path of democracy, open markets, individual liberty, and peace with their neighbors. Yet there are those who oppose America's role in the world, and who are willing to use violence against us and our friends. Our great power leaves these enemies with few conventional options for doing us harm. One such option is to take advantage of our freedom and openness by secretly inserting terrorists into our country to attack our homeland. Homeland security seeks to deny this avenue of attack to our enemies and thus to provide a secure foundation for America's ongoing global engagement.[37]

Thus, even the administration admits that our aggressive forward presence abroad spurs terrorism. Yet maintaining a global presence appears to have become an end in itself for U.S. national security strategy. As such, the Bush administration's national security strategy is less about national security and more about exercising American power (military, economic, and political) to make a better and safer world. However grand and noble the cause of spreading freedom and democracy throughout the world might be, it has little to do with protecting America against more terrorist attacks from al Qaeda — the one real threat we face.

The notion that the United States can be made more secure by spreading freedom and democracy around the world is based on two assumptions. The first assumption is that democratic nations are peaceful countries[38] and is rooted in the post–World War II reconstruction of West Germany and Japan because the two former members of the Axis were transformed from being America's mortal enemies to being close allies and economic trading partners. According to professor R. J. Rummel at the University of Hawaii, between 1816 and 1991 there were 353 wars and none of them were between two stable democracies.[39] Thus, President Bush claims, "because democracies respect their own people and their neighbors, the advance of freedom will lead to peace."[40]

Although there may be a certain amount of truth to this logic, it is not necessarily true that all future democracies will be friendly to the United States — especially democracies in Muslim countries. For example, if completely free and popular elections were held in Pakistan, Egypt, Saudi Arabia, and Jordan, the resulting governments would likely be anti-American. According to Pew Research, 50 percent of Pakistanis have a very unfavorable view of the United States and another 11 percent have a somewhat unfavorable view.[41] In Egypt — the recipient of more U.S. foreign aid for the past twenty years than any other Muslim country — only 2 percent of the population has a favorable view of the United States. In Saudi Arabia, only 4 percent of the people have a favorable opinion of America.[42] And in Jordan, only 5 percent of the population has a favorable view (compared to 67 percent who have a very unfavorable view).[43] Even a supporter of President Bush's democratic nation-building policy — Reuel Marc Gerecht at the American Enterprise Institute — admits that democracy in Arab and Muslim countries is not likely to be pro-American:

> [T]he march of democracy in the Middle East is likely to be *very* anti-American. Decades of American support to Middle Eastern dictators helped create bin Ladenism. Popular anger at Washington's past actions may not fade quickly, even if the United States were to switch sides and defend openly all the parties call-

ing for representative government. Nationalism and fundamentalism, two complementary forces throughout most of the Middle East,
will likely pump up popular patriotism. Such feelings always have
a sharp anti-Western edge to them.[44] (Emphasis in original)

So the notion of spreading democracy in the Middle East is a case of "be
careful what you wish for" in which the result is likely to be worse than the
current situation, however unsatisfying that is.

The second assumption is that the United States is hated for "who we
are" and that democratic countries would not have a reason to hate us and
breed terrorism. In his address to a joint session of Congress and the American people after the 9/11 terrorist attacks, President Bush said: "Why do they
hate us? They hate what we see right here in this chamber — a democratically
elected government. They hate our freedoms — our freedom of religion, our
freedom of speech, our freedom to vote and assemble and disagree with each
other."[45]

Certainly, suicide terrorists who fly airplanes into buildings do hate
the United States. But it would be misleading to assume that such hatred is
the primary reason and motivation for terrorism against the United States.
Throughout the world there is a deep and widespread admiration for
America and what it has accomplished domestically, including its culture
and values. But the world also has a love/hate relationship with America:
many people love what we are, but they often hate what we do. That is, anti-
American animosity is fueled more by our actions than by our existence.
According to the Defense Science Board, "Muslims do not hate our freedom,
but rather, they hate our policies. The overwhelming majority voice their
objections to what they see as one-sided support in favor of Israel and against
Palestinian rights, and the longstanding, even increasing support for what
Muslims collectively see as tyrannies, most notably Egypt, Saudi Arabia,
Jordan, Pakistan, and the Gulf states."[46]

Evidence for this can be found in various polls taken around the world.
In 2004 the Pew Global Attitudes Project reported:

In the predominantly Muslim countries surveyed, anger toward
the United States remains pervasive, although the level of hatred
has eased somewhat and support for the war on terrorism has

inched up. Osama bin Laden, however, is viewed favorably by large percentages in Pakistan (65%), Jordan (55%), and Morocco (45%). Even in Turkey, where bin Laden is highly unpopular, as many as 31% say that suicide attacks against Americans and other Western-ers in Iraq are justifiable.[47]

A Zogby International "Impressions of America" poll (of six Arab nations) in 2004 found that in most Arab countries there were favorable opin-ions about "American services and technology," "American freedom and democracy," "American people," "American education," "products," etc. On the other hand, opinion about American policy toward the Palestinians and Iraq was low (often in the single-digit range). "When we asked our Arab respondents to name the first thought that came to mind when they hear 'America,' they told us, 'its unfair policies.'"[48]

These views are not confined to countries that might somehow be in-herently predisposed to disliking the United States. A poll conducted for the Chicago Council on Foreign Relations and the German Marshall Fund of the United States showed that "a majority of people surveyed in six European countries believe American foreign policy is partly to blame for the Sept. 11 attacks."[49] The results of a Gallup International poll of thirty-six countries showed that in twenty-three countries (nine of which were Western Euro-pean countries and included Great Britain) "more people think U.S. foreign policy is negative rather than positive in its effects on their country."[50] And according to the Pew Research Center, "anti-Americanism is deeper and broader now than at any time in modern history. It is most acute in the Muslim world, but spans the globe — from Europe to Asia, from South America to Africa."[51]

The obvious conclusion American policymakers can draw based on this evidence is that the United States needs to stop meddling in the internal affairs of countries and regions around the world, except when they directly threaten U.S. national security interests — i.e., when U.S. territorial integrity, national sovereignty, or liberty is at risk.

September 11 only further highlights the need for the United States to distance itself from problems that are not truly vital to U.S. national secu-rity. Much of the anti-American resentment around the world — particularly in the Islamic world — is the result of interventionist U.S. foreign policy. Ac-cording to the 9/11 Commission, "the United States is heavily engaged in the Muslim world. . . . This American engagement is resented."[52] Such resentment breeds hatred, which becomes a steppingstone to violence, including terrorism.

Indeed, the linkage between an interventionist foreign policy and terrorism against the United States was recognized by upper levels of the U.S. government long before 9/11. According to a 1997 study by the Defense Science Board: "America's position in the world invites attacks simply because of its presence. Historical data shows a strong correlation between U.S. involvement in international situations and an increase in terrorist attacks against the United States."[53] The empirical evidence to support this conclusion is shown in appendix 1.

Thus, the United States has a strategic interest in divesting itself of any unnecessary commitments and ridding itself of any distractions to (1) be able to focus its attention and resources on the terrorist threat to America, i.e., al Qaeda, and (2) not create reasons and incentives for more people to become terrorists who would attack America.

Accordingly, the United States should withdraw its military forces from Western Europe. Currently, nearly 115,000 troops are stationed in Europe.[54] But as Ted Galen Carpenter points out, "That troop presence is an utterly obsolete commitment inherited from the Cold War. The U.S. forces are apparently on duty to prevent an invasion of Western Europe by a Warsaw Pact that no longer exists led by a Soviet Union that no longer exists."[55] President Bush recognized this reality when he spoke at the Veterans of Foreign Wars Convention in August 2004: "America's current force posture was designed, for example, to protect us and our allies from Soviet aggression — the threat no longer exists."[56]

Moreover, European countries can afford to pay for their own defense. In 2003 U.S. GDP was $10.9 trillion and total defense expenditures were 3.7 percent of that. In contrast, the combined GDP of the fifteen European Union countries in 2003 was $10.5 trillion, but defense spending was less than 2 percent.[57] Without a Soviet threat to Europe, the United States does not need to subsidize European defense spending and the European countries have the economic wherewithal to increase military spending, if necessary.

Adding to the problem of a U.S. military presence in Europe are America's obligations under NATO. The *raison d'être* for NATO — the Soviet military threat — no longer exists, so the need for NATO also no longer exists. Nonetheless, the United States is obligated — under Article 5 of the NATO

Treaty—to come to the defense another NATO country.[58] One of the newest members of NATO is the Republic of Latvia, admitted to the alliance in April 2004. Russia has expressed its concern that over 460,000 Russian-speaking Latvians were unable to vote in March 2005 municipal elections. If Russia and Latvia were to come to blows over the issue of ethnic Russian Latvians, U.S. security would clearly not be at stake but U.S. forces might be compelled to intervene. That is exactly the kind of situation the United States must avoid entangling itself in.

Second, the United States should jettison its obsolete Cold War commitments in East Asia, where nearly ninety thousand U.S. troops are deployed. The bulk of those troops are deployed in South Korea and Japan—over forty thousand and thirty-six thousand, respectively.[59] But just as the Europeans are capable of defending themselves so are America's allies in East Asia. According to the CIA, "North Korea, one of the world's most centrally planned and isolated economies, faces desperate economic conditions."[60] North Korea's GDP in 2003 was $22 billion compared to South Korea's $605 billion GDP (more than twenty-seven times North's Korea's). South Korea also outspends North Korea on defense nearly three-to-one ($14.6 billion versus $5.5 billion).[61] Japan's GDP was $4.34 trillion (more than 195 times larger than North Korea's) and defense spending was $42.8 billion for defense (almost eight times that of North Korea).[62] So South Korea and Japan certainly have the economic resources to adequately defend themselves against North Korea. They even have the capacity to act as military balancers to China (if China is perceived as a threat). In 2003 China had a GDP of $1.43 trillion and spent $56 billion on defense[63]—about the same as the combined defense spending of South Korea and Japan.

And the nearly thirty-one thousand forward-deployed U.S. ground forces in South Korea are insufficient to fight a war. Operation Iraqi Freedom—against a smaller and weaker military foe—required more than one hundred thousand ground troops to take Baghdad and topple Saddam Hussein (and more to occupy the country afterward). So if the United States decided to engage in an offensive military operation against North Korea, the thirty-one thousand U.S. troops stationed in South Korea would have to be reinforced—which would take almost as much time as deploying the entire force from scratch, if South Korea agreed to be a willing host for staging such an operation. If North Korea (with a nearly one-million-man army) decided to invade South Korea, the defense of South Korea would rest primarily with that country's seven-hundred-thousand-man military, not thirty-one thousand U.S. troops. Nor does the U.S. military presence in South Korea alter the fact that North Korea is believed to have tens of thousands of artillery tubes that can hold the capital city of Seoul hostage. At best, U.S. forces are a tripwire but clearly not a bulwark for defending South Korea.

The Bush administration's Global Posture Review is a step in the right direction. According to President Bush, "over the next 10 years, we will bring home 60,000 to 70,000 uniformed personnel."[64] But this is not a complete withdrawal from either Europe or East Asia. According to David Isenberg at the British American Security Information Council, the Global Posture Review "is not primarily about withdrawing U.S. military forces from around the world. It is about reconfiguring their military basing structure, i.e., 'global footprint.'"[65] In an act of legerdemain, two Army divisions in Germany will return to the United States and a Stryker brigade (built around the Army's new smaller, lighter combat vehicle instead of heavy armor) will be going to Germany in their stead.[66] The Pentagon admits that "there will still be a very substantial ground presence in Germany when this is done."[67] But adding new troops there defies the reason behind removing the existing forces in the first place.

Removing seventy thousand U.S. troops from Germany and South Korea is the right thing to do. But like the proverbial joke about the demise of one hundred lawyers at the bottom of the sea, it's just a good start. In fact, seventy thousand U.S. troops is only about one-third of the total deployed in Europe and East Asia — the nearly 135,000 other troops deployed in those two regions must also be withdrawn.

Finally, the U.S. military must exit Iraq as expeditiously as possible. The dilemma for any U.S. military withdrawal is Abu Musab al-Zarqawi, because he has declared his loyalty to bin Laden and al Qaeda. While Zarqawi would remain an al Qaeda threat in Iraq, he may not be a global threat. One of the points of contention between Zarqawi and bin Laden has been that Zarqawi wants to focus his efforts on attacking targets in the Middle East to topple apostate Muslim regimes while bin Laden clearly wants to target America. Indeed, bin Laden has appealed to Zarqawi to aid in planning attacks against the United States[68] — but Zarqawi seems more interested in making a stand in Iraq. In fact, many analysts still see bin Laden and Zarqawi as independent of each other rather than as allies who have combined their efforts.[69]

But removing U.S. troops from Iraq is not the same as ignoring the threat posed by Zarqawi. First and foremost, a large U.S. military presence in Iraq is not necessary for capturing or killing Zarqawi. Instead, Special Forces operating in small units are better suited to the task—and can be sent in when actionable intelligence warrants a specific operation against Zarqawi. Second, the U.S. military presence in Iraq is counterproductive because of the anti-American sentiment it engenders, creating a common enemy that the insurgents capitalize on to generate sympathy and tacit support. Ending the U.S. military occupation would remove a strong reason for many Iraqis to support or join the insurgency—and have the effect of reducing the insurgency to the Islamic jihadists who are largely foreign fighters.

As such, Iraqi popular opinion might shift from being antioccupation to being anti–foreign fighters and terrorists. Such a phenomena is not unprecedented in the Muslim world. For example, many Muslim Bosnians welcomed foreign fighters in their struggle against the Serbs, but that did not necessarily mean that they were embracing the mujahideen's version of Islam. According to Dutch journalist Emerson Vermaat, "these foreign fanatics were also hated by the local Bosnian population; most of whom preferred a more secular lifestyle, did not like growing beards, and would eat pork and drink alcohol."[70] In 1992 *Newsweek* reported:

> While Bosnians want their freedom, they worry about the price. Some fear the mujahedin haven't yet shown their extremist side. "If they want to offer the people religion, culture and language, that's good," says 27-year-old Zafir, a Muslim from Travnik who asked that his last name not be used. "But if they *insist* on it, that's not good." Bektas, the platoon leader, is concerned the mujahedin are really fighting for Islam, not Bosnia. "It's good for us that they are here," he says. "But after the war, who knows?" So far, at least, locals have been more eager to embrace Kalashnikovs than the Koran: men still drink beer unmolested, and women have resisted the chador.[71]

Iraq under Saddam was probably the most secular Muslim country in the Middle East, so many Iraqis would likely resist the extremist religious views of Zarqawi and his ilk. And even though both al Qaeda and many Shi'ites want Islamic Shari'a law in Iraq, they are not natural allies. For example, in August 2005 Zarqawi's al Qaeda-in-Iraq group issued a communiqué threatening to kill the drafters of the new Iraqi constitution, which would include religious Shi'ites. Even Shi'ite religious leader Ayatollah al-Sistani was not exempt as an infidel in helping to draft the Iraqi constitution with Iraqi president Jalal Talabani and Kurdish leader Mas'oud Barzani.[72] Perhaps more important, the extremists represented by al Qaeda embrace violent jihad and seek to reshape the Muslim world in their own mold. Iraq's Shi'ites are more concerned with exerting power and governing their own country.

Ultimately, it is a question of strategic choice for the United States. Bin Laden is clearly a direct terrorist threat to America. Zarqawi is a threat to the U.S. military and other Americans in Iraq. Going after the latter at the expense of pursuing the former (which is the current situation) is an unwise strategic choice. As is always the case in war, hard decisions must be made about which targets are more important and about allocating resources accordingly. For example, as chief of the War Plans Division during World War II, Gen. Dwight D. Eisenhower argued that Germany was the most dangerous member of the Axis and favored a "Germany-first" strategy, even though Japan was more important to America for emotional reasons because of the attack on Pearl Harbor. The United States must make the same kind of decision about Zarqawi in Iraq. We must remember that bin Laden—thought to be hiding in Pakistan—was the man behind the 9/11 attacks, not Zarqawi, and our priorities must reflect that reality.

Beyond being a dangerous distraction in the war on terrorism against al Qaeda, the costs and burdens of an ongoing U.S. military presence in Iraq cannot be ignored. In February 2003—just a few weeks before the invasion of Iraq—President Bush said, "Rebuilding Iraq will require a sustained commitment from many nations, including our own: we will remain in Iraq as long as necessary, and not a day more. America has made and kept this kind of commitment before—in the peace that followed a world war."[73] But he never addressed the question of cost, and the administration has been—and continues to be—evasive about the costs of going to war against Iraq.

In September 2002 White House economic adviser Lawrence Lindsey suggested that going to war against Iraq might cost $100 to $200 billion, significantly higher than a preliminary Pentagon estimate of $50 billion.[74] Lindsey was rebuked by Office of Management Director Mitch Daniels, who thought Lindsey's estimate was "very, very high,"[75] and chose to resign three months later. Subsequently, Daniels offered an estimate of $50 to $60 billion.[76] But even this estimate was downplayed by the White House.[77] And Defense Secretary Donald Rumsfeld defended the Pentagon's prewar vagueness about cost: "We've been asked over and over again if we would give what we thought the total costs would be, and we've all said the truth, that is to say we don't know."[78]

Although the Bush administration refuses to put a price tag on the Iraq war and subsequent occupation and reconstruction, several reputable analysts have. Lawrence Korb, assistant secretary of defense (manpower, reserve affairs, installations, and logistics) during the Reagan administration, has estimated the total cost at $500 billion.[79] According to Steven Kosiak at the Center for Strategic and Budgetary Assessments (CSBA), "If substantial numbers of US troops are required to remain in Iraq for many years beyond FY [fiscal year] 2005, total costs could approach, or possibly even exceed, $300 billion over the coming decade."[80] The Brookings Institution estimated that military and reconstruction costs in Iraq could range from $150 to $300 billion[81] (and according to Brookings' Michael O'Hanlon, "This [Iraq] has been tougher and more expensive than I ever thought."[82]). And a Council on Foreign Relations task force on post-conflict Iraq — cochaired by former Secretary of Defense James R. Schlesinger — concluded: "The scale of American resources that will be required could amount to some $20 billion per year for several years. This figure assumes a deployment of 75,000 troops for post-conflict peace stabilization (at about $16.8 billion annually), as well as funding for humanitarian and reconstruction assistance. . . . If troop requirements are much larger than 75,000 — a real possibility — the funding requirement would be much greater."[83]

To date, the Bush administration has requested three supplementals to fund military operations in both Iraq and Afghanistan. The first supplemental — in April 2003 — was for $78 billion and the second supplemental — in November 2003 — was for $87 billion. According to Kosiak at CSBA, "about $100 billion [was] to cover the cost of military operations in that country [Iraq]."[84] A third supplemental — requested in February 2005 — was for $82 billion, of which $75 billion was for military operations in Iraq and Afghanistan.[85] And the Defense Appropriations Act for FY 2005 signed by President Bush on August 5, 2004 — which totaled $417.5 billion — included an additional $25 billion for military operations in Iraq and Afghanistan.[86] So the cost of the Iraq war — so far — is approaching $200 billion. With the U.S. Army planning on keeping 120,000 soldiers in Iraq for at least two more years[87] and the cost of military operations at $5.8 billion a month,[88] Lawrence Lindsey's estimate of $200 billion will likely turn out to be overly optimistic.

And unlike the 1990–91 Persian Gulf War, which cost approximately $61 billion and was almost entirely paid for by other coalition countries,[89] the U.S. taxpayer has been stuck with the mounting bill of the Iraq war. This is in stark contrast to Deputy Defense Secretary Paul Wolfowitz's testimony before the House Committee on Appropriations in March 2003: "There's a lot of money to pay for this that doesn't have to be U.S. taxpayer money, and it starts with the assets of the Iraqi people. On a rough recollection, the oil revenues of that country could bring between $50 and $100 billion over the course of the next two or three years. We're dealing with a country that can really finance its own reconstruction, and relatively soon."[90] And according to Rumsfeld, "No one I know believes that the United States taxpayers ought to pay any significant fraction of that [Iraq reconstruction]. We do know that the funds for whatever the number may prove to be, the bulk of it's going to be paid by the Iraqi people."[91]

But the promise of Iraqi oil revenue paying for reconstruction has been more bust than boom. Although Iraq was on track to bring in $20 billion or more in oil revenue in 2005, most of the money was for Iraq's national budget of $18 billion. Of that $18 billion, about 80 percent was allocated for government salaries, food and fuel subsidies, pensions, and other government operating costs — leaving very little for reconstruction and not accounting for the problem of oil-revenue theft.[92]

The costs of the Iraq mission, though, are more than just dollars and cents. Perhaps the most important, but often overlooked, cost is that many Special Forces were diverted from Afghanistan — and the hunt for Osama bin Laden and other senior al Qaeda leaders — to Iraq. For example, in 2002 troops from the Fifth Special Forces Group with Middle East expertise were pulled out of Afghanistan in preparation for the war against Iraq and replaced with troops with expertise in Spanish cultures.[93] In early 2002 a top-secret team known as Task Force 5 — which was hunting al Qaeda along the

Afghanistan-Pakistan border—numbered about 150 commandos. But that number dwindled to as few as thirty men when members of the task force were recalled in preparation for military operations in Iraq. By early 2003 a similar task force in Iraq had swelled to more than two hundred soldiers and the two commando teams were merged and headquartered in Baghdad.[94] Retired U.S. Army Gen. Wayne Downing—recruited to head the White House Office for Combating Terrorism after the 9/11 attacks and a former U.S. Special Operations Command chief—admits that "Iraq did take focus and energy away from the Afghanistan campaign."[95] The end result of shifting Special Forces from Afghanistan to Iraq is that instead of tracking down al Qaeda, many Special Forces are training Iraq's fledgling security forces.[96]

The prolonged U.S. military presence in Iraq has also put a tremendous strain on the regular U.S. Army. To maintain unit cohesiveness and meet rotation requirements for the Iraq mission, the military must resort to the use of stop-loss orders to prevent soldiers from leaving the military when their terms of enlistment expire. In November 2003 the Army issued stop-loss orders for the 110,000 soldiers whose units were preparing to go to Iraq and Afghanistan. In December 2003 the *Washington Post* reported that "through a series of stop-loss orders, the Army alone has blocked the possible retirements and departures of more than 40,000 soldiers, about 16,000 of them National Guard and reserve members who were eligible to leave the service this year."[97] And in January 2004 stop-loss orders were issued covering 160,000 Army soldiers who were returning from Iraq, Afghanistan, and other deployments—although the Army estimated that only 7,000 of those soldiers would have their service involuntarily extended.[98]

To fill the need for critical skills, the Army has drawn increasingly from the ranks of the National Guard and reserve. For the first Operation Iraqi Freedom troop rotation (OIF-1), the force mix was 75 percent active duty and 25 percent reserves. For OIF-2, the reserves increased to 39 percent of the force, with twenty thousand reserve soldiers and thirty-three thousand National Guard. For OIF-3 (July 2005 to March 2005), the reserves comprised 42–43 percent of the troops in Iraq, with seventeen thousand reserves and thirty-seven thousand National Guard.[99]

The strain on the military is also evident in its failure to meet recruiting goals. In August 2005 deputy chief of staff Lt. Gen. James Lovelace admitted that the Army would not meet its recruiting goals for the year. In

June 2005 the Army National Guard missed its recruiting goal for the ninth straight month and was nineteen thousand soldiers short of its authorized strength.[100] Perhaps the most stark admission of the recruiting problem is that in March 2005 the Army raised the maximum enlistment age for the National Guard and reserve to thirty-nine years from thirty-four. And according to a Pentagon spokeswoman, it was possible that the enlistment age for Army reservists might be raised beyond thirty-nine.[101]

Ultimately, the U.S. military—in particular, the Army—cannot sustain the occupation of Iraq indefinitely. According to the Department of Defense, the OIF-4 rotation "continues the current force strength and structure" and "does not significantly increase or decrease troop levels in . . . Iraq."[102] Thus, the number of U.S. troops in Iraq will be about 135,000 soldiers plus about another 30,000 soldiers in Kuwait and other areas of the region supporting military operations in Iraq[103]—or a total of 165,000 U.S. troops.

The troops in Iraq and elsewhere must eventually be relieved by fresh troops. Excessively long or too frequent periods of time away from home creates the risk that soldiers will decide that a military career is too much of a hardship for them and their families, resulting in exodus rather than retention. For a professional volunteer military force to be able to retain soldiers over time, the appropriate deployment ratio seems to be somewhere between 3:1 and 5:1.[104] Although a somewhat confusing term, a 3:1 rotation ratio means that three total units are required to keep one unit on duty (*not* three units for every deployed unit). To maintain 165,000 troops in Iraq and Kuwait requires a total force size of 495,000 troops for a 3:1 rotation ratio and 825,000 troops for a 5:1 ratio. The former is just within the Army's current congressionally authorized end strength of 502,400 soldiers. But the latter far exceeds proposed legislation by Senators Jack Reed (D-RI), a member of the Senate Armed Services Committee, and Chuck Hagel (R-NE), a member of the Senate Foreign Relations Committee, to increase Army end strength to 532,400 in FY 2006.[105]

And because the Pentagon is relying so heavily on reserve and National Guard units—a total of 140,000 members of the Army Reserve and National Guard are currently mobilized and, in the past three years, more National Guard and reserve soldiers have been called to active duty than were cumulatively mobilized since the Cuban Missile Crisis (including for the Vietnam War, the Cuban refugee crisis, Haiti, Bosnia, Kosovo, and Desert Storm).[106] Plus the reserves and National Guard have a ripple effect rotation ratio problem. Because these are part-time soldiers, the rotation ratio needed to keep them enlisted is between 7:1 and 9:1.[107] The number of reserve and National Guard troops currently mobilized requires a total force of 980,000 to 1.3 million citizen soldiers—this is nearly double the size of the Army Reserve and National Guard force.

Also, the current force in Iraq may not be enough. Historically, the force ratio required for imposing stability and security is twenty troops per one thousand inhabitants; this is the ratio the British—often acknowledged as the most experienced practitioners of such operations—deployed for more than a decade in Malaysia and more than twenty-five years in Northern Ireland.[108] With a population of nearly 25 million people, to meet the same standard in Iraq would require a force of five hundred thousand troops for perhaps a decade or longer. The Defense Science Board acknowledged this possibility in December 2004: "The United States will sometimes have ambitious goals for transforming a society in a conflicted environment. Those goals may well demand 20 troops per 1,000 inhabitants . . . working for five to eight years."[109] And in February 2005 Air Force Gen. Richard Myers, then-chairman of the Joint Chiefs of Staff, acknowledged that insurgencies have generally lasted seven to twelve years and that Iraq "is not the kind of business that can be done in one year, two years probably."[110] Like Operation Market Garden during World War II—the failed British attempt to break the German lines in Arnhem, Netherlands, by securing bridges across the rivers in Holland so that the Allied army could rapidly advance into the lowlands of Germany and skirt the Siegfried line defenses—such an undertaking in Iraq would be a bridge too far (as Operation Market Garden came to be known).

Finally, the military manpower pressures being imposed by the Iraq mission raise the very real possibility of running out of or wearing out available forces[111] and the specter of another potential cost: the return of a military draft. During the 2004 presidential campaign, President Bush insisted, "We will not have a draft, so long as I am president of the United States."[112] The president is a man who means what he says and says what he means, so he should be taken at his word. But not having a draft does not preclude the possibility of mandatory national service with a voluntary military component, as is done in some European countries. In January 2003 Representative Charles Rangel (D-NY) introduced HR 163 that would have required "all young persons in the United States, including women, perform a period of military service or a period of civilian service in furtherance of the national defense and homeland security, and for other purposes";[113] the bill was ultimately rejected. The Universal Service Act of 2003 — a companion bill in the Senate introduced by Senator Fritz Hollings (D-SC) — was also defeated.

Even before 9/11, the United States needed to readjust its national security policy. The un-war now demands making changes or risking defeat. Whether they are obsolete commitments or unnecessary wars, we cannot afford distractions that otherwise divert our focus from the true threat: al Qaeda. If we are to unleash the dogs of war against the real enemy, we must first clear the decks.

4

A WAR NOT WON BY THE MILITARY

This conflict cannot be won by military means alone.

—Secretary of Defense Donald H. Rumsfeld

Good warriors do not arm.
—Lao Tzu, *Tao Te Ching*

On August 5, 2004, President Bush signed the Defense Appropriations Act for fiscal year (FY) 2005, which totaled $416.2 billion including an additional $25 billion for military operations in Iraq and Afghanistan.[1] The Defense Department had originally requested $401.7 billion,[2] which did not include funding for military operations in Iraq and Afghanistan. According to the Department of Defense, "the fiscal 2005 budget includes robust readiness and acquisition funding, important legislative authorities, and other essentials for winning the global war on terrorism."[3] And President Bush attacked Senator John Kerry's voting record during the 2004 presidential campaign in a television ad that said: "As our troops defend America in the war on terror, they must have what it takes to win. Yet John Kerry has repeatedly opposed weapons vital to winning the war on terror: Bradley fighting vehicles, Patriot missiles, B-2 stealth bombers, F-18 fighter jets."[4]

But such logic assumes that the war on terrorism is primarily a military war to be fought by the U.S. Army, Navy, Air Force, and Marines. The reality is that large, conventional military operations will be the exception rather than the rule in the war on terrorism. To be sure, U.S. military action has deprived al Qaeda of its sanctuary in Afghanistan. But al Qaeda is not an enemy in command of an opposing military force, and as a transnational, non-state terrorist organization, it does not have physical infrastructure and high-value targets that can be easily identified and destroyed by military force.

The military's role in the war on terrorism will mainly involve special operations forces in discrete missions against specific targets, not conventional warfare aimed at overthrowing entire regimes (although President Bush claims Iraq is the central front in the war on terrorism, ridding the world of Saddam Hussein's brutal regime did not eliminate an al Qaeda sanctuary or source of support for the terrorist group). The rest of the war aimed at dismantling and degrading the al Qaeda terrorist network will largely be the task of unprecedented international intelligence and law enforcement cooperation.

Therefore, an increasingly large defense budget—the Defense Department projects the budget to grow to more than $492 billion by FY 2010[5]—is not necessary to fight the war on terrorism. Nor is it necessary to protect America from traditional nation-state military threats.

According to the International Institute for Strategic Studies (IISS), in 2003 (the last year for which there is comparative worldwide data) total U.S. defense expenditures were $404.9 billion (current year dollars).[6] This amount exceeded the combined defense expenditures of the next thirteen countries and was more than double the combined defense spending of the remaining 158 countries in the world, as shown in figure 4.1. The countries closest in defense spending to the United States were Russia ($65.2 billion) and China ($55.9 billion). The next five countries—France, Japan, the United Kingdom, Germany, and Italy—are all U.S. allies. In fact, the United States outspent its North Atlantic Treaty Organization allies nearly two-to-one ($404.9 billion versus $221.1 billion). And the combined defense spending of what's left of the so-called axis of evil nations (North Korea and Iran) was about $8.5 billion—or 2 percent of U.S. defense expenditures.

From a three-year historical viewpoint, non-U.S. global defense expenditures increased from $541.8 billion in 2001 to $617.9 billion in 2003 (in constant 2005 dollars), or 14 percent. During the same period, U.S. defense expenditures increased from $335.9 billion to $422.5 billion (in constant 2005 dollars), or 26 percent—nearly twice as much as the rest of the world.[7] Or put another way, U.S. defense spending went from 38 percent of the world's

Figure 4.1
Defense Expenditures Compared, 2003

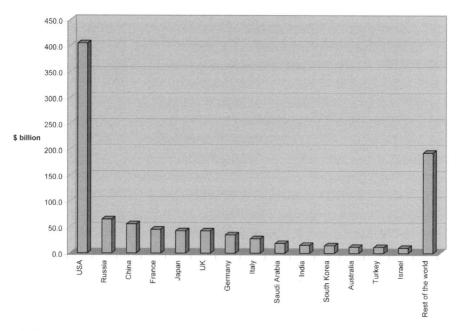

defense spending in 2001 to 41 percent in 2003. If these growth rates (approximately 4.5 percent annually for the rest of the world and 8.5 percent annually for the United States) could be sustained, in ten years U.S. defense expenditures would nearly equal what the rest of the world combined spends, as shown in figure 4.2.

The six-year trend shows that U.S. defense expenditures grew from $338.1 billion in 1997 to $422.5 billion in 2003, while the rest of the world's defense expenditures fell from $656.0 billion to $617.9 billion during the same period.[8] In other words, U.S. defense expenditures grew at about 4 percent per year while the rest of the world's expenditures declined by about 1 percent annually. If the six-year trend is used, U.S. defense expenditures would exceed what the rest of the world combined spends in eight years, as shown in Figure 4.2. While accurately predicting future defense expenditures is impossible, it is probably safe to say that the United States is on track to outspend the rest of the world combined sometime during the next ten to twenty years—especially if the trend of declining defense expenditures for the rest of the world continues.

Figure 4.2
Defense Expenditures Growth Rates Compared

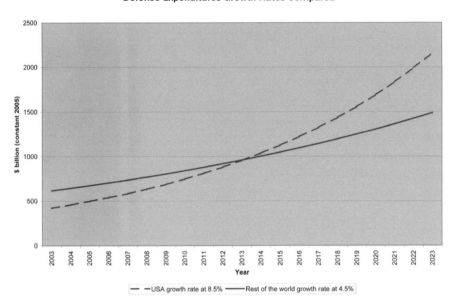

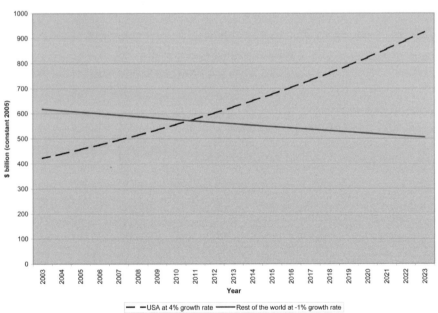

Such large U.S. defense spending must be put in perspective relative to the twenty-first-century threat environment, which is less severe than that during the Cold War. The FY 2005 defense budget (including supplemental funding for military operations in Iraq and Afghanistan) was more than $495 billion—exceeding defense spending during the Vietnam war and during the Reagan military buildup in the 1980s, as shown in figure 4.3. Yet the United States has not been confronted by a strategic military challenger since the end of the Cold War.

The key question for defense spending is: How much is enough? According to Steven M. Kosiak at the Center for Strategic and Budgetary Assessments, the FY 2005 budget is "roughly 10 percent higher than the average Cold War budget in real terms. Under the administration's long-term plan, funding for defense would increase to about 20 percent above average Cold War levels by 2009."[9] But if the United States does not face a military adversary similar to the former Soviet Union during the Cold War, is a larger defense budget necessary? Ted Galen Carpenter at the Cato Institute argues that "post–Cold War U.S. policymakers have reflexively sought to preserve the principal features of the strategy the United States pursued during the Cold War—high levels of military spending, an emphasis on U.S. global leadership, and a hypersensitive reaction to 'aggression' anywhere in

Figure 4.3
U.S. Department of Defense Budget

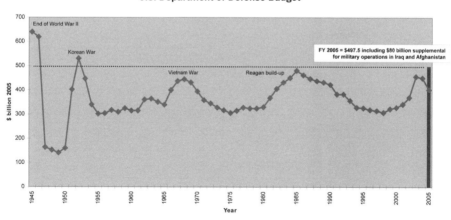

Source: Department of Defense, "National Defense Budget Estimates for FY 2005," Office of the Undersecretary of Defense (Comptroller), March 2004; Richard Wolf, "White House expected to seek $80B more for wars," *USA Today*, January 24, 2005, http://www.usatoday.com/news/world/iraq/2005-01-24-iraq-spending_x.htm?csp=34.

the world — despite the vastly altered strategic environment."[10] And Kosiak states, "Whether the requested increase in defense spending is necessary to meet U.S. security requirements adequately is unclear. . . . [I]t might be possible to meet U.S. security requirements adequately at lower budget levels by adopting a scaled-back and more transformation-oriented defense plan. In other words, the ability of the U.S. military to meet future challenges effectively is likely to have more to do with how wisely we spend our defense dollars, than on how much more we spend."[11] Ultimately, larger defense budgets are both unnecessary and unwise because they do not target the al Qaeda terrorist threat.

According to the Department of Defense, prior to Operation Iraqi Freedom the total number of U.S. active-duty military personnel was more than 1.4 million troops, of which 237,473 were deployed in foreign countries.[12] Assuming twice as many troops (deployed in the United States) are needed to rotate those deployments at specified intervals — i.e., a 3:1 ratio — then the cost to the United States of maintaining a global military presence is over 700,000 active-duty troops along with their associated force structure. But since the lack of a global military threat does not require the United States to maintain its current worldwide deployments, U.S. security against traditional nation-state military threats can be achieved at significantly lower costs.

Instead of a Cold War–era extended defense perimeter and forward deployed forces (intended to keep in check an expansionist Soviet Union), the very different twenty-first-century threat environment (in terms of traditional nation-state militaries that have the ability to attack the United States or challenge the U.S. military) affords the United States the opportunity to adopt a "balancer-of-last-resort" strategy. Such a strategy would place greater emphasis on allowing countries to build regional security arrangements, even in important areas such as Europe and East Asia. In his book *Putting "Defense" Back Into U.S. Defense Policy*, Ivan Eland argues that "the regional arrangements could include a regional security organization (such as any newly formed defense subset of the European Union), a great power policing its sphere of influence, or simply a balance of power among the larger nations of a region. Those regional arrangements would check aspiring hegemonic powers and thus keep power in the international system diffuse."[13] Instead of being a first responder to every crisis and conflict, the U.S. military would only intervene when truly vital U.S. security interests were at stake. That would allow U.S. forces to be mostly stationed in the United States, rather than forward deployed in other countries around the world. Such a posture might require prepositioning of supplies and equipment and negotiating access and base rights but would not require large numbers of troops to be stationed in foreign countries.

Historically, the U.S. military has maintained a significant overseas presence since the Korean War; this correlates strongly with the size of the defense budget, as shown in figure 4.4. In other words, a large percentage of U.S. defense spending can be attributed to overseas military deployments. However, if the United States adopted a balancer-of-last-resort strategy, virtually all U.S. foreign military deployments (except, for example, U.S. Marine Corps personnel assigned to embassies) and twice that many U.S.-based troops could be cut. Applying this rule of thumb to the various services would result in the following active-duty force size:

- U.S. Army: 189,000 (a 61 percent reduction)
- U.S. Navy: 266,600 (a 31 percent reduction)
- U.S. Marine Corps: 77,000 (a 56 percent reduction)
- U.S. Air Force: 168,000 (a 54 percent reduction)
- TOTAL: 699,000 (a 50 percent reduction)

Admittedly, this is a very top-level macro approach that assumes the current active-duty force mix is appropriate. But it is one reasonable analytic method to assess how U.S. forces and force structure could be reduced by adopting a balancer-of-last-resort strategy.[14]

The FY 2006 Department of Defense budget request was $419.9 billion,[15] which does not include funding for military operations in Iraq and Afghanistan. According to the Defense Department, the FY 2006 personnel budget for active-duty forces is $91.7 billion (out of a total of $108.9 billion for military personnel).[16] If forces were reduced as suggested above:

- the Army active-duty budget would be $11.1 billion and the total Army personnel budget would be $24.1 billion,
- the Navy active-duty budget would be $15.9 billion and the total Navy personnel budget would be $20.0 billion,
- the Marine Corps active-duty budget would be $4.0 billion and the total Marine Corps personnel budget would be $5.0 billion, and
- the Air Force active-duty budget would be $10.8 billion and the total Air Force personnel budget would be $17.1 billion.[17]

Figure 4.4
U.S. Defense Budget and Overseas Troop Deployment, 1945–2005

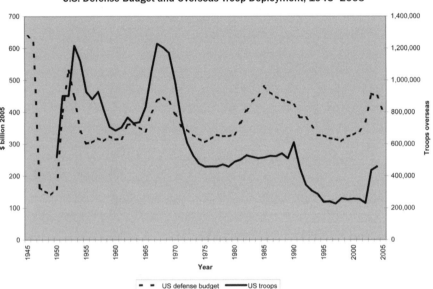

Overall, the total savings in the active-duty military personnel budget would be $42.1 billion and total military personnel spending would fall from $108.9 billion to $66.8 billion.[18]

If U.S. active-duty forces are substantially reduced, it logically follows that the associated force structure could be similarly reduced resulting in reduced operations and maintenance (O&M) costs. Using the same percentage reductions applied to active-duty forces, the O&M budget for:

- the active Army force could be reduced from $25.3 billion to $9.9 billion,
- the active Navy force could be reduced from $30.8 billion to $21.3 billion,
- the active Marine Corps force could be reduced from $3.8 billion to $1.7 billion, and
- the active Air Force could be reduced from $31.5 billion to $14.5 billion.[19]

The total savings would be $44.0 billion and the total spent on O&M would fall from $147.8 billion to $103.8 billion.

The combined savings in military personnel and O&M costs would total $86.1 billion or about 21 percent of the total defense budget. Military personnel and O&M are the two largest portions of the defense budget—26 percent and 35 percent, respectively—so significant reductions in defense spending can only be achieved if these costs are reduced. And the only way to reduce these costs is to downsize active-duty military forces.

Defense transformation is another reason U.S. military forces can be downsized. Technological advances act as force multipliers that allow U.S. forces to achieve equal or greater combat effectiveness with fewer troops. For example, both Operation Enduring Freedom and Operation Iraqi Freedom demonstrated that the U.S. military could engage and defeat on the battlefield the opposing military forces of adversaries using a significantly smaller force than was required in previous conflicts. Kenneth Adelman and Norman Augustine documented this phenomenon by calculating the manpower density on the battlefield and showing that fewer soldiers are needed to fight wars than in the past.[20] They attribute the trend of decreasing density to the increase in technology available to war fighters. Using Adelman and Augustine's methodology, Dr. J. Douglas Beason at the Los Alamos National Laboratory calculated that the battlefield density for U.S. military forces in Operation Iraqi Freedom was less than one soldier per square kilometer, as shown in figure 4.5.[21] So if fewer soldiers are needed to fight wars and U.S. security policy is to become involved only in conflicts and crises that are direct threats to core U.S. national security interests, a smaller military can be a capable and effective fighting force. And although it seems counterintuitive, even a smaller U.S. military would still be able to apply the Powell doctrine of "overwhelming force" because of the superiority achieved via advanced technology rather than sheer numbers.

Further savings could be realized by eliminating unneeded weapon systems; this would reduce both the procurement budget ($78.0 billion) and the research, development, test, and evaluation (RDT&E) budget ($69.4 billion). The Pentagon has already cancelled two major weapon systems: the Army's Crusader artillery piece and Comanche attack helicopter, with program savings of $9 billion and more than $30 billion, respectively.[22] But this is simply a good start. Other weapon systems that could be canceled include the F-22 Raptor, F/A-18E/F Super Hornet, V-22 Osprey, Virginia-class attack submarine, and DD(X) destroyer.

The Air Force's F-22 Raptor fighter/bomber was originally designed for air superiority missions against advanced, futuristic Soviet tactical fighters that were never built. The F-22 is intended to replace the best air superiority fighter in the world today, the F-15 Eagle ($55 million unit cost[23] versus

Figure 4.5
Manpower Density on the Battlefield

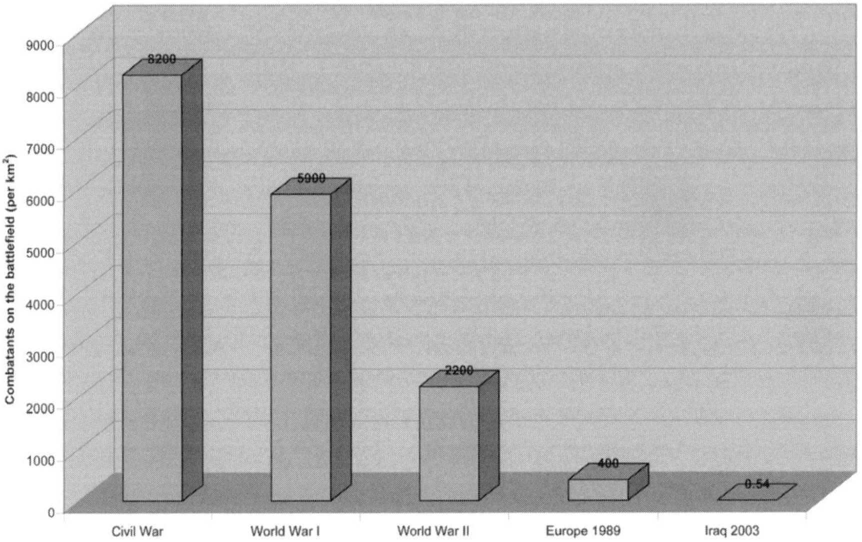

an estimated unit cost of $338 million for the F-22[24]). But the U.S. Air Force has not faced an adversary that can seriously challenge it for air superiority, as was shown when the U.S. Air Force flew virtually unopposed in the Gulf War in 1991, in the 1999 air war over Kosovo and Bosnia, enforcing the no-fly zones in northern and southern Iraq from 1991 to 2003, and in Operation Iraqi Freedom. Canceling the F-22 would save $4.3 billion in procurement and RDT&E in the FY 2006 budget.[25] The Air Force has already purchased 98 F-22s, but canceling the remaining 179 aircraft would save more than $20 billion in future program costs.[26]

Like the Air Force's F-22, the Navy's F/A-18E/F Super Hornet is another unneeded tactical aircraft: just as the Air Force's air-to-air threat environment is relatively benign, so is the Navy's. For example, according to the Office of Naval Intelligence, the F/A-18C/D Hornet is superior to China's Su-27.[27] Plus, the United States has other advantages over potential adversaries, including pilot training (according to IISS F-18 pilots average 372 flying hours compared to Chinese Su-27 pilots averaging 180 hours),[28] aircraft maintenance, and airborne fighter control.

In 1996 the General Accounting Office (GAO)[29] stated that "the F/A-18E/F would provide only a marginal improvement in capability of the older

F/A-18s at significantly greater cost."[30] According to the GAO, the unit cost for the F/A-18C/D Hornet was $28 million (in FY 1996 dollars) compared to $53 million for the Super Hornet and "the Navy could save almost $17 billion (fiscal year 1996 dollars) in recurring flyaway costs by buying 660 new F/A-18C/D model aircraft instead of 660 F/A-18E/F model aircraft."[31] These estimates now seem conservative because the current unit cost for the F/A-18E/F stands at $97 million per aircraft.[32]

The F/A-18E/F entered operational service in 1999. Boeing is currently delivering 222 Super Hornets under a five-year contract with the U.S. Navy. Boeing and the U.S. Navy signed a second multiyear contract in December 2003 (the contract runs from 2005 to 2009) for another 210 F/A-18E/Fs. The U.S. Navy plans to buy a minimum of 548 (and perhaps as many as 1,000) F/A-18E/Fs through 2010. Canceling the Super Hornet would save $2.9 billion in procurement and RDT&E in the FY 2006 budget alone.[33] If the second Boeing contract is terminated and no further Super Hornets are purchased, $20 billion in future program costs would be saved.

The V-22 Osprey is a tilt-rotor aircraft that takes off and lands vertically like a helicopter but flies like an airplane by tilting its wing-mounted rotors to become propellers. When the V-22 program entered full-scale development in 1986, the armed forces planned to build 923 aircraft, with an average unit cost of $24 million.[34] The current program plan calls for building 458 Ospreys at a total cost of $50.5 billion, or $110 million each.[35] In other words, the military will end up with fewer than half the aircraft at more than four times the original unit cost. Canceling the V-22 would save $1.8 billion in procurement and RDT&E costs in the FY 2006 defense budget[36] and more than $40 billion in future program costs.[37]

If carrying a payload at maximum speed to maximum range is the only or most critical mission, then the V-22 would seem to be a more capable choice than helicopters. But the need to be able to project power from long-range or far inland is more of a convenient justification for the V-22 than a real operational requirement. Most Marine Corps ship-to-shore operations occur at distances far shorter than the maximum range of the V-22. And long-range inland operations would still require support from slower helicopters because the V-22 cannot carry enough heavy equipment or large amounts of supplies to support the troops it would be transporting.

Instead of spending $50 billion of the V-22, equivalent lift capacity could be procured for significantly less by increasing the number of MH-60S (a Navy variant of the Army Blackhawk helicopter). Other helicopter alternatives include the Sikorsky S-92, a civilian helicopter that can be adapted for military use, or the AgustaWestland EH-101, a medium-lift helicopter in service for a number of different countries, as shown in table 4.1.

During the Cold War, U.S. submarines were developed to counter two threats: a land war in Europe and Soviet nuclear ballistic missile submarines (SSBNs) that could attack the United States with nuclear weapons. The United States feared that technologically advanced Soviet attack submarines could attack U.S. warships and convoys supporting a European war or could mount an offensive nuclear strike. Accordingly, the United States built quiet, nuclear-powered attack submarines that could hunt the Soviet submarines in the event of either scenario. But with the demise of the Soviet Union and with closer relations with Russia, the United States no longer needs the ability to perform these missions, and this obviates the need for the Virginia-class submarine.[38] And even if China is seen as a potential future threat, it only has one deployed SSBN and five Han-class nuclear attack submarines (compared to the U.S. Navy's fifty-four nuclear attack submarines).[39]

Nonetheless, the Navy is currently planning to buy thirty Virginia-class submarines costing a total of $94 billion (about $3.1 billion each).[40] Canceling the Virginia-class submarine program would save $2.6 billion in procurement and RDT&E costs in the FY 2006 budget.[41] Five submarines are already under contract so terminating the program would save approximately $77 billion in future costs.

The U.S. Navy currently has forty-four DDG-51 Arleigh Burke–class Aegis destroyers and twenty-six CG-47 Ticonderoga-class Aegis cruisers in the fleet. With 91 and 122 vertical launch system (VLS) cells each, respectively, these ships provide ample capacity (over 7,000 VLS launch cells) to dedicate a substantial portion to the land-attack mission. Thus, the U.S. Navy will have formidable land-attack capabilities that obviate the need for the new DD(X) destroyer, which is designed for major wars and, according to the Congressional Budget Office, "would be an exceptionally large and expensive ship to use for those [terrorism, drug smuggling, violations of economic sanctions, illegal immigration, and arms trafficking] missions."[42] Forgoing the DD(X) would save $1.8 billion in procurement and RDT&E costs in the FY

Table 4.1

Comparison of the V-22 to Helicopters

	Number (USMC	Unit cost ($ million)	Max speed (knots)	Range (nautical mi)	Payload (pounds)
V-22 Osprey (projected)	458	$104.9	275	515	10,000

Is proposed replacement for these helicopters no longer in production:

	Number	Unit cost	Max speed	Range	Payload
CH-46 Sea Knight	239		180	132	5,000
CH-53 Super Stallion	155		160	578	8,000

Helicopters in production as alternatives to the V-22:

	Number	Unit cost	Max speed	Range	Payload
CH/MH-60S Knighthawk		$25.2	145	380	4,000
S/H-92 Superhawk*		$16.0	151	475	10,000
EH-101**		$25.0	150	750	10,000

For the V-22 total program cost ($48 billion) which provides a total lift capacity of 4.6 million pounds, the number of helicopters that could be procured:

CH/MH-60S Knighthawk	1,906	= total lift capacity of 7.6 million pounds
S/H-92 Superhawk	3,002	= total lift capacity of 30 million pounds
EH-101	1921	= total lift capacity of 19 million pounds

Number of helicopters required to equal V-22 program total lift capacity of 4.6 million pounds:

CH/MH-60S Knighthawk	1,150	= $29 billion total program cost
S/H-92 Superhawk	460	= $7.4 billion total program cost
EH-101	460	= $11.5 billion total program cost

* S/H-92 is a Sikorsky helicopter not built under military contract, but it is designed to be used by the military as an off-the-shelf acquisition alternative. $16.0 million unit cost is based on a civilian helicopter; a military version might cost several million more.

** EH-101 is a military utility medium lift helicopter built by AgustaWestland that has a variety of configurations for different missions and in service with many countries. $25.0 million unit cost is based on a procurement of several hundred helicopters.

Source: Charles V. Peña, "$400 Billion Defense Budget Unnecessary to Fight War on Terrorism," Cato Institute Policy Analysis No. 539, March 28, 2005, 11.

2006 Defense Department budget. And if the Navy cancelled all three of its new surface ships — the DD(X) destroyer, CG(X) cruiser, and littoral combat ship — the total savings would be $30 billion, $70 billion, and $20 billion, respectively, or $120 billion in future procurement costs.[43]

Canceling the F-22 Raptor, F/A-18E/F Super Hornet, V-22 Osprey, Virginia-class attack submarine, and DD(X) destroyer would save a total of $13.4 billion in procurement and RDT&E costs in the FY 2006 budget (and probably more than $200 billion in future program costs). Combined with the military personnel and O&M savings previously discussed, the total savings would be $99.5 billion and a revised FY 2006 defense budget would be $320.4 billion, a 24 percent reduction, as shown in figure 4.6. Of course, it is not realistic that the defense budget could be reduced immediately. But the budget could be reduced in increments to this proposed level over a period of five years.

Further reductions could be realized by analyzing the utility of other weapon systems in today's security environment. For example, the Defense Department could:

- reduce the number of C-17 transport aircraft. Although a balancer-of-last-resort strategy would require airlift capacity to respond to a crisis

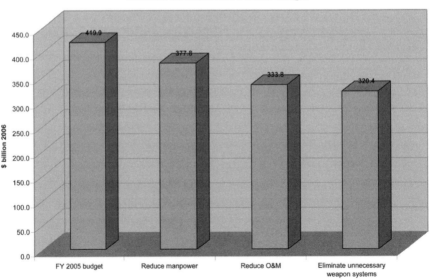

Figure 4.6
Balancer-of-Last-Resort Defense Budget

if necessary, the total number of aircraft would be less than needed to support in the current U.S. interventionist foreign policy.

- retire B-1 bombers, originally designed to evade Soviet air defenses. The B-2 is a more capable strategic nuclear bomber and the venerable B-52 is a more efficient — i.e., it has a greater payload — long-range precision weapons delivery platform.

- downsize the Trident ballistic missile submarine fleet as part of reducing the strategic nuclear arsenal per the Strategic Offensive Reductions Treaty agreement with Russia.

- cancel new aircraft carriers. A balancer-of-last-resort strategy would also allow for reducing the number of deployed carrier battle groups from the current fleet size of twelve groups.[44]

- scale back the missile defense program. A balancer-of-last-resort strategy would require theater missile defense systems that can be deployed with forces to respond to crises but would not require permanently deployed systems in foreign countries. A limited national missile defense system to protect the United States (largely as an insurance policy against small attacks or accidental/unauthorized launches) would also be appropriate for a balancer-of-last-resort strategy. But any missile defense systems must be thoroughly and realistically tested (as should be the case for any weapon system) before a procurement and deployment decision is made.

This top-down, macro-level analysis should be viewed as just one way to show how the defense budget could be reduced and the projected savings if the United States adopted a balancer-of-last-resort strategy. A bottom-up approach based on sizing the force against specific military threats and war-fighting requirements might yield a different result. Eland performed such an analysis using the requirement for the U.S. military to fight a single major theater war, which is still a relevant and realistic military requirement in the post-9/11 threat environment.[45] This requirements-based analysis used Defense Department planning guidelines for forces needed to fight a major regional war to develop a force structure comprised of:

- 5 active Army divisions
- 30 National Guard combat brigades
- 5 active Air Force wings
- 9 reserve Air Force wings
- 187 heavy bombers

- 200 total Navy ships
- 4 active aircraft carriers and air wings
- 2 reserve aircraft carriers and air wings
- 25 attack submarines
- 1 active Marine Corps division
- 1 reserve Marine Corps division[46]

The cost of this force structure was $183.9 billion (in 2002 dollars),[47] 40 percent less than the FY 2001 defense budget of $303 billion (in 2002 dollars). If a 40 percent reduction factor is applied to the FY 2006 defense budget, the resulting savings would be $167.7 billion and the defense budget would only be $252.2 billion. If Eland's proposed force structure and resulting defense budget is adjusted from 2002 dollars to 2006 dollars, then the FY 2006 defense budget would be $204.3 billion.[48] Thus, a balancer-of-last-resort strategy requires a smaller, not a larger, defense budget—perhaps as small as $204.3 billion but certainly no larger than $320.4 billion. In other words, U.S. security could still be maintained spending one-quarter to one-half less than the current budget.

The defense budget can be reduced because the nation-state threat environment is markedly different than it was during the Cold War and also because a larger military is not necessary to combat the terrorist threat. It is important to remember that the large U.S. military with its forward-deployed global presence was not an effective defense against nineteen hijackers. And the shorthand phrase "war on terrorism" is misleading because the term "war" implies the use of military force as the primary instrument of policy for waging the fight against terrorism. But traditional military operations should be the exception rather than the rule in the conflict with al Qaeda. Al Qaeda is not an army that wears uniforms and operates in a specific geographic region. Rather, it is a loosely connected and decentralized network with cells and operatives in sixty or more countries around the world. As such, the arduous task of dismantling and degrading the network will largely be the task of unprecedented international intelligence and law enforcement cooperation—not of large-scale military force. The military's involvement in the war on terrorism will be more in the form of Special Forces in discrete operations against specific targets rather than large-scale military operations.

Instead of spending hundreds of billions of dollars to maintain the current size of the armed forces and on weapons such as the F-22, F/A-18E/

F, V-22, Virginia-class submarines, and DD(X) destroyers, the United States could better serve the war on terrorism by investing in better intelligence gathering, unmanned aerial vehicles (UAVs), special operations forces (SOF), and language skills.

Better intelligence gathering about the terrorist threat will be the foundation of the fight.[49] Because the al Qaeda terrorist threat is diffuse and decentralized, intelligence is critical to knowing who comprises the threat, analyzing disparate pieces of information to understand the nature of the threat, anticipating the terrorists' next steps, and thwarting their plans. So spending on intelligence is an area that deserves greater attention. But according to the 9/11 Commission, "Even the most basic information about how much money is actually allocated to or within the intelligence community and most of its key components is shrouded from public view."[50]

Although the budgets for the fifteen agencies with intelligence gathering and analysis responsibilities[51] are veiled in secrecy, the best estimate is that the total spent on intelligence is about $40 billion.[52] As with the defense budget, it is not necessarily a question of spending more money on intelligence gathering and analysis, but of best allocating spending and resources. For example, about 85 percent of the estimated $40 billion spent on intelligence activities goes to the Defense Department, only about 10 percent is for the CIA, and the remainder is spread among the other intelligence agencies. If the war on terrorism is not primarily a military war, perhaps the intelligence budget could be reallocated between the Defense Department and other intelligence agencies—with less emphasis on nation-state military threats, since the conventional military threat environment is less severe than during the Cold War, and more emphasis on terrorist threats to the United States.

Regardless of whether $40 billion is the right amount of intelligence spending and how that money is allocated, the war on terrorism requires:

- less emphasis on spy satellites as a primary means of intelligence gathering. This does not mean the United States should abandon the use of satellite imagery. Rather, it means recognizing that while spy satellite images may have been an excellent way to monitor stationary targets, such as missile silos, or easily recognizable military equipment, such as tanks and aircraft, they may not be as capable at locating and tracking individual terrorists.
- recognition of the problems involved with electronic eavesdropping.

According to Loren Thompson at the Lexington Institute, "the enemy has learned how to hide a lot of its transmissions from electronic eavesdropping satellites."[53] The problem of finding and successfully monitoring the right conversations is further compounded by the inability to sift through the sheer volume of terrorist chatter to determine what bits of information are useful.

- greater emphasis on human intelligence gathering. Spies on the ground are needed to supplement—and sometimes confirm or refute—what satellite images, electronic eavesdropping, interrogations of captured al Qaeda operatives, hard drives on confiscated computers, and other sources are indicating about the terrorist threat. Analysis and interpretation needs to be backed up with as much "inside information" as possible. This is perhaps the most critical missing piece in the intelligence puzzle in terms of anticipating future terrorist attacks. Ideally, the United States needs a "mole" inside al Qaeda, but it will be a difficult task (and likely take many years) to place someone inside al Qaeda who is a believable radical Islamic extremist and will be trusted with the kind of information U.S. intelligence needs. The task is made even more difficult because of the distributed and cellular structure of al Qaeda and the expansion of the radical Islamic ideology that fuels the terrorist threat to America beyond the formal al Qaeda structure that existed in September 2001 into a larger, more loosely knit movement in Muslim world.

In a strange twist, the United States actually has a model for penetrating al Qaeda: John Walker Lindh. Born in Washington, D.C., and raised in affluent Marin County, California, Lindh was the "American Taliban" captured by U.S. soldiers in Afghanistan in November 2001. As shocking as it is that an American would be a soldier for the Taliban regime fighting against U.S. forces, even more remarkable is that someone like Lindh—white and middle class—would be taken in and trusted by radical Islamists. In 1997 the sixteen-year-old Lindh converted to Islam. A year later he traveled to Yemen for nine months. After returning home to California, Lindh went back to Yemen and then to Pakistan in 2000. There he enrolled in a madrassa and became interested in the Muslim fight in Kashmir. Lindh first joined the Harakat-ul Mujahideen-Al Almi—a militant Islamic group that operates in Kashmir—but then decided he wanted to join the Taliban because he thought the regime was "the only government that actually provides Islamic law."[54] But because he was not a native of Afghanistan and did not speak the local languages, Lindh was directed to the "Afghan Arabs" or al Qaeda. Beginning in June 2001, Lindh spent seven weeks at an al Qaeda training camp near Kandahar and even met with Osama bin Laden. So if someone described as a "sweet kid" from a "Birkenstock family" of Irish Catholic descent living in a community sometimes lampooned as a "hot tub haven" can join the ranks of al Qaeda, certainly America's intelligence agencies can also find a way.

As important as better human intelligence is, technology also has its proper place. For example, the potential utility of UAVs—remotely controlled airplanes—for the war on terrorism has been demonstrated in Afghanistan and Yemen. During Operation Enduring Freedom in Afghanistan, UAVs moved beyond playing a supporting role for combat aircraft (in the Balkans in the mid-1990s and then Iraq, UAVs provided aerial surveillance and later designated targets for laser-guided bombs) and became offensive weapons when armed with Hellfire missiles (a dozen UAVs launched a total of 115 missiles in Afghanistan).[55] In February 2002 a Predator UAV (armed with Hellfire missiles and operated by the CIA) in the Tora Bora region of eastern Afghanistan attacked a convoy and killed several people, including a suspected al Qaeda leader.[56] In November 2002 a Predator UAV in Yemen destroyed a car containing six al Qaeda suspects, including Abu Ali al-Harithi who was one of the suspected planners of the USS *Cole* attack in October 2000.[57]

If parts of the war on terrorism are to be fought in places such as Yemen, Sudan, Somalia, and Pakistan—especially if it is not possible for U.S. ground troops to operate in those countries—UAVs could be key assets for finding and targeting al Qaeda operatives because of their ability to cover large swaths of land for extended periods of time in search of targets. For example, a Predator UAV has a combat radius of four hundred nautical miles and can carry a maximum payload of 450 pounds for more than twenty-four hours. According to the Defense Department, "due to its vantage point, one unmanned sentry equipped with automated cuing algorithms and multiple sensors could survey the same area as ten (or more) human sentries."[58]

Armed UAVs offer a cost-effective alternative to deploying troops on the ground or having to call in manned aircraft to perform combat missions against identified terrorist targets. According to Dyke Weatherington, deputy of the UAV Planning Task Force in the Office of the Secretary of Defense, without armed UAVs "we either couldn't get strikes to the target in time or the manned aircraft couldn't find that target the UAV had found."[59] One can only wonder what might have happened if the spy Predator that took pictures of a tall man in white robes surrounded by a group of people—believed by many intelligence analysts to be Osama bin Laden—in the fall of 2000 had instead been an armed Predator capable of immediately striking the target. According to retired Gen. Wayne Downing, "We were not prepared to take the military action necessary. . . . We should have had strike forces prepared to go in and react to this intelligence, certainly cruise missiles."[60]

In addition to their utility, UAVs are particularly attractive because of their relatively low cost—especially when compared to manned aircraft. Developmental costs for UAVs are actually about the same as for a similar manned aircraft because "the engineering required to get to first flight is driven more by aerodynamics (i.e., flight control software development) and propulsion than by human factors and avionics."[61] But procurement costs for UAVs are substantially less than for manned aircraft. For example, in FY 2004 fifteen Predator UAVs were purchased for $215.7 million ($14.4 million each); in FY 2005 twelve Predators were purchased for $205.3 million ($17.1 million each); and the FY 2006 budget is for nine Predators to be purchased for $155.9 million ($17.3 million each)[62]—or an average unit cost of $16 million over three years (the increases in unit cost reflect arming more Predators with Hellfire missiles). Operations and maintenance costs for UAVs are also likely to be less than for manned aircraft. According to the Defense Department:

> The UCAV [unmanned combat aerial vehicle] weapon system performance is to be much greater and have a significantly reduced total life cycle cost. The UCAV is to have a design life [flying time] of 4,000 hours, half of which could be spent in combat operations under a form of build, store, fly CONOPS [concept of operations]. Today's SEAD [suppression of enemy air defenses]/Strike platform will spend 95 percent of its 8,000 hour inflight life conducting training sorties, accumulating some 400 hours supporting combat operations before retirement. The depreciation rate, in terms of dol-

lars per combat hour flown, of the UCAV is significantly less than that of current platforms, implying that UCAVs could suffer greater combat loss rates and still be cost effective by the standards applied to today's manned fighters.[63]

So the $10 billion in planned spending on UAVs in the next decade (compared to just $3 billion in the 1990s) is a smart investment in the war on terrorism. And even doubling the budget to $20 billion over the next ten years would make sense and would represent less than 1 percent of the annual defense budget based on a balancer-of-last-resort strategy. The bottom line is that UAVs are a very low cost weapon that could yield an extremely high payoff in the war on terrorism.[64]

But if, as President Bush has put it, "we'll have to hunt them down one at a time,"[65] we cannot rely solely on UAVs to track and find al Qaeda terrorists. U.S. SOF—units such as Navy SEALS (Sea-Air-Land) and Army Green Berets, Rangers, and Delta Force—are ideally suited for this kind of mission. Indeed, counterterrorism is the number one mission of SOF, which are "specifically organized, trained, and equipped to conduct covert, clandestine, or discreet CT [counterterrorism] missions in hostile, denied, or politically sensitive environments," including "intelligence operations, attacks against terrorist networks and infrastructures, hostage rescue, [and] recovery of sensitive material from terrorist organizations."[66]

Secretary of Defense Donald Rumsfeld has been a strong advocate of using SOF against terrorist targets. In August 2002 he issued a classified memo to U.S. Special Operations Command (SOCOM) to capture or kill Osama bin Laden and other al Qaeda leadership.[67] Rumsfeld has also proposed sending SOF into Somalia and Lebanon's Bekaa Valley because these lawless areas are thought to be places where terrorists can hide (or are thought to be hiding) and be safe from U.S. intervention.

Like UAVs, SOF is relatively inexpensive. The FY 2005 budget for SOCOM was $6.5 billion[68] or only about 1.6 percent of the total defense budget. Surprisingly—even though SOF are critical for success in the war on terrorism—the proposed FY 2006 budget request for SOF is less: $4.1 billion,[69] or just 1 percent of the total defense budget. Instead of spending less money, the budget for special operations forces could be significantly increased without adversely affecting the overall defense budget. The current size of U.S. SOF units is about thirty-four thousand active-duty and fifteen thousand reserve personnel in the Army, Navy, Marine Corps, and Air Force—or about 2 percent of all U.S. active and reserve forces.[70] Given the importance and unique capabilities of SOF relative to the regular military in the war on terrorism, it would make sense to increase the size and funding for Special Forces—perhaps doubling the force size.

In the timeless treatise of strategic thinking, *The Art of War*, Chinese military theorist Sun Tzu stressed the importance of knowing the enemy:

> Knowing the other and knowing oneself,
> In one hundred battles no danger.
> Not knowing the other and knowing oneself,
> One victory for one loss.
> Not knowing the other and not knowing oneself,
> In every battle certain defeat.[71]

To truly know the enemy, the United States must train a cadre of experts to teach and analyze the relevant languages of the Muslim world—Arabic, Pashtu, Urdu, Farsi, Dari, and Malay, to name a few. But according to a GAO report, in FY 2001 only half of the Army's eighty-four positions for Arabic translators and interpreters were filled and twenty-seven positions (out of a total of forty) for Farsi were unfilled.[72] Undersecretary of Defense for Personnel and Readiness David Chu admitted that the Defense Department is having a "very difficult time . . . training and keeping on active duty sufficient numbers of linguists."[73] As of March 2004 FBI director Robert Mueller reported that the bureau had only twenty-four Arabic-speaking agents (out of more than twelve thousand special agents).[74] At the State Department only five linguists are fluent enough to speak on Arab television (out of nine thousand foreign service and sixty-five hundred civil service employees).[75] Even if progress has been made to fill these shortfalls, clearly we are starting with a large deficit.

According to the GAO, the Pentagon estimates that it currently spends up to $250 million per year to meet its foreign language needs.[76] The GAO did not indicate whether the $250 million (about six-hundredths of 1 percent of the FY 2005 defense budget) was adequate. Whether the Defense Department (as well as other government agencies such as the CIA and FBI) is spending enough, this much is certain: language skills for the war on terrorism are in short supply. One result is that "FBI shortages of linguists have resulted in thousands of hours of audiotapes and pages of written material not being reviewed or translated in a timely manner."[77] Increasing that supply will not be easily or quickly done.

The Defense Language Institute (DLI) in Monterey, California, is the largest language school in the world and provides 85 percent of the language training for the federal government. In 2001 DLI graduated 2,083 students in basic language training in twenty languages. Such training lasts from twenty-five to sixty-three weeks depending on the difficulty of the language. Two of the four most difficult languages for Americans to learn are Arabic and Farsi. Thus, the lead time to teach native English speakers even the basics is relatively long.

Finding instructors and creating language courses are also challenges. According to DLI Chancellor Ray Clifford, "The faculty we need to find are not being produced for us by U.S. colleges and universities." And if instructors can be found, they often have to develop coursework from scratch. According to Neil Granoien, a former Russian instructor and dean of DLI's Korean school, "People have been writing Spanish grammar for a couple hundred years, French even longer. If you take a language like Uzbek, there's much work to be done, or [Pashto], for example, where there's very little work that's been done, and most of that was done in Victoria's [Queen Victoria in the nineteenth century] reign."[78]

The military's own policies may hinder its ability to train qualified linguists. For example, over a two-year period thirty-seven linguists from DLI were discharged for being gay under the military's "don't ask, don't tell" policy. One was Cathleen Glover who had mastered Arabic but could no longer cope with leading a double life and voluntarily admitted to her homosexuality. Another was Alastair Gamble—also an Arabic linguist—who was caught with his boyfriend in a surprise barracks inspection.[79] The point here is not whether the "don't ask, don't tell" policy is right or wrong (or whether the military should lift its ban on allowing homosexuals to serve), but simply to show how it has affected—and could continue to affect—the military's ability to fill the need for Arabic and other language speakers for the war on terrorism.

Almost every war sees the emergence of a weapon that is considered decisive or revolutionary. The English longbow — with its ability to kill in great numbers at long range — gave England's armies the edge in medieval wars on the continent for nearly three centuries, but advances in protective armor plating and the development of gunpowder eventually ended the longbow's effectiveness on the battlefield. The capital ships of the Royal Navy were crucial to maintaining the British Empire during the nineteenth century. During World War I, the tank restored maneuver to a battlefield brought to a stalemate by trench warfare. World War II saw the emergence of the importance of airpower with the Japanese surprise attack of Pearl Harbor, the Battle of Britain, and the D-Day invasion. The Gulf War introduced precision-guided weapons that could destroy hardened and buried targets with minimal collateral damage.

The war on terrorism will be no different. Perhaps UAVs — with their ability to locate and destroy targets remotely without putting a pilot at risk — will be the revolutionary weapon of the war on terrorism. But more important is knowing that what is truly revolutionary about the war on terrorism is that, although the military will be part of the war, it is not a war that ultimately will be won by the military.

5

YIN AND YANG OF AL QAEDA

Evidence obtained under different experimental conditions cannot be comprehended within a single picture, but must be regarded as complementary in the sense that only the totality of the phenomena exhausts the possible information about the objects.

—Niels Bohr, Nobel Prize–winning physicist

American and Western thinking tends to be binary: on or off, black or white, good or bad, and us or them. Indeed, this binary view of the world is exactly how President Bush characterized the war on terrorism in his speech to Congress and the American people after the 9/11 attacks: "Every nation, in every region, now has a decision to make. Either you are with us, or you are with the terrorists."[1] Addressing the cattle industry convention in February 2002, he said, "You've probably figured it out by now that I don't see many shades of gray in the war on terror. Either you're with us, or you're against us."[2]

Another example of how binary thinking colors our world view is President Bush's frequent use of the term "evil"—clearly meant as the antithesis to "good," dividing the world into only two parts—to describe the terrorist threat. The day after the 9/11 attacks Bush said, "This will be a monumental struggle of good versus evil."[3] In his commencement address to the cadets at West Point in June 2002, the president said, "We are in a conflict between good and evil, and America will call evil by its name."[4] Although his January 2003 State of the Union address was largely about Iraq, President Bush did say that America was "leading the world in confronting and defeating the man-made evil of international terrorism."[5] And on the third anniversary of 9/11, Bush referred to the terrorist attacks as "the struggle of good against evil . . . compressed into a single morning."[6]

By defining it as "evil," President Bush can easily expand the terrorist threat to America to include all terrorism, not just al Qaeda. For example, when the Imam Ali mosque in Najaf, Iraq, was bombed in August 2003, Ambassador Paul Bremer remarked that those responsible for the bombing had "shown the evil face of terrorism."[7] And after the Breslan, Russia, school shooting in September 2004, President Bush said, "I'm here to express my country's heart-felt sympathies for the victims and the families who suffered at the hands of the evil terrorists. The United States stands side-by-side with Russia as we fight off terrorism."[8]

But evil is not really a description of the threat to America and does not provide any useful understanding of the enemy. According to the 9/11 Commission, "the enemy is not just 'terrorism,' some generic evil. This vagueness blurs the strategy. The catastrophic threat at this moment in history is more specific. It is the threat posed by Islamist terrorism—especially the al Qaeda network, its affiliates, and its ideology."[9] The threat consists of two interrelated parts: "al Qaeda, a stateless network of terrorists that struck us on 9/11; and a radical ideological movement in the Islamic world, inspired in part by al Qaeda, which has spawned terrorist groups and violence across the globe."[10]

Knowing the twofold nature of the threat, a binary either-or construct is not an appropriate approach. Instead, the Chinese philosophy concepts of "yin" and "yang" as complementary opposites are more useful. "Yin" and "yang" originally referred to the dark and sunlit sides of a mountain, respectively, but in Taoism, they have come to mean opposites that express a pervasive unity. For example, there is no day without night, and vice versa. Therefore, yin and yang are not separate but are two parts that combine to make a unified whole.

This duality also underlies modern quantum physics.[11] According to classical Newtonian physics, light is composed of tiny particles and its behavior can be predicted via Newton's deterministic laws of motion. But in 1803 Thomas Young proved that light behaved as a wave with his now famous double-slit experiment.[12] Young thought he had definitively proved that light was a wave, not a particle. Instead, he was opening the door to what eventually became known as the wave-particle duality of light. The theory of duality holds that although waves and particles are mutually ex-clusive, both concepts are necessary to understanding light. Ultimately, we observe light either as a wave or a particle, but we must understand light as both a wave and a particle. According to Gary Zukav, who in the 1970s made the connection between physics and eastern philosophy in *The Danc-ing Wu Li Masters*:

> The wave-particle duality was (is) one of the thorniest problems in quantum mechanics. Physicists like to have tidy theories which explain everything, and if they are not able to do that, they like to have tidy theories about why they can't. The wave-particle duality is not a tidy situation. . . .
>
> For most of us, life is seldom black and white. The wave-particle duality marked the end of the "Either-Or" way of looking at the world.[13]

Al Qaeda is like wave-particle duality in quantum mechanics. It is not tidy and simple. Therefore, we must avoid using overly simple either-or explanations—however convenient or easy to understand they may be. Like physics in the first half of the twentieth century, we must make a quantum leap to a new paradigm and a more complete understanding. And first we must be able to view the world through a different lens and use the duality concept of yin and yang as an analytic metaphor to understand al Qaeda.

If yin and yang are two inseparable halves that comprise the whole, then the yin and yang of al Qaeda are structure and ideology. As something physical, the organizational structure of al Qaeda is probably best associ-ated with the concept of yang. Thus, yin is the metaphysical aspect of al Qaeda: its ideology. More important than determining which is yin and which is yang, however, is knowing that both parts are essential to understanding al Qaeda.

The Western bias was all too apparent when President Bush said, "Al Qaeda is to terror what the mafia is to crime,"[14] implying that al Qaeda is an organization with a centralized hierarchy, wholly dependent on the leader-ship for its existence and operation. Therefore, if the leadership is destroyed, then the organization can be collapsed, and progress can be measured by keeping score of the capture or killing of al Qaeda's leadership. According to terrorism analyst Peter Bergen, "President Bush reportedly keeps a scorecard in his desk of the top twenty or so terrorists, putting an X through each one when they are captured or killed."[15] In September 2003 President Bush claimed that the United States had made great progress in the war on terrorism, citing that "nearly two-thirds of al Qaeda's known leaders have been captured or killed."[16] And in his 2005 State of the Union address, he said, "The al Qaeda terror network that attacked our country still has leaders — but many of its top commanders have been removed."[17] But, as Bergen points out, "al Qaeda is not like the Gambino crime family where if you eliminate the various capos and lieutenants of the organization it eventually goes out of business."[18]

Certainly, al Qaeda has a leadership hierarchy, and it is important to capture or kill those key leaders. At the top is Osama bin Laden. His most trusted lieutenant is Ayman al-Zawahiri, an Egyptian doctor who is the architect of al Qaeda's ideology and who has been indicted in the United States for his role in the U.S. embassy bombings in Africa in 1998. Al-Zawahiri was previously a key figure in the Egyptian Islamic Jihad group that merged with al Qaeda. Some other key al Qaeda leadership presumed to be still at large include:

- Saif al-Adel, an Egyptian and bin Laden's security chief. He was a colonel in the Egyptian army and is believed to have assumed many of the responsibilities previously held by Mohammed Atef, who was killed by U.S. forces in Afghanistan. Al-Adel is linked to U.S. embassy bombings in Africa.
- Sheikh Said, an Egyptian and al Qaeda's financial controller. He is also bin Laden's brother-in-law.
- Abu Mohammed al-Masri, an Egyptian also known as Abdullah Ahmed Abdullah, who ran al Qaeda training camps in Afghanistan. He is believed to have been involved in the U.S. embassy bombings in Africa.
- Sulaiman Abu Ghaith, a Kuwaiti and nominal al Qaeda spokesman.
- Thirwat Salah Shirhata, an Egyptian who was al-Zawahiri's deputy in the Egyptian Islamic Jihad group[19]

To be sure, we are making progress against al Qaeda. Hundreds of operatives in nearly one hundred countries have been arrested. Some key al Qaeda members who have been captured or killed include:

- Mohammed Atef, believed to have been al Qaeda's military commander, was reportedly killed by a U.S. bombing raid in Afghanistan in November 2001.

- Khalid Sheikh Mohammed, a Kuwaiti who is considered the mastermind of the 9/11 attacks, was captured in Pakistan in March 2003.
- Abu Zubaydah, thought to have been bin Laden's field commander, was captured in Pakistan in March 2002.
- Ramzi Binalshibh, a Yemeni national who was a key member of the Hamburg cell (the core group that carried out the 9/11 attacks), was captured in Pakistan in September 2002.
- Mohammed Haydar Zammar, a Syrian who was living in Germany and a member of the Hamburg cell, was arrested in Morocco after he left Germany in the wake of the 9/11 attacks.
- Mohamedou Ould Slahi, a Mauritian who was living in Germany and a member of the Hamburg cell, was handed over to the United States by the government of Mauritia after 9/11.
- Abu Faraj al-Libbi, a Libyan who is blamed for masterminding two assassination attempts against Pakistan's Pervez Musharraf and may have been al Qaeda's third.[20]

But if al Qaeda is not a centralized top-down hierarchical organization (as depicted in figure 5.1), then simply taking out the leadership will not be enough to destroy it or even degrade it so that it is less effective and unable to attack the United States. The now famous "most wanted" deck of cards approach used in Iraq may work for regime change against rogue states,[21] but it would be a mistake to assume that it will yield the same results against al Qaeda. In fact, we already know that as elements of al Qaeda's leadership have either been captured or killed, new leaders have emerged. For example, in the fall of 2002 it was reported that with the main al Qaeda leadership (e.g., bin Laden, al-Zawahiri) either in hiding or on the run, new leaders were filling the void to run the network. This is evidence that al Qaeda can rapidly adapt to changing circumstances and regenerate its leadership to respond to those changes. So while dismantling al Qaeda's leadership is a necessary action, it will not be sufficient. According to one U.S. intelligence official, "The strength of the group is they don't need centralized command and control."[22] And without a single target (either an individual or part of the organization) within al Qaeda, according to a senior U.S. official, "Now, instead of a large, fixed target we have little moving targets all over the world, all armed and all dangerous. It is a much more difficult war to fight this way."[23]

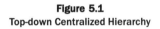

Figure 5.1
Top-down Centralized Hierarchy

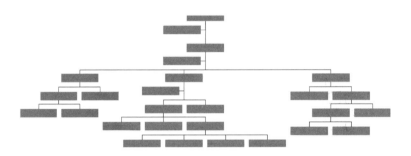

Instead of a centralized hierarchy, al Qaeda is both a decentralized and distributed organization that can be better understood as a network. "Decentralized" means complete reliance on a single node (such as al Qaeda's leadership) is not always required for the network to function. Figure 5.2 shows a centralized "star" network in which all the nodes are connected to a single central node. Clearly, if the central node, e.g., the al Qaeda leadership, is destroyed, then the remaining nodes are disconnected and the network is rendered inoperable.

In a decentralized network (shown in figure 5.3), instead of a single leadership node, there may be several different nodes, each with an ability to lead and direct the organization. As such, even if the main leadership is destroyed, the other leadership nodes can continue to operate independently because the cells connected to them are not dependent on the main leadership to function. But while a decentralized network is more robust than a centralized one, it can still be destroyed (or severely degraded) if enough of the individual leadership nodes are eliminated such that the cells of the organization are not effectively connected.

Communications engineers recognized this vulnerability in the early- and mid-1960s,[24] and they thus developed distributed networks, which are grids or mesh patterns with redundant connection paths (see figure 5.4). Depending on how redundant the network is (i.e., how many different paths

Figure 5.2
Centralized Network

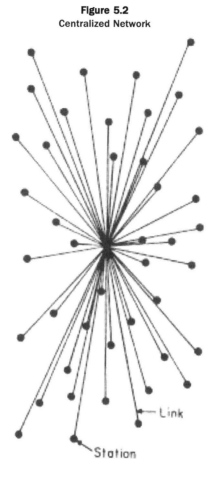

Source: Paul Baran, "On Distributed Communications," Rand
Memorandum RM-3420-PR, August 1964, Santa Monica, CA:
RAND Corporation. Reprinted with permission.

create a connected and functioning network), the more difficult it is to destroy. Thus, even if a significant number of nodes in the network are destroyed, the network can continue to function as long as the nodes can find a path between those that need to be connected.

In fact, a distributed network can theoretically be designed so that all of its nodes have to be destroyed in order to destroy the network. Paul Baran at the RAND Corporation wrote in 1964: "We will soon be living in an era in

Figure 5.3
Decentralized Network

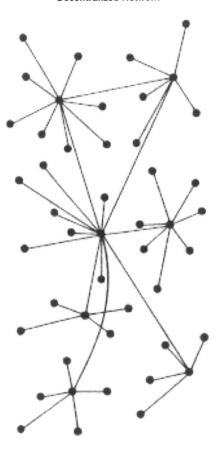

Source: Paul Baran, "On Distributed Communications," Rand
Memorandum RM-3420-PR, August 1964, Santa Monica, CA:
RAND Corporation. Reprinted with permission.

which we cannot guarantee survivability of any single point. However, we
can still design systems in which system destruction requires the enemy to
pay the price of destroying n of n stations [i.e., all the nodes]. If n is made
sufficiently large, it can be shown that highly survivable system structures
can be built."[25] Baran analyzed the survivability of distributed communications networks (as a response to nuclear war scenarios), but his work can
now be used to describe the nature of the al Qaeda network: no single opera-

Figure 5.4
Distributed Network

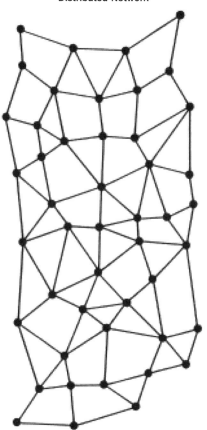

Source: Paul Baran, "On Distributed Communications," Rand
Memorandum RM-3420-PR, August 1964, Santa Monica, CA:
RAND Corporation. Reprinted with permission.

tive or cell can be guaranteed its survivability, but the network may be large
enough that destroying or severely degrading it will require the destruction
of a large number of nodes approaching the total in the network. No one
knows how large the al Qaeda network really is, but an estimated one hundred thousand Muslims passed through al Qaeda training camps in the 1980s
and 1990s.[26] Also, an estimated three thousand al Qaeda operatives have
either been captured or killed,[27] yet the organization is still considered vi-

able and threatening. Therefore, it is prudent to assume that the size of the network is sufficiently large such that it is highly survivable in the same manner as a large, multinode grid network.

Another aspect of al Qaeda that makes it a difficult organization to dismantle is its adaptivity to changes in environment. Baran credits adaptive distributed networks with this important attribute: "The links could also be cut and altered, yet the network would relearn. Each node sees its environment through myopic eyes by only having links and link status information to a few neighbors. There is no central contact; only a simple local routing policy is performed at each node, yet the overall system adapts."[28] Figure 5.5 shows how a communications network can adapt if the nodes move or are cut (in this example, all the nodes except Charlie have changed location, Dog and Easy have combined, Baker has been removed from the network, and X-Ray and Zebra are new nodes).

Al Qaeda has demonstrated this adaptiveness at different levels. For example, in November 2002 then-chairman of the Joint Chiefs of Staff, U.S. Air Force Gen. Richard Myers, commented to an audience at the Brookings

Figure 5.5
Network Adaptability to Change

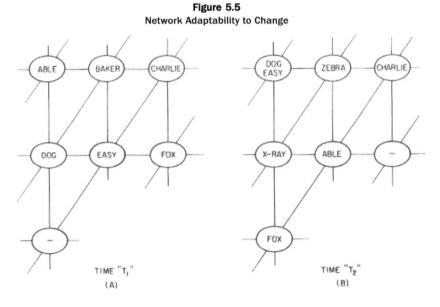

Source: Paul Baran, "On Distributed Communications," Rand Memorandum RM-3420-PR, August 1964, Santa Monica, CA: RAND Corporation. Reprinted with permission.

Institute in Washington, D.C., that the remnants of al Qaeda and the Taliban in Afghanistan had adapted more successfully to U.S. military tactics than the United States had to theirs.[29]

Even more remarkable has been al Qaeda's ability to repeatedly replace the same key individual node in the network. In December 2001 Mohammed Atef, al Qaeda's No. 3 and chief of military operations, was killed by U.S. bombing in Afghanistan. Atef's successor, Khalid Sheikh Mohammed, was captured in Pakistan in March 2003 in a raid made famous by television and front-page headlines featuring his picture, looking decidedly like John Belushi in National Lampoon's *Animal House*.[30] Next in line to assume many of Atef's duties appears to be al Qaeda's security chief, Saif Al-Adel.[31] But Atef's role in al Qaeda may have been divided within the organization because Abu Faraj al-Libbi was reported to have taken over for Khalid Sheikh Mohammed, who was his mentor. With al-Libbi's capture in May 2005, either Al-Adel has assumed all of Atef's duties or a still unknown person has succeeded al-Libbi. The bottom line is that al Qaeda has proven to be very resilient.

A better model for understanding the al Qaeda structure, then, is as a decentralized and distributed grid network connected by multiple paths rather than a strict top-down chain of command. The nodes of the network can be conceptualized at three different levels: (1) individual al Qaeda operatives, (2) terrorist cells, and (3) the countries where al Qaeda has a presence. So individual al Qaeda operatives can be connected to each other by a grid to form their own small networks, i.e., cells. In turn, these cells can also be networked together in a similar fashion. Additionally, individuals within cells can be directly networked to individuals in other cells completely apart from direct cell-to-cell connections. Finally, individual operatives and cells need not necessarily be tied to the same geographic location, so the more than sixty countries that al Qaeda is thought to be operating in can also be connected together in a gridlike fashion and overlaid on the operative and cell connections. Former foreign service officer Marc Sageman, author of *Understanding Terror Networks*, has depicted the complexity of the al Qaeda network, as shown in figure 5.6.[32]

Another way to think of the al Qaeda network is as the interlinked honeycombs (either individual operatives or cells) of a beehive with myriad paths between any two points. A beehive is a particularly appropriate rep-

Figure 5.6
Al Qaeda as a Network of Networks

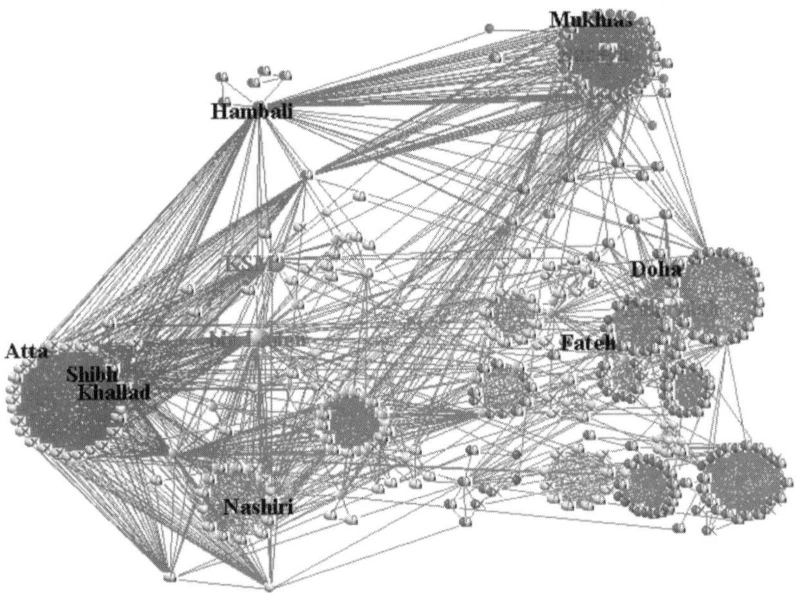

Source: Marc Sageman, "Understanding al Qaeda Networks."

resentation because, as honeycombs inside the beehive are destroyed, worker bees can rebuild them; this is an analogy for the organic nature of the al Qaeda network, i.e., its ability to adapt and regenerate.

Finally, the Internet is also a useful analytic metaphor for understanding al Qaeda's structure. In one way, the al-Qaeda-as-the-Internet metaphor is a literal description because the Web appears to have replaced Afghanistan as a virtual rather than physical sanctuary and as a means of communication for al Qaeda and other radical Muslims.[33] Also, al Qaeda can be thought of as a network of networks, which is exactly what the Internet is: a global collection of big and small networks that are connected. The Internet may also be a template for understanding how the al Qaeda network is evolving. The connections on the Internet are not hardwired in that they are not a function of individuals creating permanent physical connections between themselves. Instead, people connect to each other at times and places of their own

choosing. Moreover, the actual routing of the connection is not a predeter-
mined path—rather it is a function of finding the path of least resistance between the two points and will be different each time the connection is made.

Similarly, the al Qaeda network may not be a permanent physical structure. Connections may exist only when they need to exist. Individuals and
cells may drop in or out of the network at will or by direction. Snapshots of
the network at two different moments in time may look completely different. For example, Sageman has shown how the al Qaeda network looks different when operational links are considered versus when personal links
are considered, as shown in figures 5.7 and 5.8.

All this does not mean there is a single definitive description of and
way to understand al Qaeda as an organizational structure; it means only
that viewing the network strictly as top-down chain of command hierarchy
is not accurate. Rather—just as physicists had to learn to understand light as

Figure 5.7
Al Qaeda Operational Links

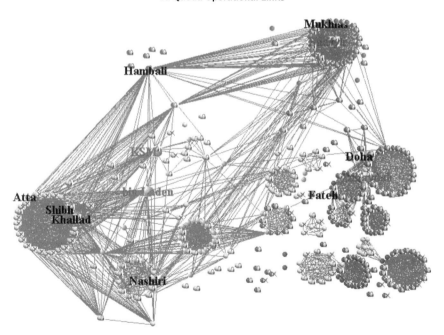

Source: Marc Sageman, "Understanding al Qaeda Networks."

Figure 5.8
Al Qaeda Personal Links

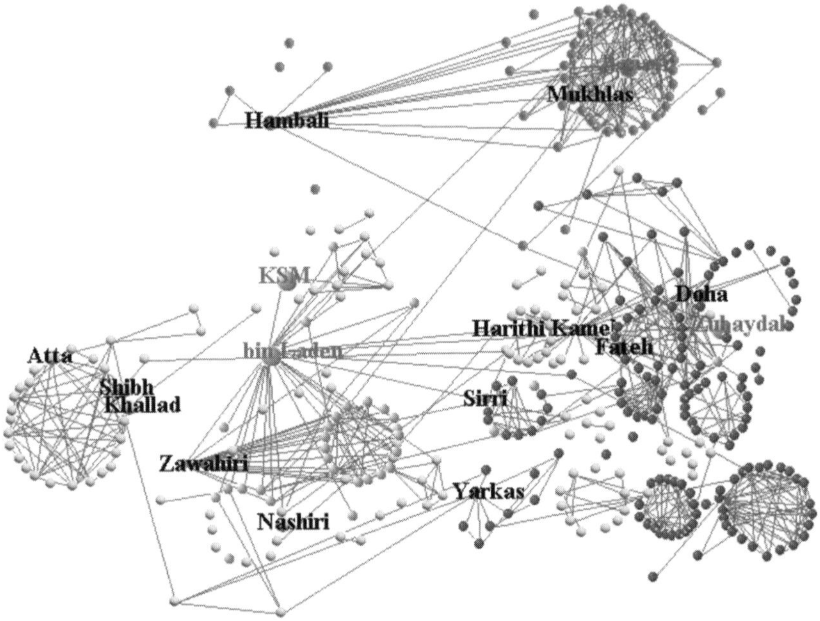

Source: Marc Sageman, "Understanding al Qaeda Networks."

both a particle and a wave, even though it could only be observed as one or the other — we must accept that there are different ways to view and understand al Qaeda. Each one may not provide a complete answer, but the sum of them will provide a more thorough, if not complete, picture.

It is also important to understand that al Qaeda is more than just a terrorist organization: it is representative of a radical Islamic ideology. Here again, President Bush has chosen to define al Qaeda's ideology in broad, sweeping terms by using the phrases "ideology of hate"[34] and "ideology of murder,"[35] which imply the binary view that al Qaeda can be explained only as the opposite of peaceful, loving, and law abiding. To be sure, terrorists who fly airplanes into buildings and kill thousands of innocent people are filled with hate and are guilty of murder. But just as "evil" is an inadequate definition of the terrorist threat to America, "hate" and "murder" are not adequate descriptors of al Qaeda's ideology, and understanding the network's ideology is a prerequisite to understanding why Muslims would sympathize with and even support al Qaeda.

First and foremost, it is important to understand that al Qaeda's ideology is not simply driven by a desire to destroy America. Because we were attacked on 9/11 and because it is human nature to think of the enemy as "not us" and "not like us," believing that Osama bin Laden is a psychopathic Muslim who only wants to murder Americans because he hates the United States is all too easy. According to Reuel Marc Gerecht of the American Enterprise Institute for Public Policy Research, "Bin Laden's criticisms of the West, and America in particular, can easily appear to a Westerner as the tirades of a loony ideologue."[36] And the conventional wisdom is that bin Laden must hate us for who we are, i.e., our way of life and our culture, as argued by Paul Bremer (ambassador-at-large for counterterrorism during President Reagan's second term and former head of the Coalition Provisional Authority in Iraq): "He [bin Laden] doesn't like America. He doesn't like our society. He doesn't like what we stand for. He doesn't like our values."[37] Amazingly enough, however, bin Laden has been rather lucid about why he has targeted America. Unfortunately, often we hear only the part about wanting to kill Americans and disregard or refuse to believe the rest of what he has to say. Yet, as Michael Scheuer—former head of the CIA's bin Laden unit and the anonymous author of the *New York Times* bestseller *Imperial Hubris: Why the West Is Losing the War on Terror*—keenly observes: "Osama bin Laden is preeminently a man of words, and a man of his word."[38]

In August 1996 the London-based newspaper *Al Quds Al Arabi* published bin Laden's "Declaration of War on the Americans Occupying the Country of the Two Sacred Places." This fatwa declared the Saudi regime to be illegitimate because of its "suspension of Islamic Shari'ah law and exchanging it with man made civil law" and "the inability of the regime to protect the country, and allowing the enemy of the Ummah—the American crusader forces—to occupy the land for the longest of years." Bin Laden claimed, "The regime is fully responsible for what had been incurred by the country and the nation; however the occupying American enemy is the principle and the main cause of the situation. Their [Muslims'] efforts should be concentrated on destroying, fighting and killing the enemy." And he exhorted, "To liberate their sanctities is the greatest of issues concerning all Muslims; It is the duty of every Muslim in the world" and "there is no more important duty than pushing the American enemy out of the holy land."[39]

In February 1998 bin Laden issued another fatwa to all Muslims claiming that "the ruling to kill the Americans and their allies—civilians and military—is an individual duty for every Muslim who can do it in any country in which it is possible to do it, in order to liberate the al-Aqsa Mosque and the holy mosque [Mecca] from their grip, and in order for their armies to move out of all the lands of Islam, defeated and unable to threaten any Muslim."[40]

Neither of these fatwas cites American or Western culture and democratic freedom as the reason for jihad against the United States. Indeed, in an October 2004 videotape bin Laden said, "Contrary to what [President George W.] Bush says and claims—that we hate freedom—let him tell us then, 'Why did we not attack Sweden?'"[41]

According to al Qaeda expert Rohan Gunaratna, "What Osama and his followers object to is not so much the American way of life, not so much Americans themselves, as what they perceive the American government, in the shape of its foreign policy, is doing to Muslim countries, including Saudi Arabia, the occupation of which is intolerable to Osama."[42] This view is reinforced by Peter Bergen, one of the few Western journalists to interview bin Laden: "What he condemns the United States for is simple: its policies in the Middle East. Those are, to recap briefly: the continued U.S. military presence in Arabia; U.S. support for Israel; its continued bombing of Iraq; and its support for regimes such as Egypt and Saudi Arabia that bin Laden regards as apostates from Islam."[43] And according to Michael Scheuer:

> There is no record of a Muslim leader urging his brethren to wage jihad to destroy participatory democracy, the National Association of Credit Unions, or the coed Ivy League universities. Many Muslims may not particularly like what and who the rest of us are, but those things seldom if ever make them hate us enough to attack us.
>
> What the United States does in formulating and implementing policies affecting the Muslim world, however, is infinitely more inflammatory. While there may be a few militant Muslims out there who would blow up themselves and others because they are offended by McDonald's restaurants, Iowa's early presidential primary, and the seminude, fully pregnant Demi Moore on *Esquire*'s cover. The focused and lethal threat posed to U.S. national security arises not from Muslims being offended by what America is, but

rather from their plausible perception that the things they love most and value — God, Islam, their brethren, and Muslim lands — are being attacked by America. . . .

Part of bin Laden's genius is that he recognized early on the difference between issues Muslims find offensive about America and the West, and those they find intolerable and life threatening.[44]

In other words, bin Laden has found some core issues that many Muslims can agree with him about in principle, even if they do not condone the killing of innocent people. This defies traditional binary thinking, which would hold that you must either endorse or condemn al Qaeda's actions and, by extension, the reasons for those actions. This example further shows that understanding al Qaeda requires something other than a binary approach. We must be able to think differently to understand why Muslims such as Dr. Saad al-Fagih, a Saudi dissident in London, who has never advocated violence against Americans or endorsed bin Laden's terrorism, can also agree with bin Laden: "I don't think there is a sensible person who believes that the Americans should stay in Saudi Arabia. . . . If you are a devoted Muslim, there is a religious obligation not to accept non-Muslims in military form staying in the country, especially the holy land."[45]

Bin Laden credibly asserts to Muslims that the United States is "occupying the lands of Islam"[46] (previously in Saudi Arabia[47] and now in Iraq) and can use the words of the Prophet Mohammed — "Let there be no two religions in Arabia"[48] — as the basis for jihad. Many Americans thus believe that al Qaeda is engaged in a holy war against the non-Muslim world. But bin Laden skillfully portrays his jihad as defensive to expel non-Muslims from Muslim countries: "We ourselves are the target of killings, destruction, and atrocities. We are only defending ourselves. This is defensive jihad. We want to defend our people and our land."[49] As Rohan Gunaratna points out, a defensive jihad is "when an enemy is expelled from the jihadist's homeland,"[50] not a wider war. Moreover, Islamic tradition holds that when Muslims are attacked, all Muslims are obligated to defend against the attack.[51] Indeed, one of bin Laden's mentors — Abdullah Azzam, who is considered one of the ideological architects of al Qaeda — wrote:

When the enemy enters the land of Muslims, jihad becomes individually obligatory, according to all jusists, mufassirin, and muhaddithin. . . . When jihad becomes obligatory, no permission of parents is required. . . . Donating money does not exempt a person from bodily jihad, no matter how great the amount of money given. . . . Jihad is the obligation of a lifetime. . . . Jihad is currently individually obligatory, in person and by wealth in every place that the disbelievers have occupied. It remains obligatory continuously until every piece of land that was once Islamic is regained.[52]

The call for jihad is not restricted to Saudi Arabia or even the Middle East. In a statement shortly after the 9/11 attacks, bin Laden claimed Muslims "are being violated in Palestine, in Iraq, in Lebanon, in Sudan, in Somalia, in Kashmir, in the Philippines, and in every place."[53] Al Qaeda spokesman Suleiman Abu Ghaith justified the 9/11 attacks as "but a tiny part of the exchange for those killed in Palestine, Somalia, Sudan, the Philippines, Bosnia, Kashmir, Chechnya, and Afghanistan."[54] This does not mean that every Muslim in all these countries will agree with bin Laden and answer his call to arms. According to British journalist Jason Burke, "The problem for bin Laden and others is that the vast majority of Muslims, though they may feel profound sympathy with the Palestinians, oppose the invasion and occupation of Iraq, feel humiliated by the presence of American troops elsewhere in the Middle East and are concerned by burgeoning Western cultural and political hegemony, do not sympathize with his methods and reject his extremism."[55] But the problem for the United States is that nothing in Islamic law or tradition prevents Muslims from taking up defensive jihad. Moreover, bin Laden's assertion that the United States is occupying Islamic countries is factually correct. Although the U.S. military has withdrawn from Saudi Arabia, American forces are deployed in Afghanistan (where the mujahideen fought and expelled the Soviets) and Iraq (which is described by bin Laden as "a former capital of Islam").[56] So it is easy to understand why al Qaeda's message is not completely rejected by Muslims.

Bin Laden also links America and apostate regimes in his call for jihad. For example, in a tape broadcast on Al Jazeera television just prior to the U.S. invasion of Iraq, bin Laden enjoined, "True Muslims should act, incite, and mobilize the nation in such great events, hot conditions, in order to break free from the slavery of these tyrannic and apostate regimes, which is enslaved by America, in order to establish the rule of Allah on earth. Among regions ready for liberation are Jordan, Morocco, Nigeria, the country of the two shrines [Saudi Arabia], Yemen, and Pakistan."[57] An al Qaeda training manual declares that "Sadat, Hosni Mubarak, Gadhafi, Hafez Assad, Saleh, Fahed" are "all apostate Arab rulers."[58]

Bin Laden also makes clear that Muslims who support the United States are, by definition, apostate. In a 1999 interview, he stated, "Now infidels walk everywhere on the land where Mohammed was born and where the Koran was revealed to him. The situation is serious. The rulers have become powerless. Muslims should carry out their obligations, since the rulers of the region have accepted the invasion of their countries. These countries belong to Islam and not to the rulers."[59] And in his pre–Iraq war tape: "Whoever supported the United States, including the hypocrites of Iraq or the rulers of Arab countries, those who approved their actions and followed them in this crusade war by fighting with them or providing bases and administrative support, or any form of support, even by words, to kill the Muslims in Iraq, should know that they are apostates and outside the community of Muslims."[60]

The linkage between the United States and apostate Islamic regimes reveals that although bin Laden has declared war on America, al Qaeda's real war is within the Muslim world—it is not the Muslim world versus America or the West. According to Gunaratna, "Al Qaeda targeted the secular rulers of the Middle East for failing to create Islamic states and for suppressing Islamists. Osama highlighted not only the victimization of Muslims by non-Muslim regimes but also the persecution of religious scholars and others fighting for the restoration of Islam."[61] Thus, jihad against America to expel a foreign presence in Muslim countries and displacing apostate regimes is a means to a larger end: establishing an Islamic state or caliphate. In a speech posted to a number of Islamist Internet forums in July 2003, bin Laden states, "In order to establish the Islamic state and the religion, there must be . . . jihad."[62]

That the core of al Qaeda's ideology is the reestablishment of Islamic rule in Muslim countries should come as no surprise given the influence of prominent Islamist scholars, such as Sayyid Qutb, on bin Laden's thinking. In the 1950s and 1960s Qutb was a key figure in the development of Muslim fundamentalism and an active member of the Muslim Brotherhood in Egypt (where he was tried and sentenced to death in 1966 on charges of attempting to assassinate President Nasser). According to Middle East historian Bernard Lewis:

> The main thrust of Sayyid Qutb's writing and preaching was directed against the internal enemy—what he called the new age of ignorance, in Arabic *jahiliyya*, a classical Islamic term for the period of paganism that prevailed in Arabia before the advent of the Prophet and of Islam. As Sayyid Qutb saw it, a new *jahiliyya* had engulfed the Muslim peoples and the new pharaohs—rightly seen as an allusion to the existing regimes—who were ruling them.[63]

Most important, Qutb declared that "all existing so called 'Muslim' societies are also jahili societies"[64] and that "the position of Islam in relation to all these jahili societies can be described in one sentence: it considers all these societies un-Islamic and illegal."[65] Furthermore, the intention of Islam is "to abolish all those systems and governments which are based on the rule of man over men and the servitude of one human being to another,"[66] and for Muslims, it is "a God-given right to step forward and take control of the political authority so that it may establish the Divine system on earth."[67]

Thus, the list of Muslim countries that could be considered apostate by bin Laden—and therefore legitimate targets for al Qaeda—includes Saudi Arabia, Iraq (under Saddam Hussein previously and under the new Iraqi government currently because it is seen as cooperating with the United States), Egypt, Kuwait, Qatar, United Arab Emirates, Oman, Libya (probably more so now that the regime has negotiated a more normal relationship with the United States), Syria, Yemen, Nigeria, Morocco, Turkey, Bosnia, Pakistan, the Philippines, and Indonesia. It should come as no surprise, then, that post-9/11 terrorists have attacked Saudi Arabia, Egypt, Morocco, Turkey, Bosnia and Herzegovina, Pakistan, Indonesia, and the Philippines.[68]

All of the above attacks have been attributed to Islamic terrorists, but not necessarily directly to al Qaeda. For example, the Moro Islamic Liberation Front claimed responsibility for the March 4, 2003, attack in Davao, Philippines, that killed twenty-one people (including one U.S. citizen). The May 2003 bombings in Casablanca, Morocco, that killed forty-two people are blamed on al-Sirat al Mustaqim. Jemaah Islamiya is believed to be responsible for the Marriott hotel bombing in Jakarta, Indonesia, in August

2003 that killed thirteen people, as well as the October 2002 Bali bombings that killed more than two hundred people (although the group's alleged leader, Indonesian cleric Abu Bakar Bashir, was acquitted in March 2005 of involvement in both bombings). And two bombings just five days apart in November 2003 in Istanbul, Turkey, that killed fifty-five people are thought to be the work of the Abu Hafez al-Masri Brigades.

The common thread between these and other terrorist attacks by Islamic militants is potential linkage of the different groups to al Qaeda. But if these attacks were not carried out by al Qaeda under Osama bin Laden's direction (and all the available evidence suggests most of them were not), this points to yet another aspect of al Qaeda's ideology: it may have a life of its own outside of the direct control of bin Laden. According to Omar Bakri Mohammed, the London-based leader of the radical Islamic group al-Muhajiroun, "Al Qaeda is no longer a group. It's become a phenomenon of the Muslim world resisting the global crusade of the U.S. against Islam."[69]

As a result, even without any direct connection to or contact with al Qaeda (e.g., planning, training, financing), individuals or groups may conduct terrorist attacks citing al Qaeda's ideology. According to Bergen, "al Qaeda has now mutated into an ideology with many adherents who may have never traveled to bin Laden's Afghan training camps. . . . Rather, al Qaeda, the organization, has also evolved into an ideology of 'bin Ladenism' or 'al Qaedaism.'"[70] This appears to be the case in the July 2005 London tube bombings.

Thus, al Qaeda, which means "the base" in Arabic, has become something more than a terrorist group that serves as physical or structural base (as it did in Afghanistan) for Islamic extremists. According to Burke, al Qaeda is an ideology that radical Muslims can subscribe to and act upon on their accord: "In very broad terms they share the key ideas, and the key objectives, of bin Laden and the 'al Qaeda hardcore.' They subscribe, whether involved in a radical group or not, to the 'al Qaeda' worldview."[71]

Just like yin and yang, al Qaeda as an organization and as an ideology cannot be separated. They are inextricably intertwined with each other. Al Qaeda exists as both an organization and an ideology. To focus only on al Qaeda as an organization is to miss the larger picture and to misunderstand the nature of the threat. The al Qaeda organization is representative of a larger radical Islamic jihadist ideology. In effect, al Qaeda is the vanguard of a larger movement and a source of inspiration. Other Muslims — either individuals or groups — do not have to be a part of al Qaeda formally, but simply have to believe in the ideology and be willing to carry out attacks in the name of al Qaeda in what amounts to a kind of reverse franchise effect. The ideology is the basis for expanding the organization, even if no direct links connect bin Laden and the al Qaeda leadership. In turn, the organization perpetuates the ideology.

And like yin and yang, al Qaeda — and the relationship between organization and ideology that defines al Qaeda — is not static. As physicist Fritjof Capra explains, "The Taoists saw all changes in nature as manifestations of the dynamic interplay between the polar opposites yin and yang, and thus they came to believe that any pair of opposites constitutes a polar relationship where each of the two poles is dynamically linked to the other."[72] Such is the case for al Qaeda as it evolves and adapts to an ever-changing environment. The al Qaeda that existed on September 11, 2001, is not the same al Qaeda that exists today. Similarly, the al Qaeda that exists today will be different tomorrow.

If non-Western thinking, such as the Chinese concepts of yin and yang, provides a useful frame of reference for a more complete understanding of al Qaeda, then the Chinese book of practical wisdom, *Tao Te Ching*, offers some sage advice: "No calamity is greater than underestimating opponents."[73] To persist in thinking about al Qaeda as a mafia crime family–like organization driven by hatred of American freedom and culture would be the greatest calamity because such thinking misunderstands and misconstrues the threat facing America and is a recipe for failure.

6

TAO OF STRATEGY

Blunt the sharpness
Untie the knot

— Lau Tzu, *Tao Te Ching*

If al Qaeda can be thought of as comprised of yin and yang components, then it logically follows that an appropriate strategy would be twofold. Just as Chinese philosophy helps us to understand al Qaeda, we can draw on Chinese philosophy—in this case Lau Tzu's *Tao Te Ching*—to help shape a strategy against al Qaeda. "Tao" means the "way" or "path" in Chinese. Relating the concept of tao to strategy is appropriate because tao can be thought of as knowing where to go and how to get there; and this is the essence of strategy.

Lau Tzu wrote: "Do nondoing."[1] Such a paradoxical statement is typical of Taoist thought and the ideas of "doing" and "not doing" are essential to crafting a strategy against al Qaeda. To the extent that individuals who are part of what we know as the al Qaeda terrorist organization are threats to America, the "doing" part of strategy requires that we capture or kill the terrorists who would do us harm. But at the same time, there is a "not doing" aspect of strategy: ensuring that we do not create more terrorists. The paradox is that some actions intended to kill terrorists may result in creating new terrorists. The art of the un-war, then, is to do the former and not do the latter.

As a result of Operation Enduring Freedom, al Qaeda has lost its physical sanctuary in Afghanistan. Consequently, the organization is now more diffuse; it is thought to be present in as many as sixty countries around the world.[2] According to the 9/11 Commission, some of the places al Qaeda has dispersed to include:

- western Pakistan and the Pakistan-Afghanistan border region
- southern and western Afghanistan
- the Arabian Peninsula, especially Saudi Arabia and Yemen, and the nearby Horn of Africa, including Somalia and extending southwest into Kenya
- Southeast Asia, from Thailand to the southern Philippines to Indonesia
- West Africa, including Nigeria and Mali
- European cities with expatriate Muslim communities, especially cities in central and eastern Europe where security forces and border controls are less effective.[3]

But going after al Qaeda in these and other countries does not necessarily require the same kind of military action the United States took in Operation Enduring Freedom in Afghanistan. Indeed, in many cases the United States may be constrained in its ability to take direct action and will have to rely on the cooperation of other governments.

If we believe that the Osama bin Laden and the remnants of al Qaeda's senior leadership are in hiding in Pakistan (most likely in the lawless border areas between Pakistan and Afghanistan), then Pakistan represents the belly of the beast. To date, we have relied on President Pervez Musharraf's government to hunt down al Qaeda in Pakistan. And some of the bigger successes in the war on terrorism have been in Pakistan. In early April 2002 Abu Zubaydah—described as a "key terrorist recruiter and operational planner and member of Osama bin Laden's inner circle"[4]—was apprehended in a raid by Pakistani and U.S. security forces. In September 2002 Ramzi Binalshibh—one of the members of the Hamburg cell—was captured in Karachi by Pakistani security forces. In March 2003 Khalid Sheikh Mohammed—who, according to al Qaeda expert Rohan Gunaratna, was a "highly experienced organizer of terrorist attacks across international borders, one of an elite group capable of such events"[5]—was netted in Pakistan. And in May 2005 Abu Faraj al-Libbi—thought by many analysts to be Khalid Sheikh Mohammed's successor[6]—was captured by the Pakistani military. In each of these cases, the U.S. military or intelligence was involved in some way.

But when left to their own devices, the Pakistanis have sometimes acted a bit like the Keystone Kops. For example, in mid-March 2004 the Pakistani military claimed that they had surrounded some two hundred al Qaeda fighters, including a "high-value target,"[7] according to Musharraf. This high-value target was thought to be Ayman al-Zawahiri, al Qaeda's second in command. But when the dust settled from the helicopter gunships and artillery used to bombard the area in South Waziristan, al-Zawahiri was not found. Although the Pakistani military claimed to have sealed off a twenty-square-mile cordon around the area and was confident that no one escaped, either al-Zawahiri slipped the noose or was never there to begin with.[8]

It was déjà vu all over again in late March 2004, when Pakistani intelligence officials claimed that al Qaeda's spy chief Abu Mohammed al-Masri (aka Abdullah Ahmed Abdullah, one of the FBI's most wanted terrorists for his involvement in the August 7, 1998, bombings of the United States embassies in Tanzania and Kenya) was killed. One day after making that announcement, however, the Pakistanis admitted that it had been a case of mistaken identity and that the slain militant was only a local operative. To add insult to injury, in addition to coming up empty handed with al-Masri and al-Zawahiri during this spring 2004 operation, the Pakistanis suffered the loss of twelve soldiers killed and fifteen wounded when an army convoy was ambushed.[9]

Although capturing or killing bin Laden and other senior al Qaeda leaders will not win the war on terrorism, they are nonetheless important targets — too important to be delegated to the Pakistanis if they are unable or unwilling to mount a serious effort to hunt them down. The latter is a very real concern. According to Gary Schroen (a former CIA officer who oversaw agency operations in the region until August 2001 and still works on contract for the CIA), the Pakistanis are not engaged in a serious hunt for bin Laden. Schroen believes that Musharraf fears a horrendous Islamic backlash if he arrests the man seen as Robin Hood by many in the Muslim world but that Musharraf is willing to hand over lesser al Qaeda figures. According to *Newsweek*'s Michael Hirsch:

> As evidence, Schroen says that it took the Pakistanis five months to act against al-Libbi after the Americans delivered intelligence on the whereabouts of a Qaeda suspect who could not, at the time be specifically identified; Schroen believes the Pakistanis acted only after determining that the suspect was not bin Laden but a smaller

fish. "We gave them information on Libbi back in December," says Schroen, who has written a new book on his work with the CIA in Afghanistan [*First In: An Insider's Account of How the CIA Spearheaded the War on Terror in Afghanistan*, Novato, CA: Presidio Press, 2005]. "They didn't want to do it."[10]

Further evidence that the Pakistanis may not be serious about the hunt for bin Laden is that twice they have called for suspending military operations in South Waziristan — the very area where al Qaeda's leadership is thought to be hiding. In late April 2004 — after the embarrassment of having to retract claims of capturing al-Zawahiri and killing al-Masri — the Pakistani army said it had reached an agreement to halt military operations against tribesmen in return for a pledge not to harm Pakistan's interests. At the same time, however, the tribal elders announced ending their hunt for al Qaeda militants and their supporters.[11]

Again in late November 2004, the Pakistani government reportedly reached an agreement with the region's five most-wanted militants to stop their resistance and not harbor foreign militants in exchange for clemency for the five militants, compensation for property damage, and releasing prisoners. The Pakistani government also agreed to remove all military checkpoints from Wana in South Waziristan.[12] In reaction to these news reports the Pakistani government issued a statement that military operations would continue and security forces would remain in the area until all foreign terrorists and their local facilitators were eliminated from South Waziristan.[13]

In an Oval Office meeting between President Bush and Musharraf in early December 2004, Musharraf briefed Bush that the Pakistani Army's focus was moving to North Waziristan. But in April 2005, when Lt. Gen. David Barno — the outgoing commander of U.S. troops in Afghanistan — suggested that Pakistani forces were planning a new offensive in North Waziristan, Lt. Gen. Safdar Hussain responded that "It is only speculation that terrorists are in North Waziristan"[14] and that such an operation was "a figment of his [Barno's] imagination. There is no bloody operation going on."[15]

But if Pakistan is going to claim to be an ally in the war on terrorism, such soap-opera farce cannot continue. If — for whatever reasons — the Pakistani government is not prepared to mount a serious effort against al Qaeda, then the United States must be willing to take matters into its own hands.

This does not mean a large-scale military incursion of Pakistan. Rather, simply that U.S. Special Forces — acting on verifiable and corroborated intelligence — conduct operations against specific al Qaeda targets. Officially — for understandable reasons — the Musharraf government may not be able to sanction U.S. troops in Pakistan. But unofficially, the government needs to allow U.S. forces to conduct covert operations into Pakistan against al Qaeda when we have actionable intelligence.

Admittedly, this is easier said than done. On the one hand, the United States does not want to take actions that would destabilize the Musharraf regime because a likely successor government could be radical Islamists who inherit Pakistan's nuclear weapons. But at the same time, the United States cannot embrace Musharraf as an unequivocal ally in the war on terrorism if his government is unwilling to make a serious effort to hunt down bin Laden and other senior al Qaeda leaders.

While hunting down al Qaeda in Pakistan may require the U.S. military to take more direct action, most of the rest of the war on terrorism in other countries around the world requires the United States to rely on foreign governments to take up the hunt. This is especially true in Muslim countries because a U.S. military presence would not likely be welcomed by the local population and would be cited by the Islamic radicals as evidence that America is waging a war against and invading Islam.

For example, Saudi Arabia is a country with an al Qaeda presence that cannot be ignored, but putting U.S. troops in the country is not the appropriate course of action. After all, bin Laden cited the five thousand U.S. troops stationed in Saudi Arabia after the Gulf War as a foreigner occupation of the "lands of Islam in the holiest places,"[16] one of his reasons for declaring war on the United States. Now that those troops have been withdrawn from Saudi Arabia, it is unwise for them to return — even if their mission is to root out al Qaeda.

The first real sign that the Saudi government would cooperate in the war on terrorism came in June 2002 when thirteen people with suspected ties to al Qaeda were arrested (seven of whom were thought to be involved in a failed effort to shoot down a U.S. military jet with a shoulder-fired missile at Prince Sultan Air Base). But it took the May 12, 2003, bombing in Riyadh — that killed thirty-five people, including ten Americans, and wounded two hundred — to jump-start a more serious effort. A little more than two weeks after the bombing, eleven suspects were taken into custody, including Abd al-Rahman al-Faqasi al-Ghamdi, who was thought to be a top al Qaeda operative in Saudi Arabia and the mastermind of the bombing.

Subsequently, there have been more bombings—in November 2003 in Riyadh against a residential compound resulting in 11 dead and 122 injured and in April 2004 against government buildings in Riyadh that killed 50 and wounded more than 150—and other terrorist attacks, but also hundreds of arrests. The Saudis claim that seventeen of the twenty-six most-wanted militant leaders in the country have been arrested or killed and that three of four known al Qaeda cells have been dismantled.[17] Perhaps even more important, because many of the attacks have resulted in Saudi deaths, there may be a mild backlash against al Qaeda—even from those who are otherwise critical of the government. According to Mansour Nogaidan, a radical who has moderated his views but is nonetheless a vocal critic of the Saudi government, "People want government reforms and changes, but they are more scared of al Qaeda extremists. . . . The common people—those people who thought their life might improve if the government changed—they are not ready to lose all this for what some young teenagers have in their minds as a utopia."[18] A backlash against al Qaeda, if indeed there is one, would be a welcome turn of events because Saudi Arabia is thought to be rife with al Qaeda sympathizers and supporters.

The key to success in Saudi Arabia and other countries, such as Jordan, Egypt, Bahrain, United Arab Emirates, the Philippines, and Indonesia, will be to ensure that the al Qaeda threat in those countries is not used as an excuse to crack down on what should be legitimate government opposition.

For example, the Muslim Brotherhood is a banned political party in Egypt, but candidates that the group supports (serving as independents) currently hold 13 seats in the 454-seat legislature—the largest government opposition bloc. Although the Brotherhood currently represents itself as a pillar of moderate Islam—mainstream, nonviolent, and condemning recent terrorist attacks in Egypt—its history is rich with radical Islamism. Among the Brotherhood's creations is Hamas, which the group still considers a legitimate guerrilla movement against Israeli occupation. Al Qaeda's Ayman al-Zawahiri was once a member of the Muslim Brotherhood. So, Egyptian president Hosni Mubarak might target the Muslim Brotherhood as part of a crackdown on al Qaeda—especially since the brotherhood's current leader,

Mohammed Mahdi Akef, has endorsed the Iraqi insurgency, rejected Israel's right to exist, and called America a "Satan" that is out to dominate the Islamic world.[19]

But without evidence that the Muslim Brotherhood is an al Qaeda threat, Mubarak would not help the war on terrorism by seeking to wipe out the group simply because it represents a political challenge to his regime. At least for now, Mubarak and the brotherhood seem to have reached an understanding:

> Political analyst Diaa Rashwan [at the Al-Ahram Center for Political and Strategic Studies in Cairo] holds out two palms. He's explaining the Egyptian compromise the way the government and the Muslim Brotherhood wound up in this delicate balance.
>
> One palm represents the government's decision not to try to wipe out the Brotherhood despite Mubarak's deep distrust of the group. The reason: fear that more radical and dangerous groups would step into the vacuum. . . .
>
> The other palm is the Brotherhood leaders. Their part of the deal: Continue to denounce violence and avoid any true challenge to Mubarak's 24-year hold on power.[20]

It is also important that the governments of those countries target real al Qaeda threats. For example, U.S.-trained Philippine security forces have focused most of their attention on the Abu Sayyaf guerillas on the island of Basilan. But the Abu Sayyaf are a small (less than one hundred) group of militant Islamic separatists in the Philippines who are more kidnappers for money than international terrorists[21] —and it would be hard to prove that the Abu Sayyaf are supporting al Qaeda or were involved in the 9/11 attacks.[22] According to Maria Ressa, CNN's lead investigative reporter in Asia, the Philippines has "separatist groups that are often lumped together but in fact can vary from mafia-like shakedown artists to true Muslim extremists."[23]

If there is a potential al Qaeda threat in the Philippines, it is more likely the Moro Islamic Liberation Front (MILF)—a group substantially larger than the Abu Sayyaf with some twelve thousand members. According to Ressa, the MILF "has emerged as a much closer associate of al Qaeda."[24] The possible connection between the MILF and al Qaeda is Jemaah Islamiya (JI)—

the group held responsible for the October 2002 suicide bombing in Bali and the August 2003 bombing of the Marriott hotel in Jakarta and thought to be linked to al Qaeda. JI is suspected of training in MILF camps in Mindanao, where the MILF has a substantial presence. The MILF denies any ties to JI, and even the Philippine government has downplayed any links between the two groups. Filipino National Security Adviser Roilo Golez responded to the claim of a JI presence in the Philippines by stating, "That's wrong. Very, very wrong. I can bet my future, my career and my life that it's not true."[25] The MILF insists that its goal is to achieve independence for Mindanao's Muslims, not to wage jihad against the United States. According to Al Haj Murad, MILF's vice chairman for military affairs who fought the Soviets as a mujahideen in Afghanistan and met bin Laden in the 1980s, the MILF's struggle is domestic: "for the aspiration of the Mindanao people."[26]

The U.S. government is concerned about the MILF but so far has not included the group on its official list of terrorist organizations.[27] So the jury is still out on whether the MILF is a direct terrorist threat to America and a legitimate al Qaeda target. The Philippine government has been engaged in peace talks with the MILF, but whether a negotiated peace with the MILF is the right choice for the war on terrorism remains to be seen. If the MILF is linked to al Qaeda, then the Philippine government will have wasted time negotiating peace with a group that should instead be dismantled. On the other hand, if the MILF is simply a Muslim separatist movement and not part of the al Qaeda network, part of a successful peace agreement should be that the MILF helps the Philippine government to hunt down any JI or al Qaeda using Mindanao as a safe haven.

The Philippines is likely a minor player in the war on terrorism in Southeast Asia. The two countries that warrant the most attention are Malaysia and Indonesia, the latter having the largest Muslim population in the world — over 200 million Muslims out of a total population of nearly 242 million.[28] Among those 200 million is a significant number of JI. Although there is disagreement over the extent of the linkages — some analysts believe JI to be the Southeast Asian operational wing of al Qaeda, while others believe it to be more operationally and organizationally distinct — most agree that there are links between JI and al Qaeda (relationships that were likely forged while JI operatives attended al Qaeda training camps in Afghanistan). JI has been implicated in a number of terrorist attacks, including the

October 2002 bombing of a nightclub in Bali, the August 2003 bombing of the Marriott in Jakarta, and the September 2004 bombing outside the Australian embassy in Jakarta.

Prior to the October 2002 Bali bombing, the government of Indonesia denied the existence of JI. But subsequently Indonesia's then-president, Megawati Sukarnoputri, stepped up efforts against JI. Following Malaysia's lead, Indonesia formally banned JI. JI's alleged spiritual leader, Abu Bakar Bashir, was arrested a week after the Bali bombing. After a series of trials, he was found guilty of "sinister conspiracy against the state"[29] — but not guilty of any terrorism charges — and sentenced to thirty months in prison.

Although more than two hundred actual and suspected JI members and supporters have been arrested throughout Southeast Asia, far and away the biggest catch so far has been Hambali, who was arrested in Thailand in August 2003 and was subsequently transferred into U.S. custody. Hambali is thought to be the mastermind of the Bali bomb attack. More importantly, he may have arranged a meeting between two of the 9/11 hijackers and other al Qaeda figures in Malaysia in January 2000 and is accused of helping the men who bombed the USS *Cole* in Yemen in October 2000.

While the United States must rely on the government in Indonesia and many other governments in the Muslim world to hunt down al Qaeda one by one, a few countries — like Pakistan — might require a more active U.S. approach. Countries such as Sudan, Yemen, and Somalia are potential candidates for such action. All three countries have been linked to al Qaeda in varying degrees. Bin Laden established a headquarters in Khartoum, Sudan, for five years during 1990s before being asked to leave by the government and taking up residence in Afghanistan. The USS *Cole* was attacked by al Qaeda while in port in Yemen in October 2000, resulting in seventeen U.S. Navy members killed and another thirty-nine injured. According to the FBI, bin Laden issued a fatwa directing that U.S. troops stationed in the Horn of Africa, including Somalia, should be attacked and claimed responsibility for the eighteen U.S. troops killed during Operation Restore Hope in 1994,[30] the incident depicted in the movie *Blackhawk Down*.

Perhaps more important than past connections to al Qaeda is the fact that all three of these countries have weak central governments. Since each of these governments is unable to exert control over all areas of its respective country, terrorist groups — including al Qaeda — are in a position to take advantage of relative lawlessness to hide and operate. In each case, the government may not be able to mount effective operations against al Qaeda. But if al Qaeda is discovered in Sudan, Yemen, or Somalia, the prescription for Somalia offered by James Phillips at the Heritage Foundation should apply in all three instances:

> Rather than take a sledgehammer approach, which would radicalize Somalis and win bin Laden greater support, the United States should attack isolated targets with small units operating stealthily at night. Lightning "snatch and grab" commando operations should be launched from bases outside of Somalia to limit the presence of foreign troops on the ground. Wherever possible, the United States should use Somali surrogates trained by the CIA and minimize the involvement of Americans on the ground. Moving large numbers of U.S. troops into Somalia would be a lightning rod that would provoke attacks and give al-Qaeda more targets without appreciably increasing the effectiveness of the anti-terrorism campaign.[31]

According to al Qaeda expert Rohan Gunaratna, "Al Qaeda is established in most countries with indigenous or migrant Muslim communities; its infiltration is evident wherever Muslims live and work."[32] Therefore, the hunt for al Qaeda also includes enlisting the cooperation of our long-standing European allies because so many European countries have large Muslim populations—France has nearly 6 million Muslims (10 percent of the total population), Germany has 3 million (almost 4 percent of the total population), England has about 1.5 million (more than 2 percent of the total population), and Italy has more than 1 million (more than 2 percent of the total population).[33] Although the vast majority of these Muslim (largely immigrant) populations are peaceful and law abiding, these groups may be vulnerable to radicalization, the first step toward becoming a terrorist. As such, how Muslims are assimilated into society may be the single-most important issue for these countries. Thus, the French decision to ban religious dress in schools—including Muslim headscarves—is not trivial. French leaders argued that the ban was needed to protect the principle of secularism that underpins French society and to counteract rising Islamic fundamentalism. The fierce desire to keep France a secular society that separates church and state is certainly understandable given that country's history. But Islamic fundamentalism per se is not the problem, and if the ban on headscarves actually radicalizes French Muslims, then it will do more to create a potential terrorist threat rather than dissipate it.

More than anything, the United States must remember that the Europeans are important allies in the war on terrorism—despite any differences of opinion about the Iraq war. Unlike Operation Enduring Freedom, Operation Iraqi Freedom did not enjoy the full support of all North Atlantic Treaty Organization (NATO) countries. The Czech Republic, Denmark, Hungary, Iceland, Italy, the Netherlands, Poland, Portugal, Spain, Turkey, and the United Kingdom supported the coalition. But only the United Kingdom provided combat forces during the war. And Turkish support was more illusory than real: the Turkish parliament voted against allowing U.S. ground troops to deploy from Turkey, depriving the United States of a second front in northern Iraq and causing the Fourth Infantry Division to become a nonfactor in the war. France and Germany were the most vocal European governments opposing the Iraq war. Former German chancellor Gerhard Schroeder—who won reelection with an anti-American campaign—flatly stated, "Germany will not participate."[34] French president Jacques Chirac made it clear that France would not vote for a second UN Security Council resolution that, in his view, would automatically authorize war: "Whatever the circumstances, France will vote no."[35] France and Germany (along with Belgium and Russia) also sought to block prewar NATO efforts to protect NATO ally Turkey in the event of war with Iraq.

U.S. Secretary of Defense Donald Rumsfeld was dismissive of France and Germany: "Germany has been a problem, and France has been a problem. But you look at vast numbers of other countries in Europe. They're not with France and Germany on this, they're with the United States."[36] Rumsfeld also antagonized Germany by including it with two countries designated as state sponsors of terrorism—Cuba and Libya. When asked on Capitol Hill about potential allied cooperation in the event of war, Rumsfeld replied: "And then there are three of four countries that have said they won't do anything. I believe Libya, Cuba and Germany are the ones that I have indicated won't help in any respect."[37]

As a result of the impasse at the UN Security Council, French bashing became a new American pastime. Some of the scathing phrases in American newspaper headlines included: "Axis of Weasels," "Rabid Weasels," "Cheese-eating surrender monkeys," and "Standing with Saddam."[38] President Bush ended a late February 2003 telephone conversation with President Chirac by saying that if France did not support the United States on military action against Iraq: "President Chirac, we will not forgive and we will not forget."[39]

The anti-French absurdity peaked when U.S. representatives Bob Ney (R-OH) and Walter Jones (R-NC) spearheaded a move to change "french fries" to "freedom fries" in the three House office building restaurants as a culinary rebuke for France's refusal to support the U.S. position on Iraq. According to Ney: "This action today is a small, but symbolic effort to show the strong displeasure of many on Capitol Hill with the actions of our so-called ally, France."[40] But childish behavior serves no strategic purpose and impedes important trans-Atlantic cooperation. According to Ted Galen Carpenter at the Cato Institute:

> There is an urgent need for greater realism as well as greater calm on both sides of the Atlantic. Americans and Europeans could continue the unproductive and demeaning spectacle of transatlantic name-calling until bitterness grows to the point that there is little hope of effective co-operation even on those issues where there are common interests.
>
> It would be far better for both sides to acknowledge that the United States and Europe are two regions with overlapping but frequently different interests and perspectives, and that the divergence is likely to grow rather than diminish. In the future, America and its traditional allies may have to agree to disagree on some important issues. Above all, they must learn to disagree without becoming disagreeable.[41]

The reality is that the United States needs Europe (both old and new) in the war on terrorism more than Europe needs the United States. This does not mean that the United States must bend to the wishes of France, Germany, or any other country; we must simply recognize that even a superpower needs friends. Petty differences cannot be allowed to devolve into deep fissures. Freedom fries are not worth the risk of another al Qaeda terrorist attack in the United States.

Thankfully, such absurdity has not yet hindered European cooperation in the hunt for al Qaeda. For example, in December 2002 — at a time when American anti-French sentiment was riding high — the French arrested Marwan Ben-Ahmed, a French-Algerian who had trained in al Qaeda's Afghanistan camps. Ben-Ahmed was thought to be planning a bomb attack against the U.S. embassy in Paris, and authorities discovered a military-issue nuclear-chemical-biological suit and bottles of toxic chemicals in Ben-Ahmed's apartment, which led them to believe that perhaps Ben-Ahmed was planning a chemical attack.[42] In June 2003 — after the U.S. decision to invade Iraq and with both the French and U.S. governments still critical of each other about the war — French authorities arrested two suspected al Qaeda members.[43] In 2004 French authorities arrested 101 suspected Islamic militants, up from 77 in 2003.[44]

Europe's assistance and cooperation is also important because terrorism is not new to many European countries. According to the State Department, there have been 241 terrorist attacks in Western Europe since 1997.[45] The British have more than thirty years experience dealing with terrorism and the Irish Republican Army in Northern Ireland. Attacks in France by Algerian terrorists date back to de Gaulle's rule in the 1950s. The Basque separatist group Euskadi Ta Askatasuna was founded in 1959 and has a history of terrorist attacks — against both Spanish and French interests — beginning in the early 1960s. During the Cold War, Germany was home to three left-wing terrorist groups: Red Army Faction (more commonly known as the Baader-Meinhof Gang), Movement 2 June, and Revolutionary Cells.

The United States needs to be able to draw from the European experience combating terrorism, to learn from and adapt that experience to fighting al Qaeda, and to enlist the help and support of the European community. In short, the United States *needs* Europe if it is to have a fighting chance of winning the war on terrorism.

The Balkans also deserves attention because more than 2 million Muslims live in Albania, Bosnia-Herzegovenia, and Yugoslavia, respectively,[46] and Muslims who trained in al Qaeda's Afghanistan camps are believed to be in the Balkans. But because the Balkans is an area of long-standing dispute between Muslims and other ethnic populations who disagree over which groups should control certain territories, ethnic conflict should not be misconstrued to automatically mean an al Qaeda terrorist threat.

The situation in Russia, which has more than 27 million Muslims[47] and a Muslim separatist movement in Chechnya, is similar to the Balkans. In both the Balkans and Russia, the mistake the United States must avoid is supporting actions taken against Muslim populations that are unrelated to the al Qaeda terrorist threat. For example, Chechnyan terrorist violence is more rooted in nationalist aspirations and centuries of repression rather than embracing radical Islamic fundamentalism. So while the United States needs Russia to go after any al Qaeda that may be seeking refuge in Chechnya, that does not mean that severe Russian military actions — such as the destruction of entire villages — should be accepted as legitimate in the war on terrorism.

As Secretary of Defense Rumsfeld said to the World Affairs Council of Philadelphia in May 2005, this much should be very clear: "this struggle can't be won by any single country."[48] But no matter how successful we are working with countries around the world to dismantle the al Qaeda terrorist organization and network, we cannot possibly hope to capture or kill all of al Qaeda. According to Rumsfeld, "Despite the successes, new terrorist leaders continue to step forward, and new networks emerge. Madrassas around the world continue to turn out new recruits."[49] So U.S. strategy for the war on terrorism must directly address giving Muslims less reason and motivation to become terrorists who would attack the United States. This is especially true in the Middle East, which is an incubator and recruiting pool for radical Islamist terrorists. At heart, this means a willingness to reassess U.S. foreign policy.

Three important points should be made about the role of U.S. foreign policy in strategy for the war on terrorism. First, while it is not enough to think about targets simply as people or things, as we ordinarily would when it comes to war, there is some usefulness to Clausewitz's admonition that "a certain center of gravity develops, the hub of all power and movement, on which everything depends. That is the point against which all our energies should be directed."[50] According to Michael Scheuer,

> Bin Laden has no center of gravity in the traditional sense — no economy, no cities, no homeland, no power grids, no regular military, et cetera. Bin Laden's center of gravity rather lies in the current list of U.S. policies toward the Muslim world because that status quo enrages Muslims around the world — no matter their view

of al Qaeda's view of martial actions—and gives Bin Laden's efforts to instigate a worldwide defensive jihad virtually unlimited room for growth.[51]

Second, although U.S. foreign policy may enrage Muslims, resolving the Israeli-Palestinian conflict is not the key to calming that rage—yet that is the commonly held perception. That perception is grounded in the fact that Muslims around the world identify with the Palestinian's situation, but fixing the Israeli-Palestinian problem will not fix grievances that other Muslims have in their native countries. Thus, it is important to remember what former speaker of the U.S. House of Representatives Tip O'Neill once said: all politics are local. So while peacefully resolving the differences between the Israelis and the Palestinians would certainly help, it is naïve to expect that achieving such a peace will solve other problems in other countries.

On October 7, 2001, as the U.S. began military operations against the Taliban and al Qaeda in Afghanistan, Al Jazeera television aired a videotape from bin Laden that cited the plight of the Palestinians:

> Israeli tanks and tracked vehicles also enter to wreak havoc in Palestine, in Jenin, Ramallah, Rafah, Beit Jala, and other Islamic areas and we hear no voices raised or moves made. . . .
> I swear by Almighty God who raised the heavens without pillars that neither the United States nor he who lives in the United States will enjoy security before we can see it as a reality in Palestine.[52]

Thus, the conventional wisdom is that the United States must resolve the Israeli-Palestinian conflict—something that each administration since Lyndon Johnson's has tried to do, and each has failed. But the United States cannot be an honest broker in the mediation process. This is most apparent given the amount of financial aid the United States provides to Israel. According to a Congressional Research Service Issue Brief for Congress:

> Since 1976, Israel has been the largest annual recipient of U.S. Aid and is the largest recipient of cumulative U.S. assistance since World War II. From 1949 through 1965, U.S. aid to Israel averaged about $63 million per year, over 95% of which was economic development

assistance and food aid. A modest military loan program began in 1959. From 1966 through 1970, average aid per year increased to about $102 million, but military loans increased to about 47% of the total. From 1971 to the present, U.S. aid to Israel has averaged over $2 billion per year, two-thirds of which has been military assistance.[53]

For FY 2003, the United States provided $2.1 billion in military grants, $600 million in economic grants, and $60 million in refugee assistance to Israel. And as part of the first Iraq war budget supplemental, another $1 billion in military grants and $9 billion in loan guarantees to Israel were approved.[54]

By comparison, in the same fiscal year the United States provided only $200 million in indirect assistance channeled either through the UN or non-governmental organizations to the Palestinians. In a historic move, the United States for the first time also gave $20 million directly to the Palestinian Authority for social service projects.[55] Nonetheless, U.S. aid to the Palestinians pales in comparison to support for Israel.

The issue is not whether the United States should be pro-Israeli or pro-Palestinian or whether the United States should provide more aid to the Palestinian Authority. Rather, the United States needs to take a more even-handed approach with both the Israelis and Palestinians. Ultimately, a true peace can only be achieved when both parties are serious about wanting peace and are willing to take all the necessary steps to achieve peace. Instead of improperly presenting itself as an honest broker and failing to produce peace, the United States should be less involved in trying to arbitrate and impose a peace settlement. If the United States remains active in the peace process and it fails, the Palestinian terrorists could use U.S. bias toward Israel as an excuse for the failure to find resolution and as a reason to make America a target for terrorism.

The net result of U.S. aid to Israel is that many Palestinians believe that the United States is underwriting the military equipment the Israelis use to attack the Palestinians,[56] as well as financing the establishment of Jewish settlements in the occupied territories (although a stipulation of U.S. aid to Israel is that the money cannot be used in the occupied territories—but since money is fungible and there is no accounting for how U.S. aid funds are used, there is no way to really know). In other words, from the Muslim perspective, U.S. support to Israel results in harm to Palestinians. As such, the common Palestinian perception is that the United States will always favor Israel in any peace negotiations.

At a minimum, the United States should condition the enormous amount of aid it provides to ensure that Israel takes steps that are conducive to moving toward peace. If peace is viewed as serving U.S. interests, such a policy would simply be common sense. Indeed, such an approach would be entirely consistent with the Bush administration's philosophy behind the Millennium Challenge Account for development aid, which rewards nations for good policies that are likely to promote economic progress based on relatively objective criteria.[57] A similar concept could be applied to aid given to Israel, as well as any given to the Palestinian Authority, to reward good policies that are likely to promote peace. And if a peace is forged between the Israelis and the Palestinians, then the need for any aid would be obviated.

Although Israel is a U.S. friend and ally, we should not equate Israeli security with American security. Making Israel a centerpiece of U.S. national security policy and strategy provides motivation for recruiting terrorists and increases the risk of terrorist attack against the United States. The United States should not risk making Israel's war against the terrorists who attack that country part of America's war against al Qaeda. As terrible and unjustifiable as the attacks by anti-Israeli terrorists are, groups such as Hamas, Hezbollah, and Islamic Jihad do not currently attack the United States or U.S. targets in the Middle East. But if such groups feel they are being lumped in with al Qaeda as part of the war on terrorism, then they might not have any disincentive to refrain from attacking the United States.

Finally, a paradox must be understood: although the United States needs the cooperation of governments such as Saudi Arabia and other Muslim countries to hunt down al Qaeda within their borders, American foreign policy should not necessarily be directed toward creating cozy relationships with the ruling regimes, treating them as if they were long-standing allies, like the Europeans under NATO, forged by the more than fifty years of the Cold War. Hence the appropriateness of Taoist thought in the war on terrorism; the Eastern philosophy is filled with paradoxical statements, such as:

> The most difficult things in the world
> must be done while they are easy;

the greatest things in the world
must be done while they are small.
Because of this sages never do great things;
that is why they can fulfill their greatness.[58]

One of the primary motivating factors for Osama bin Laden's call for jihad was the presence of U.S. forces in Saudi Arabia. Belatedly recognizing the link between the U.S. military presence and terrorism (but using the rationale that the threat posed by Iraq to Saudi Arabia is gone[59]), those forces have since been withdrawn. But the United States must do more than simply remove forces from Saudi Arabia. According to Secretary of Defense Rumsfeld: "We do intend to maintain a continuing and healthy relationship with the Saudis."[60] The close U.S.-Saudi relationship, however, must be reassessed in light of inflaming Islamic extremists and encouraging future terrorist attacks.

Saudi Arabia is treated as a close U.S. ally for one essential reason: oil. The popular myth is that the United States is dependent on Saudi oil, hence a close relationship is necessary. To be sure, Saudi Arabia sits atop the world's largest known oil reserves (264 billion barrels or more than one-fourth of the world's total) and is the world's leading oil producer and exporter, and one of the lowest-cost producers of oil.[61] And the United States depends on imported oil for more than half of the oil it uses. But even though Saudi Arabia is the second largest source of imported crude oil and petroleum products to the United States (1.5 million barrels per day), Saudi oil makes up less than 15 percent of the total (10.1 million barrels per day). The other three major suppliers of U.S.-imported oil are from the Americas: Canada (1.6 million barrels per day), Mexico (1.6 million barrels per day), and Venezuela (1.3 million barrels per day). In fact, nearly half of the oil imported into the United States comes from North and South America. And further underscoring the misconception of U.S. dependence on Middle East oil is the fact that only about 24 percent of U.S.-imported oil comes from the Persian Gulf.[62]

Even more important than the percentage of oil imported by the United States is the fact that oil is a commodity traded openly on the worldwide market; this means that Saudi Arabia is not in a position to wield oil as a weapon against the United States. With no other meaningful source of revenue, the Saudis must sell their oil. Once the oil is sold on the world market, the Saudis cannot control where it ends up. As Massachusetts Institute of Technology economist Morris Adelman points out: "The world oil market, like the world ocean, is one great pool. The price is the same at every border. Who exports the oil Americans consume is irrelevant."[63]

Of course, the Saudis could affect the short-term price of oil by cutting back on production. The likely market reaction would be that other countries would increase production. But the myth of oil as a weapon is based on the false assumption of a "fair and reasonable price" for oil. The reality is that the price of oil is determined by supply and demand, not by some perception of what it should cost. Thus, according to Adelman: "Those who want the United States to produce its way out of the 'problem,' and those who want Americans to conserve their way out, are both the victims of an illusion. There is no shortage or gap, only a high price."[64] And even a higher price of oil is not an absolute certainty as other nations might increase their outputs in an effort to increase their revenues. Indeed, even Organization of Petroleum Exporting Countries (OPEC) members cheat by increasing production over their quotas to increase revenues even as the organization tries to constrain the supply of oil to maximize price.

The possibility of completely cutting off oil supplies is even more far-fetched according to Adelman:

> If the Arabs ever attempted to cut off the United States for political reasons, the non-Arab members of OPEC would simply divert shipments from non-American customers to American. Not for love and not for fun (though they would enjoy spiting the Arabs) but for money. Whereupon the Arabs would ship more to Europe and Asia and the net result would be simply a big confusing costly annoying switch of customers and no harm otherwise. If this is common sense, it is also the lesson of experience. In 1967 a boycott of the United States and also of Great Britain and Germany, whose dependence on imported oil was greater than the United States ever be, failed miserably.[65]

Thus, the realities of oil economics do not justify the U.S. obsession with Saudi oil and the need for a special relationship with the regime in Riyadh to secure access to the oil. But the United States has other good reasons to distance itself from Saudi Arabia. Although spreading democracy is not a sound basis for a national security strategy, liberal democracies themselves are certainly good. Conversely, U.S. support of authoritarian regimes purportedly friendly to American interests—especially while extolling the virtues of democracy—is not only hypocritical but can undermine U.S. national security. Saudi Arabia is a case in point. According to Doug Bandow, a former special assistant to President Ronald Reagan:

> Saudi Arabia is an absolute monarchy, an almost medieval theocracy, with power concentrated in the hands of senior royalty and wealth concentrated among some 7,000 al-Saud princes (or more, by some estimates). Political opposition and even criticism are forbidden. In practice there are few procedural protections for anyone arrested or charged by the government; the semiautonomous religious police, or *Mutawaa'in*, also intimidate and detain citizens and foreigners alike. The government may invade homes and violate privacy whenever it chooses; travel is limited. Women are covered, cloistered, and confined, much as they were in Afghanistan under the Taliban.[66]

Highlighting the hypocrisy of the U.S.-Saudi relationship, the *National Security Strategy of the United States of America* states:

> The United States must defend liberty and justice because these principles are right and true for all people everywhere. No nation owns these aspirations, and no nation is exempt from them. Fathers and mothers in all societies want their children to be educated and to live free from poverty and violence. No people on earth yearn to be oppressed, aspire to servitude, or eagerly await the midnight knock of the secret police.
>
> America must stand firmly for the nonnegotiable demands of human dignity: the rule of law; limits on the absolute power of the state; free speech; freedom of worship; equal justice; respect for women; religious and ethnic tolerance; and respect for private property.[67]

Thus, as Bandow observes: "The American commitment to the Saudi royal family is a moral blemish and a practical danger. It has already drawn the United States into one conventional war and has helped make Americans targets of terrorism, which generated far more casualties in one day than did the Gulf War, Kosovo conflict, and Afghanistan campaign (so far) combined."[68]

Although the Saudi government is now making a more serious effort against al Qaeda, U.S. interests and Saudi interests are not always one and the same. For example, the September 2002 *Joint Inquiry Into Intelligence Community Activities Before and After the Terrorist Attacks of September 11, 2001*, hinted at possible Saudi involvement in 9/11. One of the people named in the unclassified section of the report, entitled "Persons Known to the FBI With Whom September 11 Hijackers May Have Associated in the United States," is Omar al-Bayoumi, a Saudi national. The 9/11 report states that al-Bayoumi had a "somewhat suspicious meeting with the hijackers [al-Hazmi and al-Midhar]" and that he "gave them considerable assistance,"[69] allowing the hijackers to stay at his apartment, helping them find an apartment, cosigning their lease, and paying their first month's rent and security deposit. The report also stated that "since September 11, the FBI has learned that al-Bayoumi has connections to terrorist elements. He has been tied to an imam abroad who has connections to al-Qaeda."[70] The possible Saudi connection is that "al-Bayoumi's salary from his employer, the Saudi Civil Aviation authority, was approved by Hamid al-Rashid. Hamid is the father of Saud al-Rashid, whose photo was found in a raid of an al-Qa'ida safehouse in Karachi and who has admitted to being in Afghanistan between May 2000 and May 2001."[71] A direct connection to the Saudi government was also raised in the 9/11 report:

> Despite the fact that he was a student, al-Bayoumi had access to seemingly unlimited funding from Saudi Arabia. For example, an FBI source identified al-Bayoumi as the person who delivered $400,000 from Saudi Arabia for the Kurdish mosque in San Diego. One of the FBI's best sources in San Diego informed the FBI that he thought that al-Bayoumi must be an intelligence officer for Saudi Arabia or another foreign power.[72]

The *New York Times* reported that "the classified part of a Congressional report on the terrorist attacks on Sept. 11, 2001, says that two Saudi citizens who had at least indirect links with two hijackers were probably Saudi intelligence agents and may have reported to Saudi government officials." According to the *Times*: "Two Saudi citizens, Omar al-Bayoumi and Osama Bassnan, operated in a complex web of financial relationships with officials of the Saudi government. The sections that focus on them draw connections between the two men, two hijackers, and Saudi officials."[73]

The president claimed that declassifying the 9/11 report "would help the enemy" and "would reveal sources and methods that will make it harder for us to win the war on terror."[74] But two former chairmen of the Senate Intelligence Committee — Bob Graham (D-FL) and Richard Shelby (R-AL) — believed more of the report should be made public. Graham claimed that declassifying the report would have permitted "the Saudi government to deal with any questions which may be raised in the currently censored pages, and allow the American people to make their own judgment about who are our true friends and allies in the war on terrorism."[75] In Shelby's judgment, "they could have declassified a lot more of this report and let the American people see it."[76] Continuing to keep the section about possible Saudi involvement in 9/11 secret only makes it seem that there is indeed something to hide and that the administration is protecting the Saudi monarchy. Although the public will probably never know the truth, Senator Shelby perhaps said it best: "You're getting more than bits and pieces, and the American people will put most of it together."[77] The reality is that the Saudis are playing both sides down the middle. They take advantage of the misperception that the United States is dependent on Saudi oil to reap the benefits of being a security ward of the U.S. military against external threats. But they also help fuel Islamic extremism as one way of proving their legitimacy in the Muslim world to protect against internal threats. Both serve the interests of the ruling Saudi monarchy; neither serves U.S. interests.

What American policymakers need to put together is that U.S. security interests are not well served by a needlessly cozy relationship with the Saudi royal family and pictures of President Bush holding Crown Prince Abdullah's hand at the president's Texas ranch.[78] At best, the relationship is an alliance of convenience — but even then it's for the wrong reason: oil. At worst, it's American hypocrisy — supporting an oppressive, theocratic monarchy in Riyadh that does not comport with American values.

During the Cold War, the United States backed all manner of unsavory regimes simply because they claimed to be "anticommunist," which was often mistaken for being "pro-American." At that time such a strategy may sometimes have been necessary to contain the spread of Soviet influence, but continuing to support otherwise corrupt and undemocratic regimes in the Muslim world is counterproductive to U.S. national security. Saudi Arabia is just one example of U.S. support of a supposedly friendly Arab or Muslim regime that is actually detrimental to national security, but there are others.

Since 1975 Egypt has received $25.6 billion in assistance from the United States.[79] Although Egypt is ostensibly a constitutional democracy, according to the State Department's *Country Reports on Human Rights Practices*:

> The National Democratic Party (NDP), which has governed since its establishment in 1978, has used its entrenched position to dominate national politics and has maintained an overriding majority in the popularly elected People's Assembly and the partially elected Shura (Consultative) Council. In 1999 President Hosni Mubarak was reelected unopposed to a fourth 6-year term in a national referendum. The President appoints the Cabinet and the country's 26 governors and may dismiss them at his discretion. The judiciary is generally independent; however, this independence has been compromised by the State of Emergency legislation in force, under which the range of cases subject to its jurisdiction has been compromised due to the improper use of State Emergency Security Courts and military courts for inappropriate cases.[80]

Thus, Egypt is a democracy largely in name only. Indeed, the State Department asserts that Egyptian "citizens did not have a meaningful ability to change their government."[81]

U.S. support to an autocratic Egyptian regime masquerading as a democracy is the same hypocrisy—and carries the same great risks—as U.S. support for the monarchy in Saudi Arabia. From the Arab and Muslim perspective, the United States is "supporting a regime that crushes dissent and restricts individual liberties because to do so suits America's interests."[82] According to Mohammed Zarei, founder of the Human Rights Center for the Assistance of Prisoners: "[I]f there was democracy in Egypt, and people would be free to choose, probably [Mubarak's NDP party] would not be in power. The Islamists would control parliament and government, and that is against what America wants."[83]

As is the case with Saudi Arabia, America's support for Egypt cannot be reconciled with the Bush administration's own vision of championing "aspirations for human dignity" and "building the infrastructure of democracy."[84] According to Ruth M. Beitler and Cindy R. Jebb, both at the U.S. Military Academy: "It is clear that stability supercedes our commitment to democracy in Egypt. The United States' pursuit of stability in the absence of democracy ignores the long-term implications of its actions."[85] For example, while President Bush has demanded an immediate reform of the Palestinian regime, he has encouraged a more gradual approach to reform with Egypt, Saudi Arabia, and Jordan—countries deemed friendly to the United States. According to *Washington Post* editorial page editor Jackson Diehl: "The irony will not be lost on the people in the region, of course—Egyptians and Jordanians will once again conclude that the United States cares about democratic values only when it is strategically convenient."[86] In other words, Egyptians, Arabs, and Muslims can clearly see the hypocrisy in American policy, which is volatile fuel for radical Islamists and foments anti-American attitudes that are the basis for terrorist motivation.

The problems associated with U.S. support for the Mubarak regime are further exacerbated by the unsubtle connection between U.S.-Egyptian policy and U.S.-Israeli policy. According to Beitler and Jebb: "A crucial United States concern is the question of what happens to Egypt if Islamists gain power. Since the Islamists do not hide their disdain for the Jewish State, many in the U.S. government assert that if the Islamic groups achieve power, they would almost certainly terminate the peace with Israel."[87] But Israeli security should not be equated with U.S. national security and certainly should not be the basis for continued U.S. support of an undemocratic regime in Egypt.

Like Egypt, Pakistan claims to be a democracy, even though Gen. Pervez Musharraf came to power by overthrowing a democratically elected government and has used very undemocratic methods to control Pakistan. Although Pakistan has returned to more civilian rule with the election of a National Assembly and a Senate in October 2002 and February 2003, respectively,[88] and a prime minister, Zafarullah Khan Jamali, represents the government, Pakistan only has the veneer of a democratic government. Musharraf continues to wield extraordinary power as president, chief of army staff, and defense minister. Indeed, the Legal Framework Order that Musharraf implemented via executive decree after the referendum naming him president in October 2002 gives him a five-year term as president without a popular election, the power to dissolve the parliament, and assures a role for the military in Pakistani politics by creating a National Security Council with authority to "monitor the process of democracy and governance in the country."[89]

Thus, by supporting the Musharraf regime, the United States is subject to the same potential risks that may arise from supporting Saudi Arabia and Egypt. If America is seen as supporting an illegitimate, oppressive, or corrupt regime, then it becomes a potential target for militant Islamists who would otherwise direct their rage only at the regime. And Pakistan has no short supply of extremist groups, including Harakat-ul-Mujahideen-Al Almi (HUM), Lashkar-e-Tayyiba (LT), Jaish-e-Mohammed (JEM), Sipah-e-Sahaba Pakistan, Tehrik-i-Jafria Pakistan, and Tehrik-i-Nifaz-i-Shariat-i Mohammadi. HUM, LT, and JEM are designated by the State Department as foreign terrorist organizations. According to the State Department, the current leader of HUM, Farooz Kashmiri Khalil, "has been linked to bin Laden and signed his fatwa in February 1998 calling for attacks on U.S. and Western interests."[90]

And the United States cannot turn a blind eye (as it seemingly does with Saudi Arabia) to the fact that Pakistan may be enabling and facilitating al Qaeda terrorists. Indeed, although it is important to consider the source, India has accused the Pakistani Inter Services Intelligence Agency (ISI) of aiding al Qaeda.[91] Given the ISI's involvement with the mujahideen in Afghanistan in the 1980s and their previous support for the Taliban, such allegations cannot be blithely dismissed. But even if they are not true, they raise the larger issue of whether the United States should pursue a policy goal in Pakistan similar to its goal in Egypt: status quo. According to foreign affairs analyst Subodh Atal:

> U.S. policy toward Pakistan has failed to consider the cumulative dangers that nation presents. America continues to pump billions of dollars of aid into Pakistan, without accounting for its fate. Few questions about possible ISI links to September 11 attacks, the

organization's role in sheltering al Qaeda, or Pakistan's nuclear proliferation activities have been asked, let alone answered.

U.S. policy appears to be frozen, concerned only with the preservation of Pakistani dictator Musharraf and overlooking the larger goal of fortifying U.S. national security.[92]

As is the case with Saudi Arabia and Egypt, U.S. national security would be better served by a more arm's length relationship with Pakistan rather than embracing the Musharraf regime as a close ally and providing unqualified support.

The same is true for the U.S. relationship with the Islam Karimov government in Uzbekistan, which is a repressive government with a lack of tolerance for dissent and religious freedom. According to the State Department's *Country Reports on Human Rights Practices*:

- Uzbekistan is an authoritarian state with limited rights.
- The Government's human rights record remained very poor. . . . Citizens could not exercise the right to change their government peacefully. The Government permitted the existence of opposition political parties but harassed their members and refused either to register the parties or to allow them to participate in elections. . . . Police and NSS [National Security Service] arbitrarily arrested persons, particularly Muslims suspected of extremist sympathies.
- The Government severely restricted freedom of speech and the press. . . . The Government restricted freedom of religion and harassed and arrested hundreds of Muslims it suspected of extremism.[93]

Yet despite these acknowledgments, the ties between the United States and Uzbekistan grew closer, including five bilateral agreements, as a result of Operation Enduring Freedom in Afghanistan.[94]

The lesson that should have been learned from each of these cases is that cozy relationships with dictators or autocratic regimes in the Islamic world are strategically unsound. After the Gulf War of 1990, the United States maintained military bases in Saudi Arabia to enforce the postwar agreements with Iraq but also to help secure the kingdom and ensure stability and a continued flow of Saudi oil. The alliance between America and the Saudi royal family has generated the enormous ill will toward the United States of thousands of Saudis who despise their government. The same can be said for America's relationship with Egypt's President Hosni Mubarak. It was no wonder, then, that al Qaeda exploited that hostility to murderous ends: fifteen of the nineteen suicide-hijackers on September 11, 2001, were Saudi nationals and their ringleader, Mohammed Atta, was an Egyptian.

Therefore, we cannot turn a blind eye to Karimov's totalitarian state that quashes dissent and religious expression. The totalitarian nature of the state was made all too evident in May 2005 when violence erupted in Andijan during a violent government crackdown. Uzbekistan president Islam Karimov claimed the Islamic terrorists sparked the clash and that Uzbek troops had to use force to suppress a violent uprising. By contrast, many Uzbeks and human rights groups claimed Karimov's forces opened fire on a group of nonviolent protesters opposing the president's authoritarian rule. An Uzbek opposition leader, Nigara Khidoyatova, who heads the Free Peasants party, claimed that more than seven hundred people were killed by government troops. The Uzbek government claimed that fewer than two hundred people were killed and, according to the country's top prosecutor Rashid Kadyrov, "only terrorists were liquidated by government forces"[95]— a chilling use of words that betrayed the Karimov regime's Soviet roots and showed that the government will play the "terrorist card" for all it is worth in an effort to blunt U.S. criticism.

But the United States cannot afford to be uncritical about or to provide unqualified support for a country in which religious political parties are banned and Muslims—who comprise 90 percent of the population—are allowed to pray only at government-sanctioned mosques. American support for the Karimov regime and the regime's use of the terrorism issue to crack down on the opposition (including the apparent indiscriminate use of violence in Andijan in May 2005) could contribute to Muslim animosity toward the United States. Moderate Muslims in Uzbekistan, who are repressed by a government supported by the United States, could become radicalized and drawn toward groups such as the extremist Islamic Movement of Uzbekistan and thus become anti-American terrorists.

In November 2005 the United States withdrew from Uzbekistan, ostensibly because of the Karimov regime's violent suppression of the Andijan demonstrators. The reality, however, is that U.S. forces were evicted by the Uzbek government. The fact that the United States did not voluntarily sever its relationship with the Karimov regime will likely not be lost on Muslims, who will see the United States as only unwillingly ending its ties with an oppressive Muslim regime that it otherwise would have continued supporting.

Egypt, Pakistan, and Uzbekistan are just three examples, but they highlight the problems associated with U.S. support for countries—especially Muslim countries with autocratic regimes—without regard to whether they share common core values (beyond, for example, claiming to be anti-Islamist or antiterrorist). Such support may be a necessary evil in the short term but should be narrowly focused, done only out of necessity, and of limited duration. The United States must avoid lapsing into a Cold War mindset— just as America funneled millions of dollars to authoritarian regimes around the world because they were considered "anticommunist," America should be wary about providing ongoing support to countries simply because they profess to be "anti-Islamist" or "antiterrorist." If history is any guide, such support does not guarantee a more democratic government. Even worse, when the United States supported undemocratic and unpopular regimes during the Cold War simply because they were friendly to us, and when those regimes were overthrown, the results were often virulently anti-American successor governments (e.g., Iran and Nicaragua). Ultimately—and paradoxically—U.S. support for countries such as Egypt, Pakistan, and Uzbekistan could end up doing more to breed terrorism than to prevent it.

A final word about U.S. foreign policy: the problem is not one of communication. According to Secretary of Defense Rumsfeld:

> Anti-American messages and images of hate quickly find their way across the world via the Internet and other advanced technologies.
>
> Yet for decades, the international community's response to this ideological battle has been inadequate. In particular, the standard U.S. government public affairs operation is still rooted in the era of daily and weekly news cycles, rather than the 24-hour global maelstrom of instant coverage on cable news, talk radio, and the Internet.
>
> Communications operations may well require substantial innovation, greater agility and the speed that accompanies a transformed military. We will need to develop considerably more sophisticated ways of using the many new communication channels available to reach diverse audiences critical to success in this new world—and to do so near instantaneously.

This will require developing better access to the non-mainstream media around the world — as their influence continues to grow and as the influence and reach of more traditional channels continue to decline.[96]

But the problems of U.S. foreign policy in the Islamic world will not be repaired by a better communications or public relations or public diplomacy effort. Muslims see U.S. foreign policy for exactly what it is. A better foreign policy — not better spin — is what is needed. Deeds, not words, are what matter.

7

THE LAST LINE OF DEFENSE

When did Noah build the ark, Gladys?
Before the rain. Before the rain.

— *Spy Game* (2001)

A paramount responsibility of the federal government as set forth in the Constitution is to "provide for the common defense." Doing less in terms of American foreign policy may be the best way to reduce the risk of terrorism, but failing to defend the homeland would be unacceptable in the post-9/11 world. Therefore, the U.S. government should focus on reasonable and prudent means to provide protection for the homeland itself. In taking on this task, it is important to recognize the hard truth: providing absolute and perfect defense against any and all potential terrorist attacks is impossible. The nature of terrorism is to morph and adapt, to flow around obstacles, and to find the path of least resistance. A determined terrorist enemy will eventually find a way to exploit gaps in defenses and security — precisely what al Qaeda did on 9/11. So rather than trying to do everything, and doing nothing well, a more realistic approach to homeland security is to focus on a handful of key areas that will make another terrorist attack less easy and raise the opportunity costs for terrorists to be successful in inflicting catastrophic damage on the United States.

Accordingly, homeland security efforts must focus on those threats that pose the most catastrophic consequences and for which there are cost-effective defenses. First and foremost, that means not focusing on the last attack. The March 2004 Madrid train bombings are proof enough that we should not be obsessed with hijacked airplanes. But since 9/11, much of the focus of airport security has been on passengers — who are subject to greater inspection, including a requirement to remove their coats and routinely take off their shoes and belts to pass through security — and considerable resources have been devoted to increased airport security to prevent future hijackings. Less attention has been paid to security for airport operations, especially for those people with access to aircraft (e.g., ground crews, baggage handlers, etc.) who could also pose a hijacking threat and a potential direct threat to aircraft, if the intent is simply to blow a plane up or cause some other in-flight mishap. In that regard, although the Transportation Security Agency (TSA) now screens 100 percent of checked baggage for explosives, cargo — which is routinely loaded on passenger aircraft — is not screened. So while it may be more difficult for passengers to hijack aircraft to use as missiles, aircraft nonetheless remain vulnerable to terrorist attack.

Perhaps the most glaring vulnerability for aircraft is the threat posed by shoulder-fired antiaircraft missiles — also known as man portable air defense systems (MANPADS). MANPADS are a known clear and present danger. An estimated five hundred thousand to seven hundred thousand MANPADS have been produced worldwide,[1] and they are thought to be in the military inventories of at least fifty-six countries.[2] So containing their proliferation is a relatively moot point — especially since according to the RAND Corporation, "SA-7s and other Russian made models can be purchased in arms bazaars in a number of Middle Eastern and Central Asian countries. In some of these markets, such systems are sold for as little as $5,000."[3]

The biggest concern about the MANPADS threat is that they are known to be in the possession of non-state actors. According to a U.S. government estimate, six thousand MANPADS are outside the control of any government.[4] Over two dozen terrorist groups probably possess these weapons.[5] Al Qaeda is reported to have both first-generation former Soviet SA-7s and second-generation U.S. Stinger missiles (supplied to the mujahideen by the CIA to fight the Soviets in Afghanistan).[6] So the MANPADS terrorist threat is real, not hypothetical. Moreover, MANPADS have been used to attack civil aircraft. Table 7.1 shows various estimates for the number of MANPADS attacks and the deaths attributed to those attacks. Table 7.2 shows the reported use of MANPADS by non-state actors.

Although the loss of life from a single MANPADS attack would be considerably less than that on 9/11 (perhaps several hundred killed rather

Table 7.1
MANPADS Attacks on Civil Aircraft

Organization	Period Covered	Number of Attacks	Number of Deaths
TSA	1979–2003	35	640
CIA	1977–1996	27	400
FBI	1970s–2003	29	550
RAND	1975–1992	40	760
Jane's	1996–2000	16	186

Source: Loren B. Thompson, "MANPADS: Scale and Nature of the Threat," November 12, 2003.

than thousands), the terror spread by such an attack could be just as profound. Even an unsuccessful terrorist attack against a U.S. commercial aircraft would likely have a chilling effect on airline travel. The consequences of shutting down commercial air traffic after the 9/11 hijackings serve as a useful baseline for estimating the potential effects of a shoulder-fired missile attack against a commercial airliner.

Even though the airline industry was facing significant challenges prior to 9/11, the sharpest decline in industry revenues in history—35 to 40 percent in the last quarter of 2001 due to corporate travel freezes and cancellation of leisure trips—is attributed to the terrorist attacks.[7] But the economic consequences rippled beyond the airline industry. According to a study by the Milken Institute, the lost U.S. economic output in the immediate aftermath of the attacks was $47 billion and the loss of stock market wealth (after the end of the first week of trading after the attack) was more than $1.7 trillion.[8] The immediate cost to the insurance industry was estimated at $36 billion to $54 billion, the largest insured losses in history.[9] The economic losses associated with the attacks probably led to the loss of over 145,000 jobs in thirty-four states in 2001 and 2002.[10] Admittedly, accurately measuring the total costs of the 9/11 attacks may be impossible. But it is sobering that Dr. Robert Keleher, chief macroeconomist for the Joint Economic Committee, concluded that "terrorism's long-term costs may be more severe than suggested by many existing estimates."[11]

A MANPADS attack would have similar repercussions throughout the economy. A RAND Corporation study concluded that the "demand for

Table 7.2
Reported Non-State Use of MANPADS, 1996–2001

Date	Non-State Group	Missile Type	Killed/Injured	Aircraft	Notes
23 Oct 00	Tamil Tigers (LTTE)	Stinger	4/0	Mi-24 Hind	Shot down near Trincomalee harbour, Sri Lanka.
04 Oct 00	Chechen rebels	Stinger	1/0	Su-24	Shot down near Urus-Martan, Chechen Republic.
04 Oct 00	Chechen rebels	Stinger	Unknown	Su-25	Shot down on reconnaissance mission.
10 Aug 00	LTTE	Unknown	0/0	Fighter jet	Aircraft fired at. No damage.
25–30 Aug 00	Chechen rebels	SA-7	0/0	Unreported	Helicopters fired on. All missiles miss.
07 May 00	Chechen rebels	Unknown	2/0	Su-24	Shot down in southern Chechnya.
31 Mar 00	LTTE	Unknown	40/0	An-26	Transport craft downed, possibly by MANPAD.
10 Nov 99	Revolutionary Armed Forces of Columbia (FARC)	Unreported	5/0	DC-3	FARC mistakenly downs civilian craft, press says.
04 Apr 99	Hezbollah	SA-7	0/0	F-16s	Two missiles fired on Israeli F-16s. Both miss.
06 Mar 99	Kurdistan Workers Party (PKK)	Unknown	20/0	Puma helicopter	Helicopter shot down in southern Turkey.
02 Jan 99	United Front for the Total Independence of Angola (UNITA)	Unknown	14/0	C-130	UN plane shot down in central Angola.

Date	Group	Missile	Fired/Hit	Aircraft	Description
26 Dec 98	UNITA	Unknown	9/0	C-130	UN-chartered plane shot down in central Angola.
15 Dec 98	UNITA	Unknown	10/0	An-12	An-12 struck by missile en route to Luanda.
10 Oct 98	Tutsi rebels	Possible SA-7	40/0	Boeing 727	Airplane struck over DR of Congo
13 Aug 98	LTTE	Unknown	0/0	Kfir fighter/surveillance Aircraft	Missiles fired by rebels. No damage.
01 Dec 97	Kosovo Liberation Army (KLA)	Strela 2M	5/0	Yugoslav Air Transport	Serb reports KLA shootdown craft near Pristina.
07 Oct 97	LTTE	Unknown	0/0	Mi-17 transports	Missiles reportedly fired from Tamil rebel boats
10 Nov 97	LTTE	Unknown	2/2	Mi-17 transports and Mi-24 Hind	Missiles fired at helicopter convoy.
20 Aug 97	LTTE	Stinger (reported)	0/0	Kfir fighters	Miss over Puliyankulam
18 May 97	PKK	SA-7	2/0	Super Cobra	Shot down during operations in Iraq.
May 97	PKK	SA-7	11/0	Cougar Transport	Shot down during operations in Iraq.
22 Jan 96	LTTE	Unknown	39/0	Mi-17	Unconfirmed MANPAD.
30 Apr 96	LTTE	Unknown	94/0	Unknown	Two air force transports downed.
Apr 96	Hezbollah	Unknown	0/0	UAV	Unconfirmed MANPAD.

Source: Thomas B. Hunter, "The proliferation of MANPADS," *Jane's Intelligence Review*, November 28, 2002.

air travel could fall by 15–25 percent for months after a successful MANPADS attack on a commercial airliner in the United States. A weeklong system wide shutdown of air travel could generate welfare losses of $3–4 billion, and when losses from reduced air traffic in the following months are added in, the result could exceed $15 billion."[12] The study estimated that if airlines were shut down for one month, the total loss could be more than $70 billion.

It is also worth noting an important difference between the 9/11 hijackings and a MANPADS attack. After 9/11 the federal government was able to implement security measures designed to prevent future hijackings. Regardless of the efficacy of these measures, they provided some level of assurance to the general public that it was safe to fly. But if a shoulder-fired missile is used to attack a passenger aircraft (even if the attack is unsuccessful), it may be much more difficult to convince the public that it is safe to fly — regardless of new security measures.

Just as it is impossible to prevent the proliferation of MANPADS (because they are already proliferated) as a way to counter the threat, airport perimeter security is also an inadequate solution to a possible terrorist attack. For example, the RAND Corporation determined that the SA-7 MANPADS threat to Los Angeles International Airport would allow a terrorist to be anywhere within an 870-square-mile area of the airport.[13] Based on the 2000 census, the City of Los Angeles had a population density of 7,873 persons per square mile and 2,850 housing units per square mile.[14] If protecting Los Angeles International Airport requires securing an 870 square mile area around the airport, that means a dedicated police effort in an area containing about 6.8 million people and 2.5 million housing units. It is not surprising, therefore, that the RAND Corporation concluded that "*completely* preventing an attack solely through the use of enhanced security perimeters would be impractical, considering the large urbanized areas involved, the cover provided by urban structures, and the availability of multiple freeways for quick access to attack and getaway" (emphasis in original).[15]

Thankfully, there has not yet been a terrorist missile attack against a U.S. commercial airliner. But as the RAND Corporation concluded, "as measures are taken to preclude 9/11-style attacks (e.g., improvement in screening at airports, deployment of air marshals on aircraft, strengthening of cockpit doors), attacking aircraft with MANPADS will unavoidably become more attractive to terrorists."[16] We may be living on borrowed time.

The Last Line of Defense

        Technical countermeasures against MANPADS—used on military aircraft—are available now[17] and could be adapted for civilian commercial use. These countermeasures are not perfect and are not cheap, but they are better than leaving aircraft vulnerable to a known and predictable threat. The RAND Corporation estimated the cost for installing laser direct infrared countermeasure (DIRCM) systems—which use beams of light to emit signals that scramble the MANPADS infrared seeker, causing the missile to miss its target—on sixty-eight hundred commercial aircraft would be $11.2 billion for procurement and $2.7 billion for annual operating and support costs, and $38.2 billion for total ten-year life-cycle cost (LCC), which included various other costs.[18]

        Although the Department of Homeland Security's $41.1 billion budget may not be large enough to support a new $11 billion project, the focus should not be just on DHS. If the federal government's primary responsibility is to provide for the common defense, the costs must be viewed in a larger perspective. The Bush administration's FY 2006 budget request for the U.S. government is $2.6 trillion.[19] So the $11 billion estimated cost for aircraft-mounted MANPADS countermeasures is less than one-half of 1 percent of the total federal budget—a modest amount for the government to spend to fulfill its primary responsibility. So it is hard to believe that we can't find $11 billion within that budget to protect ourselves from a serious threat.

        According to Citizens Against Government Waste (CAGW), in 2004, congressional appropriators stuck 10,656 projects in thirteen appropriations bills for a total of $22.9 billion in pork-barrel spending[20]—more than twice what's needed to procure the type of countermeasures cited in the RAND report. The biggest purveyor of government pork-barrel spending, according to CAGW, was the Department of Defense ($11.5 billion) followed by combined Transportation and Treasury projects ($4.4 billion).[21] CAGW also made 592 recommendations that, if enacted, would trim the FY 2005 budget by $217 billion and save $1.65 trillion over the next five years. Some recommended cuts include canceling the international space station program ($9.3 billion savings over five years), eliminating community development block grants ($24.5 billion savings over five years), reducing the federal gas tax and eliminating highway trust funds ($62 billion savings over five years), and eliminating the Natural Resource Conservation Service ($12.9 billion savings over five years).[22]

The Defense Department spent nearly $500 billion in 2005, including the funds for military operations in Iraq and Afghanistan. The $11 billion for MANPADS countermeasures would represent about 2 percent of the Pentagon's spending. As with the total federal budget, money could be saved in the Defense Department's budget to pay for MANPADS countermeasures. According to a 1997 Business Executives for National Security study, "by adopting modern business practices, the Department of Defense could realize savings conservatively estimated at $15 billion to $30 billion."[23] The bottom line is that the MANPADS terrorist threat is serious enough to warrant the government taking protective action and more than enough money could be found in the federal budget to pay for appropriate countermeasures.

But we must not be preoccupied with aircraft-related threats. Another high priority for homeland security must be to prevent terrorists from entering the country. This is the single most important thing that the DHS can do to reduce the likelihood of another terrorist attack. It is important to remember that all nineteen hijackers entered the United States via known points of legal entry, as millions of visitors to the United States do annually. Thus, tracking terrorists more effectively does not necessarily mean adding more border guards. Rather, it means making sure systems and procedures are put in place so that known or suspected terrorists can be stopped at the border by the appropriate authorities. The most crucial aspect is ensuring that information from the appropriate agencies (e.g., CIA, FBI, Interpol) about known or suspected terrorists is made directly available in real time to those people responsible for checking passports, visas, and other immigration information.

The Visitor and Immigrant Status Indicator Technology (US-VISIT) program is supposed to screen foreign visitors as they enter the United States to make sure that they are not would-be terrorists. At its unveiling at Hatfield-Jackson Atlanta International Airport at the beginning of January 2004, then–DHS Secretary Tom Ridge proclaimed that US-VISIT was "part of a comprehensive program to ensure that our borders remain open to visitors but closed to terrorists." One would think that means comparing passengers' names to a database of known and suspected al Qaeda operatives and persons with suspected ties to al Qaeda. But according to Ridge, "While processing more than 20,000 travelers . . . , US-VISIT has matched 21 hits on the FBI Criminal Watch List, including potential entrants with previous convictions for statutory rape, dangerous drugs, aggravated felonies, and several cases of visa fraud."[24] So the few people snared are exactly who one would expect to catch: criminals, not terrorists. Indeed, how many terrorists' fingerprints does the FBI have in its Criminal Watch List? It's probably a good guess that Osama bin Laden and other top al Qaeda operatives are not included. But in a world where anyone can type keywords into Google with a nearly instantaneous response, being able to cross-check a person's name, passport number, and photo against U.S. and foreign terrorist databases should not be an insurmountable problem.

The U.S. no-fly list (implemented in November 2001, although the TSA denied its existence for a year) is also intended to keep terrorism suspects from entering the United States (as well as to protect aircraft from potential terrorist attack) by preventing people deemed to pose a threat from boarding commercial airline flights. TSA compiles the list from data supplied by the FBI, the CIA, and the government's terrorist screening center. In April 2004 the American Civil Liberties Union (ACLU) filed a class-action lawsuit against DHS and TSA, claiming that the no-fly list is "not maintained with sufficient accuracy, relevance, timeliness, or completeness to ensure that innocent passengers are not incorrectly and unfairly stopped, interrogated, detained, searched, or subjected to other travel impediments."[25] The facts that Senator Ted Kennedy (D-MA) was stopped twice in August 2004 because his name was on the no-fly list[26] and that infants have been stopped from boarding airplanes because their names are the same or similar to names on the no-fly list[27] certainly lends credence to the ALCU's allegations.

But even if the no-fly list was maintained with perfect accuracy, there are some very real operational problems with implementing it—as was made evident in May 2005 when two overseas flights to Boston were diverted to Bangor, Maine, within days of each other. The first was Air France flight 322 from Paris.[28] The second was Alitalia flight 618 from Milan.[29] In both cases, a passenger's name on the flight manifest matched a name on the U.S. government's no-fly list. This was not the first time flights have been diverted to Bangor. In September 2004 a United Airlines London-to-New York flight carrying the singer formerly known as Cat Stevens was forced to land in Bangor because the name Stevens took after converting to Islam—Yusuf Islam—is on the no-fly list (Islam denies any terrorist connections).[30] The question is: If it is supposed to be a no-fly list, how is it that people on the list are able to actually get onto airplanes and fly?

Airlines are supposed to check passengers against a no-fly list before they are allowed to board, but the airlines do not always have the most current no-fly list. Current U.S. law requires airlines to transmit the passenger lists of flights bound for the United States to the DHS within fifteen minutes of takeoff. DHS officials then check the names against the no-fly list. The problem is that the names are not transmitted until after takeoff; this means people are actually flying. But even if the no-fly list is sent to DHS within fifteen minutes after takeoff, why is it not apparently checked until the aircraft is almost ready to land in the United States—several hours into its flight? Would it not make more sense to check the list and make the decision about a passenger almost immediately after takeoff, when—in theory—it poses less of a risk?

Since passengers cannot go through security to get to their departure gate without first having a boarding pass, would it not make sense for those names to be transmitted to DHS on a rolling, real-time basis to be continuously checked? Such a procedure is certainly not beyond the capabilities of modern technology. More important, it would be a way to actually prevent people whose names are on the no-fly list from flying—sparing all the other passengers the major inconvenience of a detour to Bangor and the airlines the not-so-trivial cost of an unscheduled landing and departure.

The no-fly list problem goes beyond the basic issue of this list not being checked until after an aircraft has already taken off. The larger problem is knowing whether the person in question is the same person on the no-fly list. In both the Air France and Alitalia cases, the problem was mistaken identity.

But mistaken identity should not be a problem since the US-VISIT program requires practically all visitors to apply for a visa in their country of origin before entering the United States. That application process includes providing biographic and biometric information—two index finger scans and a digital photograph. Common sense says that people who apply for visas should be cross-checked against the no-fly list and any other terrorist watch lists to determine if they are a potential threat.

In the case of the Air France flight, although the passenger in question had the same name and birth date as someone on the no-fly list, he had been issued a visa and he did not match the physical description of the person on the no-fly list. In other words, there was no real reason to divert the 169 passengers aboard Air France flight 332 and delay their arrival in Boston.

And there was no real need to embarrass and humiliate the man, his wife, and two children by escorting them off the plane, detaining them, and subjecting them to questioning.

Because the prospect of terrorists using weapons of mass destruction (WMD) is something that must be taken seriously, in addition to dangerous people, homeland security must seek to prevent unauthorized dangerous cargo from entering the United States. According to Stephen Flynn, director of the Independent Task Force on Homeland Security cochaired by former U.S. senators Gary Hart and Warren Rudman, "although the CIA has concluded that the most likely way weapons of mass destruction (WMD) would enter the United States is by sea, the federal government is spending more every three days to finance the war in Iraq than it has provided over the past three years to prop up the security of all 361 U.S. commercial seaports."[31]

It is not a question of protecting those seaports per se, but of implementing screening and security measures to prevent the transit of WMD. The problem is that more than fifteen thousand containers enter the United States via ship and twice that many via truck on a daily basis, so screening each and every container without bringing the U.S. economy to a grinding halt would be impossible. The Container Security Initiative (CSI), introduced in January 2002, provides a more rational approach. In an effort to extend the security zone outside of U.S. borders rather than only at ports of entry, CSI:

- uses intelligence and automated information to identify and target containers that pose a risk for terrorism;
- prescreens those containers that pose a risk at the port of departure before they arrive at U.S. ports;
- uses detection technology to quickly prescreen containers that pose a risk; and
- uses smarter, tamper-evident containers.

Containers that might pose a terrorist risk include those shipped from or transiting through countries where terrorists are known to operate, those shipped on vessels with suspect ownership, those whose entire manifest cannot be adequately accounted for, or those shipped on vessels on which there is suspicious crew activity.

Although much of such an effort needs to be directed at WMD, focusing exclusively on actual *weapons* of mass destruction would be a mistake. Ships, trains, and trucks carrying hazardous materials could be potential bombs, as demonstrated by the foiled April 2004 terrorist plot in Jordan that involved truck bombs loaded with tons of chemicals and explosives.[32] Of course, not every ship, train, or truck is a threat, and the need for security must be balanced by the need to ensure the free flow of goods, which is vital to the health of the U.S. economy. For example, the total value of trade between the United States and Canada (by all surface transportation modes and for all commodities) was over $341 billion in 2002 ($194 billion in imports and $146 billion in exports).[33]

And as the MANPADS threat demonstrates, a myopic focus on only the WMD threat could overlook other threats that could inflict potentially catastrophic results. While terrorists would certainly like to procure WMD, they are not likely to focus all their efforts on obtaining and using WMD to the exclusion of other low-tech means. In other words, there are opportunity costs associated with acquiring WMD and, on the flip side of the coin, there are opportunity costs to defend against WMD.

Homeland security must also focus on protecting potential targets against terrorist attack—acknowledging that there are too many targets to protect and myriad ways in which they can be attacked. Instead of trying to protect every potential target against every possible attack, we must prioritize targets to defend. For example, the 104 nuclear power plant reactors at sixty-four locations operating in thirty-one states should get high priority. But protecting the nuclear reactors—as is the case with ports—is not simply a matter of providing increased security per se. The first concern is to safeguard nuclear material so that it can't be stolen for building a weapon (in this case, a radiological dirty bomb, since none of the U.S. reactors produce weapons-grade uranium or plutonium). Second, the power plant itself must be protected to prevent terrorists from creating a disaster along the lines of Chernobyl. Similarly, security for chemical and biological facilities must be designed to prevent terrorists from creating an accident such as the 1984 Union Carbide chemical pesticide plant accident in Bhopal, India, that killed more than three thousand people.

Another target set that deserves attention are dams. There are more than seventy-nine thousand dams in the United States,[34] and protecting all of them from terrorist attack would be impossible. But some dams, such as Hoover Dam (which contains Lake Mead, the largest reservoir in the United States) and Glen Canyon Dam (which contains the second largest reservoir in the United States, Lake Powell), must be protected. Lake Mead and Lake Powell supply water to Colorado, Wyoming, New Mexico, Utah, Arizona, Nevada, California, and even northern Mexico. Hoover Dam power supplies account for 19 percent of the power for Arizona, 23 percent for Nevada, and 15 percent for Los Angeles. Destruction of either or both of these dams would likely have catastrophic consequences — in terms of both actual damage to life and property and the economic impact of disrupting the water supply and electrical power. While Hoover and Glen Canyon may be the two most important dams on the Colorado River, there are more than fifty dams along that river, and destroying dams up river could achieve the same result as a direct attack simply because of the release of water — whether all of them can and need to be protected is part of creating a threat matrix for homeland security to prioritize the allocation of resources.

Prioritizing targets to defend also means deciding which targets should fall outside the federal government's purview — either because of cost or feasibility. For example, in June 2004 a Columbus, Ohio, man (originally from Somalia) — Nuradin Abdi — was indicted on charges that he conspired to bomb a shopping mall in the Columbus area.[35] Whether Abdi and his coconspirator, Iyman Faris (who pled guilty in June 2003 to providing material support to al Qaeda and admitted plotting to sever the cables of the Brooklyn Bridge in New York and to derail trains in New York or Washington, D.C.), turn out to be al Qaeda terrorists remains to be seen. But the charges demonstrate that shopping malls are a potential terrorist target. Yet although a bomb detonated in a shopping mall would probably kill tens — if not hundreds — of people and would likely have a devastating effect and possible severe economic consequences (shopping centers accounted for $1.98 trillion in retail sales in 2003[36]), protecting the nearly forty-seven thousand shopping malls and centers in the United States would be impossible.[37] Private security at malls could be increased, but they would still remain vulnerable targets; the public must accept a certain level of inherent risk.

If it is important to do certain things — such as preventing terrorists from entering the country and protecting certain critical targets — for homeland security, it is also important to know what not to do. First and foremost, homeland security actions should not needlessly raise the anxiety level of the general public. Unfortunately, this has largely been the history of the color-coded homeland security alert system.

For the first six months after it was created in March 2002, the homeland security alert system was flatlined on yellow or elevated, meaning a significant risk of terrorist attack. This despite the fact that during that time several different warnings were issued about the terrorist threats. In April 2002 the FBI issued a warning that banks in the northeast United States were targets of possible terrorist attacks.[38] In May 2002, after rhetoric of pending terrorist attacks by Vice President Dick Cheney, FBI Director Robert Mueller, Homeland Security Director Tom Ridge, and Secretary of Defense Donald Rumsfeld,[39] the FBI alerted New York City authorities about possible terrorist attacks against city landmarks, such as the Statue of Liberty and the Brooklyn Bridge. The Department of Transportation also issued a warning about possible attacks against subway and rail systems. And nuclear power plants were put on alert. But the homeland security alert level remained at yellow.

In June 2002 Attorney General John Ashcroft announced an alleged dirty bomb plot in connection with the arrest of U.S. citizen Jose Padilla. The Coast Guard issued an alert for ports and harbors.[40] And the FBI warned about fuel tanker attacks against Jewish schools and synagogues. Yet the alert level was not raised.

In July 2002 TSA warned small airports and private pilots to be on the lookout for suspicious persons, activities, and operations.[41] The Senate Select Committee on Intelligence stated that al Qaeda was regrouping and working secretly inside the United States,[42] and U.S. intelligence agencies claimed that the al Qaeda infrastructure in the United States could be as many as five thousand terrorists and supporters.[43] "Intelligence chatter" raised serious concerns that terrorists would try to strike again sometime during the summer.[44] An al Qaeda spokesman claimed that Osama bin Laden was still alive and that more attacks were being organized.[45] Still the alert level stayed at yellow.

On the one-year anniversary of the 9/11 terrorist attacks, the warning status was elevated to orange, or a high risk of terrorist attack. Yet the threat remained as vague as it was before. According to President Bush, "We have no specific threat to America."[46] Attorney General Ashcroft claimed that the heightened terror alert was prompted by "specific intelligence" pointing to threats against U.S. interests in South Asia and the Middle East.[47] But if there was no threat to the U.S. homeland, why was the homeland security advisory system level raised? Even more absurd was a joint statement by

Ashcroft and Ridge when the alert level was lowered two weeks later: "Detained al Qaeda operatives have informed U.S. intelligence and law enforcement officials that al Qaeda will wait until it believes Americans are less vigilant and less prepared before it will strike again."[48] But—by definition—lowering the alert status meant we were less vigilant and prepared.

Proof that the homeland security advisory system does little—if anything—to fulfill its mandate to "provide a comprehensive and effective means to disseminate information regarding the risk of terrorist acts to . . . the American people"[49] was the FBI's warning in October 2002 that al Qaeda might be planning to attack passenger trains. Not only did the alert level remain at yellow, but an administration spokesperson urged Americans to "continue to ride our nation's rails."[50]

The homeland security alert level has been raised from yellow to orange a total of five times: on the anniversary of 9/11; in February 2003 in conjunction with the Muslim holiday the Hajj; for the Iraq war; during Christmas 2003; and in August 2004 specifically for financial targets in New York, New Jersey, and Washington, D.C. But there have also been countless warnings about possible terrorism that didn't change the alert level. So it's hard to determine how warnings about possible terrorist attacks relate to the actual alert level. Given that there haven't been any terrorist attacks regardless of the alert level, it's also difficult to know if the alert level makes any difference at all. And it's not clear what the relationship is between the alert level and the threat. For example, when the alert level was lowered back to yellow in November 2004 for the financial sectors in New York, New Jersey, and Washington, D.C., Deputy Secretary of Homeland Security James M. Loy said that the decision was based on improved security not because the threat itself had diminished.[51]

Ultimately, it seems that the color-coded homeland security advisory system is more a way for the federal bureaucracy to be seen as "doing something" to prove to the public that politicians and government officials are not asleep at the wheel—if something actually does happen, they can claim they gave fair warning. Indeed, after stepping down as the secretary of homeland security, Tom Ridge admitted, "More often than not we [DHS] were the least inclined to raise it. . . . Sometimes we disagreed with the intelligence assessment. Sometimes we thought even if the intelligence was good, you don't necessarily put the country on (alert). . . . There were times when some people were really aggressive about raising it, and we said, 'For that?'"[52] But the system is of little use for the general public, who have been told to go about their normal, everyday lives when the alert level has been raised. For example, when the alert level was raised in conjunction with military action in Iraq in March 2003, Ridge said, "As on the other occasions when the national threat level has been increased, we encourage members of the public to continue their daily work, family and leisure activities."[53] So the homeland security alert system is largely sound and fury signifying nothing.

Second, whatever actions are taken to defend against possible terrorist attacks, homeland security officials must consider civil liberties implications. We must heed Benjamin Franklin's admonition that "they that can give up essential liberty to obtain a little temporary safety deserve neither liberty nor safety."[54] The rule of thumb should be that before the government infringes civil liberties, it must demonstrate that proposed new powers are essential, that they would be effective, and that there is no less-invasive way to accomplish the same security goal. This was certainly not the case when the Uniting and Strengthening America by Providing Appropriate Tools Required to Intercept and Obstruct Terrorism (USA PATRIOT) Act was passed. For example, when then–House Majority Leader Dick Armey (R-TX) called for separate votes on various measures contained in the PATRIOT Act, he was overruled by congressional leaders who did not want to be criticized by the White House for appearing to be weak on terrorism. Instead, a 342-page omnibus act that amended fifteen existing federal legislative packages was passed in five weeks with minimal debate because the normal process of interagency review and committee hearings was suspended (the Senate voted 98 to 1 and the House vote was 356 to 66).

Certainly, the entire PATRIOT Act is not objectionable or controversial — but some parts represent a serious threat to civil liberties. For example, section 213 allows the federal government to delay giving notice of a warrant when they conduct a search.[55] The PATRIOT Act thus undermines the protection of the Fourth Amendment that requires the government to both obtain a warrant and to give notice before conducting the search.[56] Section 215, which allows federal agents to seize any tangible items from a person's home as part of a terrorism investigation, directs that a judge "shall grant" such orders at the executive branch's request — meaning that Department of Justice does not necessarily have to show probable cause. Moreover, these orders do not have to disclose why and for what purpose they are being issued. Finally, Section 215 contains a gag provision making it a crime for anyone to speak out about its use.[57]

Fortunately, the provisions of the PATRIOT Act have not gone unchallenged. In September 2004 a federal court struck down Section 505 of the PATRIOT Act, which allowed the use of so-called national security letters that gave the Justice Department administrative subpoena power without requiring probable cause or judicial oversight.[58] Ruling that Section 505 violated Fourth Amendment protections against unreasonable searches, U.S. District Court Judge Victor Marrero wrote, "democracy abhors undue secrecy. Hence, an unlimited government warrant to conceal . . . has no place in our open society."[59] He also warned, "Under the mantle of secrecy, the self-preservation that ordinarily impels our government to censorship and secrecy may potentially be tuned on ourselves as a weapon of self-destruction."[60]

The importance of protecting civil liberties was also evident in the Supreme Court's decision regarding the Yaser Hamdi case. Hamdi—a U.S. citizen—was apparently a Taliban fighter captured in Afghanistan during Operation Enduring Freedom. He was subsequently held for more than two years in a military brig in Charleston, South Carolina. Classified as an "enemy combatant" by the Bush administration, Hamdi was not allowed to have any contact with any visitors, including his family and lawyer. In July 2004 the Supreme Court ruled that Hamdi could be held as an enemy combatant but that he could also use the U.S. courts to challenge the legality of his detention and treatment. Justice Sandra Day O'Connor wrote, "As critical as the government's interest may be in detaining those who actually pose an immediate threat to the national security of the United States during ongoing international conflict, history and common sense teach us that an unchecked system of detention carries the potential to become a means for oppression and abuse of others who do not present that sort of threat."[61]

We also need to be wary of any homeland security proposals that cast a wide net in an effort to snare a few potential terrorists. One such proposal was the Terrorism Information and Prevention System (TIPS). As a sort of nationwide neighborhood watch, TIPS would have enlisted truck drivers, cable installers, utility employees, and others whose jobs regularly take them to a variety of places to report on suspicious activities. Ignoring whether any of these people would have been qualified to detect suspicious activities, the information they provided would have been stored in a Department of Justice database — regardless of whether any of the people they were reporting on were charged or guilty of any wrongdoing. And as Lee Strickland — a retired CIA analyst and currently director of the Center for Information Policy at the University of Maryland — points out, "Since you don't know what information is being shared and how it is being stored, or how it is coded or accessed, and since you don't know what the government is looking for, there is always a possibility that it could be factored into other decisions."[62] Fortunately, the bill that created the new DHS in November 2002 also eliminated TIPS.[63]

Another misguided proposal was Total Information Awareness (TIA), which was developed under the auspices of the Defense Advanced Research Projects Agency (DARPA) and claimed "to protect U.S. citizens by detecting and defeating foreign terrorist threats before an attack."[64] The premise behind TIA was to build a database of public and private records to be analyzed for patterns indicative of terrorist activities.

TIA essentially depended on the law of large numbers or what marketing companies call data mining, a means of developing profiles of people who should be good customers for a particular product or service. A large pool of people who fit the profile is targeted, knowing that only a small fraction will actually be customers. TIA used the same concept but instead of potential customers, the profiles would be for would-be terrorists. The problem was that, like commercial data mining, only a small fraction of the pool of people who fit the profile of a terrorist would, in fact, be actual terrorists.

A "back-of-the-envelope" analysis demonstrates that TIA was bad math. Assume a population of 240 million adults (i.e., children are not would-be terrorist candidates). Assume we believe there are five thousand terrorists lurking among us. Assume a 99.9 percent probability (i.e., near perfect and very highly unlikely) of correctly identifying a suspect as an actual terrorist — that is, if you suspect someone is a terrorist, he is actually a terrorist. And assume a 99.9 percent probability (again, highly unlikely) of correctly identifying a suspect as an innocent person. The results would be:

- 244,990 people would be identified as suspected terrorists (and remember that this is with near-perfect accuracy of being able to correctly identify terrorists and innocent people).
- 239,995 innocent people would be misidentified as terrorists.

- The probability of finding a real terrorist is 2 percent.[65]

Even if the number of people subjected to TIA was reduced the results would not necessarily be any better. For example, assume we were looking for nineteen hijackers among 3.6 million U.S. male Muslims. And assume the same near perfect 99.9 percent accuracy as in the above example. How hard would it have been to find the hijackers and potentially avert 9/11?

- 3,619 people would have been identified as suspected terrorists.
- 3,600 innocent people would have been misidentified as terrorists.
- The probability of finding a real hijacker would have been about one-half of 1 percent.

Finally, we have to be careful not to engage in policies that could potentially radicalize the American Muslim community—either by needlessly eroding civil liberties or making Muslims a target. In February 2005 FBI Director Robert Mueller said his top concern was "the threat from covert operatives who may be inside the U.S., who have the intention to facilitate or conduct an attack." Mueller expressed his worry that al Qaeda could "exploit radical American converts and other indigenous extremists"[66] and named three successful FBI efforts: the indictment of Mohammed Ali al-Timimi, the spiritual leader of the Virginia Jihad training group; the arrest in Minneapolis of Mohamad Kamal El-Zahabi, a Lebanese citizen who admitted serving in Afghanistan and Chechnya as a sniper; and in New York, the arrest of Yassin Muhiddin Aref on money laundering charges connected to a possible plot to kill a Pakistani diplomat.

The threat of the so-called enemy within has been the subject of at least two books: *American Jihad: The Terrorists Living Among Us* by Steven Emerson (New York: Free Press, 2002) and *Holy War on the Home Front: The Secret Islamic Terror Network in the United States* by Harvey Kushner and Bart Davis (New York: Sentinel, 2004). But if there is a large terrorist threat from Muslims in America—as Emerson, Kushner, and Davis believe—then the obvious question is: Why haven't we been attacked again since 9/11?

At least part of the answer lies in how Muslims are assimilated into society. Muslims in the United States seem to be more integrated into mainstream American society, whereas European Muslim communities are generally enclaves—more apart from than a part of their adopted countries. None of the 9/11 hijackers were recruited from the Muslim American community. In contrast, we know that the Hamburg cell became the field marshals of the 9/11 attacks and many of those thought to be involved in the Madrid 3/11 attacks were European Muslim immigrants.

The lesson for American Muslims — particularly those who are newly immigrated to the United States — is to not fall into the same trap as Muslims in Europe. The more Muslims are separate from their community, the greater the likelihood that they will be susceptible to radicalization. And the more likely it is that they will be viewed with suspicion, however unwarranted. It is worth noting that the Lackawanna Six — six young men who attended an al Qaeda training camp and pled guilty to terrorism charges (although were not found guilty of plotting any attacks) — were from a tightly knit Yemeni community and lived within blocks of each other.

And the lesson for America is to not engage in policies and actions that would radicalize Muslims — both abroad and at home. So when a U.S. prosecutor claims that Ahmed Omar Abu Ali — a twenty-three-year old from Virginia accused of conspiring with al Qaeda to assassinate President Bush — "turned his back on America and joined the cause of al Qaeda,"[67] we must remember that the principle of innocent until proven guilty is an important foundation of the American legal system and that the charge must be proven in a court of law with due process, not in the media or by public opinion.[*]

In at least one instance, even a conviction in court was a rush to judgment. In June 2003 three Detroit-area Muslims (all Moroccan immigrants) were convicted of being a terrorist sleeper cell in a decision hailed by the Bush administration. However, a year after the trial a U.S. federal judge threw out the convictions on the grounds of widespread prosecutorial misconduct. According to Judge Gerald Rosen, the Justice Department's overzealousness to obtain a conviction "overcame not only its professional judgment, but its broader obligations to the justice system and the rule of law."[68] In fact, the Justice Department admitted, "In its best light, the record would show that the prosecution committed a pattern of mistakes and oversights that deprived the defendants of discoverable evidence (including impeachment material) and created a record filled with misleading inferences that such material did not exist."[69] In a retrial, the worse the suspects may be guilty of is document fraud.

---

[*] Abu Ali was convicted in November 2005, but the case will be appealed because Abu Ali contends Saudi interrogators tortured him and forced him to give a false confession.

In the post-9/11 world we cannot ignore the possibility that a potential enemy may be lurking inside our borders. But we also cannot afford to engage in a witch-hunt that makes the entire Muslim American community suspect. According to the Transactional Records Access Clearinghouse (a nonpartisan data-gathering and research organization), of the more than 6,400 individuals charged by the federal government in terrorism-related cases in the two years since 9/11, only 879 have been convicted—but just 341 (about 5 percent) of those convictions involved actual acts of terrorism.[70] Casting such a wide net could end up doing more to radicalize American Muslims than to catch actual terrorists.

In the post-9/11 environment Americans understandably want to be protected against terrorism and some—perhaps many—people may be willing to grant the government expansive powers believed to provide that protection, such as TIPS—which would have made us a nation of snoops and snitches—and TIA—which would have made us a nation of suspects. But the government's responsibility to provide for the common defense involves more than just protecting life and property. Its ultimate responsibility is to protect the Constitution and the fundamental principles upon which American society rests. The lesson to be learned from the PATRIOT Act, the Hamdi case, TIPS, and TIA is that the Constitution is not an impediment to fighting the war on terrorism. Rather, it is what fighting the war on terrorism is all about.

The lesson for homeland security is best summed up by what the Irish Republican Army told the British after their failed assassination attempt against Prime Minister Margaret Thatcher in 1984: "Today we were unlucky, but remember, we only have to be lucky once—you will have to be lucky always."[71] On 9/11 we were unlucky. Thankfully, we have been lucky since. But eventually our luck will run out because no matter how much we spend on homeland security, how many defensive measures we implement, and how carefully we protect civil liberties, in the final analysis we cannot build a perfect defense against every potential terrorist attack.

The paradox of homeland security is that we must build defenses against terrorist attacks, but defending against terrorism is a Maginot line: a determined terrorist will eventually find ways to circumvent the defenses. And it is unrealistic to believe that we can kill each and every al Qaeda terrorist. These two realities only accentuate the imperative to change U.S. foreign policy. If the United States does not change its policies to stem the growing tide of anti-American sentiment overseas — particularly within the Islamic world — all the time, effort, and money spent on other aspects of homeland security will be wasted because the pool of terrorist recruits will grow and the United States will continue to be a target. No matter how successful the United States is in homeland security and dismantling al Qaeda, it will not stop terrorism unless its foreign policy changes. More than anything else, U.S. foreign policy is the cause of the virulent anti-Americanism that is the basis for terrorism. Changing U.S. foreign policy may not guarantee victory in the war on terrorism, but not changing it will certainly spell defeat.

Afterword

There's a hole in the world tonight
There's a cloud of fear and sorrow
There's a hole in the world tonight
Don't let there be a hole in the world tomorrow

—"Hole in the World," The Eagles

More than four years after the 9/11 terrorist attacks one question lingers: Are we safer?

In his 2005 State of the Union address, President Bush said:

In the three and a half years since September the 11th, 2001, we have taken unprecedented actions to protect Americans. We've created a new department of government to defend our homeland, focused the FBI on preventing terrorism, begun to reform our intelligence agencies, broken up terror cells across the country, expanded research on defenses against biological and chemical attack, improved border security, and trained more than a half-million first responders. Police and firefighters, air marshals, researchers, and so many others are working every day to make our homeland safer.[1]

At the beginning of May 2005 the *Washington Post* reported that, according to intelligence and law enforcement officials, "terrorist threats against the United States are at their lowest level since the attacks of Sept. 11, 2001."[2] But a news story flew below the radar screen in April: the State Department would stop publishing its annual *Patterns of Global Terrorism* report. Critics charged that the nineteen-year-old report was eliminated because the 2004 statistics didn't support the Bush administration's frequent claim that we were winning the war on terrorism. According to a Knight-Ridder report, the National Counterterrorism Center reported 625 "significant" attacks in 2004 (not including attacks on U.S. troops in Iraq) compared to 175 such incidents in 2003, which was the highest number in two decades.[3]

America is certainly a country with more physical security to defend against terrorism. We have made buildings more secure by erecting barricades, prohibiting parking and other access, deploying armed personnel, and instituting identity and vehicle checks. Although such measures certainly raise the threshold for a successful attack, they do not provide absolute protection against suicide terrorists (the detonation of two makeshift grenades at the British Consulate in New York in early May 2005 was evidence that we remain vulnerable to terrorism[4]). It's probably safe to say that Baghdad has more security than the average U.S. city, but that has not stopped the onslaught of terrorist attacks. So increased security is no guarantee of being safer from terrorism.

Although we can and should take comfort in the fact that America has not been attacked again, all of the actions we have taken did not necessarily prevent another attack. Perhaps al Qaeda has not chosen to attack. Unfortunately, we are at a loss for the explanation. Unlike during the Cold War when we had spies in the Soviet Union, we have not penetrated the al Qaeda network or the larger radical Islamic movement. So we are still on the outside looking in without any way to confirm if our analysis of the intelligence we are able to collect is in the ballpark, let alone on the mark.

And while President Bush is right that we need to go after "the terrorists abroad so we do not have to face them here at home,"[5] we must also understand that simply killing terrorists — however necessary — will not make us safer. If we want to be safer, then we need to address the reasons people choose to become terrorists and want to kill innocent Americans. This requires understanding that the growing tide of anti-American Muslim hatred — which is the basis on which the radical Islamists draw Muslims to their ranks — is fueled more by what we do, i.e., U.S. policies, than who we are. In other words — as the 9/11 Commission concluded and numerous polls conducted throughout the Islamic world show — radical Islamists do not hate us for our freedoms, way of life, culture, accomplishments, or values.

Yet while the 9/11 Commission understood that point, they ultimately did not prescribe any real change from the course U.S. foreign policy has charted since the end of the Cold War. According to the 9/11 Commission:

> American foreign policy is part of the message. America's policy choices have consequences. Right or wrong, it is simply a fact that American policy regarding the Israeli-Palestinian conflict and American actions in Iraq are dominant staples of popular commentary across the Arab and Muslim World. That does not mean U.S. choices have been wrong. It means those choices must be integrated with America's message of opportunity to the Arab and Muslim world.[6]

But if we are unable to admit that some of our policy choices are wrong, how can we hope to correct them? Such refusal results from not wanting to be accused of blaming America for 9/11. This is understandable; certainly nothing justifies those terrorist attacks. But with more than one billion Muslims in the world, we cannot continue to ignore addressing the underlying reasons why so many of them have a growing hatred of the United States.

According to Shibley Telhami, a member of President Bush's advisory group on public diplomacy, our so-called hearts and minds campaign to dissuade Muslims from becoming terrorists is "worse than failing. Failing means you tried and didn't get better. But at this point, three years after September 11, you can say there wasn't even much of an attempt, and today Arab and Muslim attitudes toward the U.S. and the degree of distrust of the U.S. are far worse than they were three years ago."[7] If that's the case, we may be killing terrorists abroad and Americans may be better protected at home but we are actually less safe.

While killing terrorists abroad and protecting Americans at home are certainly necessary, these actions are not enough to make the United States safer against terrorism. Ultimately, without blaming America, we must be willing to look in the mirror to examine and understand how our own policies—both foreign and domestic—may affect the dynamics and evolution of the Muslim terrorist threat. The task, then, is to avoid the famous quote by Walt Kelly's comic strip character Pogo: "We have met the enemy and he is us."

Appendix 1:

Terrorist Attacks Caused by an Activist U.S. Foreign Policy

Source: Ivan Eland, "Does U.S. Intervention Overseas Breed Terrorism? The Historical Record," Cato Institute Foreign Policy Briefing No. 50, December 17, 1998[*]

- 1915 — Senate Reception Room in the U.S. Capitol was damaged by a homemade bomb built by Erich Muenter. He was a former Harvard professor who was upset by sales of U.S. munitions to the Allies in World War I.

- June 5, 1968 — Senator Robert F. Kennedy, former attorney general and senior policy adviser to President John F. Kennedy, was assassinated by Sirhan Sirhan. Sirhan had grown up on the West Bank and regarded Kennedy as a collaborator with Israel.

- March 1971 — A bomb exploded in a U.S. Senate restroom, causing extensive damage. The bombing came at a time of rising opposition to U.S. policies in Vietnam.

---

[*] This list shows the most prominent acts of terrorism against the United States in retaliation for its interventionist foreign policy. The list is by no means exhaustive. The sources for the list are as follows: International Policy Institute for Counterterrorism database (www.ict.org.il/inter_ter/attackresults.cfm); Louis Mizell Jr., Target USA: The Inside Story of the New Terrorist War (New York: John Wiley & Sons, 1998), 179–200; Beau Grosscup, The Newest Explosions of Terrorism: Latest Sites of Terrorism in 90s and Beyond (New Jersey: New Horizon Press, 1998), 1–34, 123–145, 263–319, 363–410; Leroy Thompson, Ragged War: The Story of Unconventional and Counter-Revolutionary Warfare (London: Arms and Armor Press, 1996), 156–175; Defense Science Board, The Defense Science Board 1997 Summer Study Task Force on DoD Responses to Transnational Threats (Washington, DC: U.S. Department of Defense, October 1997), vol. 1, Final Report, 13–20; Edwin P. Hoyt, America's Wars and Military Excursions (New York: McGraw-Hill, 1987), 525–529; J. Robert Moskin, The U.S. Marine Corps Story (Boston: Little, Brown, 1992), 727–741.

- November 4, 1979—Supporters of the Ayatollah Ruhollah Khomeini seized the U.S. embassy in Tehran to protest the longtime U.S. support for the shah. The hostages were not freed until January 1981.
- December 1979—Iranians sacked and burned the U.S. embassy in Tripoli, Libya. Iranian sponsored terrorism against the United States was a result of U.S. support for the shah and Israel.
- During the 1980s—Hezbollah kidnapped nineteen American diplomats, educators, businessmen, clergy, journalists, and military personnel and killed at least four.
- July 22, 1980—Ali Akbar Tabatabai, a former press counselor at the Iranian embassy in the United States during the shah's reign, was assassinated by the Islamic Guerrillas of America (IGA) at his home in Bethesda, Maryland. He had supplied U.S. officials with a manifesto of the IGA that advocated strategically planned terrorism on U.S. soil and assassinations of U.S. officials and Iranian dissidents. The manifesto stated: "Any American can be targeted . . . no American is innocent . . . as long as U.S. foreign policies are to the detriment of the Islamic community." The document was especially critical of U.S. support for Israel. Tabatabai knew that that IGA had 230 members operating in the United States. Tabatabai's assassin fled to Iran and became part of an Islamic assassination squad.
- April 8, 1983—The anti-American, Iranian-sponsored Hezbollah (some sources also implicate the Islamic Jihad) bombed the U.S. embassy in Beirut, Lebanon. Information gathered by the American, French, and Israeli intelligence agencies indicated that the Iranian government funded and provided the explosives for the attack that killed seventeen Americans. The intelligence information also showed that Syrian military experts directed the assembly and emplacement of the bombs that Hezbollah used. All attacks by Hezbollah in Lebanon around this time were retaliation for U.S. military presence there. The Americans were supporting the Christian government against the Muslim militias by training and arming the Lebanese National Army (LNA). Later, the U.S. Marines even began patrolling with the Christian LNA, and the Navy and Marines began shelling the Muslims to support the LNA.
- October 23, 1983—A suicide truck bomber from Hezbollah (some sources also implicate the Islamic Jihad) attacked the U.S. embassy and

destroyed the U.S. Marine barracks in Beirut (killing 290 people and wounding 200 more). Intelligence information gathered by the American, French, and Israeli intelligence agencies indicated that Iran funded and provided the explosives used in the attack. Apparently, Syrian military experts directed the assembly and emplacement of the bombs that Hezbollah used. The U.S. Marines were later withdrawn from Beirut. A terrorist spokesman bragged that two "martyrs" had forced the Marines out of Lebanon: one who died to blow up the embassy and the other who drove the truck that destroyed the Marine barracks.

- September 1984—Hezbollah (some sources also implicate Islamic Jihad) bombed the U.S. embassy annex in East Beirut. Twenty-three people were killed and four Marine guards were wounded.

- Mid-1980s—Lebanese Revolutionary Army Faction leader Georges Ibrahim Abdallah was accused of complicity in the deaths of American military attaché Lt. Col. Charles Ray and Israeli diplomat Yacov Barsimantov. The suspect was held by the French government. The most likely motive for the attack was the U.S. military presence in Lebanon.

- April 5, 1986—Libyan leader Moammar Qaddafi sponsored the bombing of the La Belle nightclub in West Berlin, which was frequented by U.S. servicemen. The bombing killed an American soldier and a Turkish woman. The bombing seemed to be in retaliation for two specific prior incidents: (1) Ronald Reagan had accused Libya of aiding Palestinian Abu Nidal in bombing the Rome and Vienna airports. (The United States had no jurisdiction over those terrorist incidents.); (2) in late March 1986 the largest peacetime American naval armada had sailed across the "line of death" that Qaddafi said marked Libyan territorial waters in the Gulf of Sidra. Qaddafi had threatened to attack any invader. Fulfilling the predictions of American defense analysts, he shot missiles at the armada. The United States destroyed a missile site and three Libyan naval craft.

The La Belle bombing was part of a more general "war" between the Reagan administration and Qaddafi that started after a Reagan administration review of U.S. policy toward Libya in the summer of 1981, shortly after taking office. The Reagan administration pursued ways to get rid of Qaddafi, or failing that, to isolate him politically and economically. Reagan believed Qaddafi acted as a Soviet agent and was heavily involved in terrorism against the West. Some analysts argue that the Reagan administration inflated the threat that Qaddafi posed to garner support for increased defense spending. The "war" began with an attempt by the Reagan administration to provoke Qaddafi by skirting Libyan territorial waters and air space during war games in the Mediterranean. In August 1981 U.S. jets — to challenge Libya's extension of its territorial waters and air space over the Gulf of Sidra — entered the gulf and shot down two Libyan aircraft that intercepted them.

The United States retaliated for the La Belle bombing with air strikes — from air bases in the United Kingdom and from U.S. aircraft carriers in the Mediterranean — against Tripoli and Benghazi, Libya, on April 15, 1986 (two weeks after the line of death incident in late March). The air strikes apparently aimed to kill Qaddafi. According to the Defense Science Board, contrary to popular belief, the air strikes did not cause Qaddafi to shrink from using terrorism. In fact, he began a secret campaign of terrorism against the United States in retaliation for the air strikes (see the next eight entries). Prior to 1986 there is little evidence that Libyan agents harmed Americans. Ronald Reagan had interpreted Qaddafi's terrorism as anti-American, but Western European nations had been the major target. Beginning in April 1986 State Department analysts linked Libyan agents to an average of one attack per month against U.S. targets.

- April 1986 — In retaliation for the U.S. air strikes on Libya, an American hostage in Lebanon was sold to Libya and executed.
- July 1986 — In retaliation for the air strikes, Libyans attempted to blow up the U.S. embassy in Lome, Togo.
- September 1987 — In retaliation for U.S. air strikes, Abu Nidal, working for Libya, hijacked Pan Am Flight 73 in Karachi, Pakistan. The hijacking caused the death of several Americans.
- 1988 — Libyan bombings of U.S. library facilities in Peru, Colombia, and Costa Rica. The bombings were part of Qaddafi's retaliation campaign.
- April 12, 1988 — A Japanese Red Army operative was arrested in New Jersey with three antipersonnel bombs that were intended for a terrorist attack on a military base in the United States. The attack was to

have been timed to coincide with the second anniversary of the U.S. air strikes on Libya.

- April 14, 1988 — The Japanese Red Army, under contract from Abu Nidal, planted a bomb at the USO military club in Naples, Italy, to coincide with the same anniversary. The blast killed five people.
- December 1988 — Two Libyan intelligence agents allegedly bombed Pan Am Flight 103. The bomb killed 270 people, 200 of whom were Americans. This bombing was also part of Libya's retaliation campaign for U.S. air strikes in 1986.
- September 1989 — Libyans recruited a Chicago street gang to attack U.S. airliners with shoulder-fired weapons. This plot was foiled. The scheme was part of Libya's retaliation campaign.
- March 10, 1989 — A pipe bomb exploded beneath a van owned by Sharon Rogers, wife of Will Rogers III, commander of USS *Vincennes*. The bombing was related to the July 3, 1988, incident in which the *Vincennes* shot down an Iranian airliner over the Persian Gulf (killing 290 civilians) during U.S. participation in the "tanker war" against Iran.
- March 31, 1990 — Four terrorists attacked a U.S. Air Force bus in Tegucigalpa, Honduras. Eight people were injured. The Moranzanist Patriotic Front claimed responsibility. The attack was most likely related to U.S. military presence in Honduras.
- May 1990 — A group of religious extremists led by Ramzi Yousef assassinated Rabbi Meir Kahane, radical leader of the Jewish Defense League in the United States. The murder was first treated as a mere homicide but was later discovered to be a part of a larger revenge campaign against U.S. foreign policy that included the World Trade Center bombing in 1993.
- May 13, 1990 — New People's Army assassins shot two U.S. Air Force airmen to death near Clark Air Base in the Philippines. The killings came on the eve of the U.S.-Philippine exploratory talks on the future of U.S. military bases in the Philippines. Most likely, the attack was perpetrated to protest U.S. presence in the Philippines.
- June 13, 1990 — An American Peace Corps worker was kidnapped from his home in the Philippines. The New People's Army was responsible. He was released unharmed on August 2 even though no ransom was paid. Coming around the time of U.S.-Philippine exploratory talks on

the future of military bases in the Philippines and exactly a month after the killing of two Air Force airmen at Clark Air Base, the attack was most likely a protest against U.S. presence in the Philippines.

- January 2, 1991—A U.S. military helicopter was shot down by the Farabundo Marti National Liberation Front militants (FMLN Marxist guerillas) in San Miguel, El Salvador. The two crewmen were then executed. The crewmen were most likely targets because the United States was providing military aid and advisers to the government of El Salvador.

- Mid-January to late February 1991 (during the Persian Gulf War)— 120 terrorist attacks hit American targets all over the world (compared to 17 over the same period in 1990). Terrorism analysts labeled those incidents "spontaneous" or "free-lance" Iraqi-inspired terrorism. The following are examples of such terrorism:

  – In late January 1991, two incidents occurred in Adana, Turkey: A car exploded next to the U.S. consulate and Bobbie Mozelle, an American customs official, was murdered outside a NATO air base. Dev Sol (Revolutionary Left), a Turkish group that analysts said had no links to Iraq, claimed responsibility for the incidents. The group claimed that Mozelle was a CIA agent and that the bombing campaign was to retaliate for the Turkish government's approval of U.S. air strikes on Iraq being launched from Turkish air bases.

  – During the same period of time, a bomb exploded across the street from an American Express office in Athens, Greece. U.S. involvement in the Persian Gulf War was probably the reason for the attack.

  – February 2, 1991—Dev Sol shot and killed a U.S. civilian contractor that worked at Incirlik air base in Adana, Turkey.

  – February 28, 1991—Dev Sol shot a U.S. Air Force officer as he entered his residence in Izmir, Turkey.

- March 12, 1991—A U.S. Air Force sergeant was blown up by a remotely controlled bomb placed at the entrance of his residence in Athens, Greece. A group called November 17 claimed responsibility. November 17, the deadliest terrorist group in Greece, attacked U.S. targets because of "American imperialism-nationalism." The timing of the attack indicated that it was most likely related to U.S. involvement in the Gulf War.

- March 28, 1991 – Three U.S. Marines were shot by an Arab while driving near Jubial, Saudi Arabia. This incident was most likely related to U.S. involvement in the Persian Gulf War or continued U.S. presence in Saudi Arabia.
- October 28, 1991 – The Turkish Islamic Jihad claimed responsibility for a car bomb that killed a U.S. Air Force sergeant. Like the other incidents in Turkey around this time, this bombing was probably related to U.S. use of Turkish air bases during the Gulf War.
- June 10, 1992 – A U.S. Army vehicle was raked with gunfire between Panama City and Colon, Panama. The driver was killed and a passenger and nearby civilian bystander were wounded. This incident was mostly likely related to U.S. military presence in Panama and U.S. control of the Panama Canal Zone.
- October 12, 1992 – A U.S. soldier serving with the UN in Umm Qasr, Iraq, was stabbed and wounded. Most likely, the stabbing was in retaliation for U.S. intervention in Iraq.
- December 29, 1992 – An explosion occurred at the Gold Mihor Hotel in Aden, Yemen. About one hundred U.S. soldiers, part of Operation Restore Hope in Somalia, had been staying in Aden since mid-December.
- January 23, 1993 – Mir Aimal Kansi, a Pakistani, opened fire on CIA employees on the highway outside the agency's headquarters in Virginia. Kansi allegedly told a roommate that he was angry about the treatment of Muslims in Bosnia and was going to get even by shooting up the CIA, the White House, and the Israeli embassy.
- February 26, 1993 – A group of Islamic extremists detonated a massive van bomb in the garage of the World Trade Center in New York City. The Egyptian perpetrators were trying to kill 250,000 people by collapsing the towers. Ramzi Yousef, the leader of the terrorists, said the intent was to inflict Hiroshima-like casualties to punish the United States for its policies in the Middle East. The perpetrators considered augmenting the explosion with radiological or chemical agents that would have increased the casualties.
- March 3, 1993 – Terrorists exploded a bomb in front of the U.S. embassy in Belgrade. This attack was most likely directed at U.S. policy toward Serbia and Bosnia.
- April 15, 1993 – Seventeen Iraqis were arrested by Kuwaiti authori-

ties as they tried to infiltrate Kuwait. A large car bomb and weapons were confiscated. The group was charged with being part of an Iraqi government plot to assassinate former President George Bush on a visit to Kuwait. According to the U.S. government, Saddam Hussein was attempting to assassinate President Bush in retaliation for his direction of the Gulf War against Iraq. Saddam was carrying out a threat he had made during the war. President Clinton later retaliated militarily against Iraq for this assassination plot by attacking Iraqi intelligence headquarters with cruise missiles.

- June 1993 — Sheik Omar Abdul Rahman — a militant Egyptian cleric — and other radical Muslims conspired to destroy New York landmarks and kill numerous people in one day. On July 4, as a follow-up to their bombing of the World Trade Center, the group planned to blow up UN headquarters, the Lincoln and Holland tunnels under the Hudson River, the George Washington Bridge, and the federal government's main office building in New York. The group also planned to assassinate Senator Alfonse D'Amato and others. Funding for the operation apparently came from Iran and was funneled through Sudan. Two intelligence officers from Sudan were planning to place the bombs in the UN building. At the time they were arrested, the conspirators were mixing fertilizer and diesel fuel to create a bomb like the one used to blow up the World Trade Center. Rahman and nine others were convicted of the plot on October 1, 1995. As in the World Trade Center bombing, the plotters were attempting to punish the United States for its policies in the Middle East.

- July 1, 1993 — Terrorists fired two rockets at the U.S. Air Force base at Yokota, Japan. The incident happened a few days before President Clinton arrived at the base. The incident most likely resulted from opposition to U.S. military presence in Japan.

- July 7, 1993 — Six days later terrorists fired four projectiles at the headquarters of the U.S. Air Force in Japan at Camp Zama, Japan. Again, the incident was most likely related to opposition to U.S. military presence in Japan.

- October 3, 1993 — Osama bin Laden's operatives trained Somali tribesmen who conducted ambushes of U.S. peacekeeping forces in Somalia in support of clan leader Mohamed Farah Aideed. The ambushes culminating in the downing of two helicopters, the death of eighteen American Army Rangers, and the dragging of dead American soldiers through the streets of Mogadishu. An indictment of his followers alleged that bin Laden's organization, al Qaeda, believed that the United States—an infidel nation—had a nefarious plot to occupy Islamic countries, as demonstrated by its involvement in the peacekeeping operation in Somalia and the Persian Gulf War. This incident led to the withdrawal of U.S. forces from Somalia. Bin Laden called the Somalia operation his group's greatest triumph.

- October 21, 1994—Members of the Abu Nidal Organization were convicted of plotting to kill Jews in the United States, blow up the Israeli embassy in the United States, and kill anyone who exposed their plots. These attacks were likely directed at U.S. support for Israel.
- February 7, 1995—Ramzi Yousef, mastermind of the World Trade Center bombing, was arrested in Pakistan. The arrest foiled a plan he had already set in motion to bomb twelve U.S. jumbo jets in flight and kill the four thousand passengers. Yousef wanted to punish the United States for its policies in the Middle East.
- Shortly before Easter 1995—Authorities were tipped off by Japanese police that members of the Aum Shinrikyo (Supreme Truth) religious cult planned a nerve gas attack at Disneyland in Anaheim, California. The group planned to attack during a fireworks celebration when attendance at the park would reach maximum capacity. U.S. authorities apprehended the men at the Los Angeles airport before they could launch the attack. The plan also included an attack on petrochemical facilities in Los Angeles. Aum Shinrikyo earlier used Sarin nerve gas to attack the Tokyo subway (March 20, 1995). According to the group's belief system, the last years of the millenium would give rise to an Armageddon between Japan and the United States. Aum Shinrikyo believed that attacking the Tokyo subway would hasten the Armageddon. The group was hoping to kill tens of thousands of people.
  In its belief system, the cult chose the United States—a friendly nation—as Japan's adversary, rather other regional nations that were much more likely to be future rivals of Japan in East Asia—China, Russia, or North or South Korea. Such beliefs indicated how easily an interventionist superpower could be vilified by conspiratorially

minded groups even in a friendly nation.

The cult had assets of $1.2 billion and the capability to produce Sarin, VX, anthrax, botulism, and radiological weapons. The group was listed as a designated foreign terrorist organization in the last published *Patterns of Global Terrorism* (April 2004).

- August 18, 1995 — The Manuel Rodriguez Front (FPMR) claimed responsibility for a bomb explosion at an office building that housed the American company Fluor Daniel in Santiago, Chile. The group stated that the incident was carried out in solidarity with Cuba and against the American economic blockade of that island.

- September 13, 1995 — A rocket-propelled grenade was fired at the U.S. embassy in Russia. Authorities suspect the attack was in retaliation for U.S. involvement in NATO air strikes against Bosnian Serb targets.

- November 13, 1995 — A car bombing of a military complex in Riyadh, Saudi Arabia — which housed a U.S. military advisory group — killed seven people (including five Americans) and wounded forty-two others. Muslim militants seeking to topple the Saudi monarchy and push the "infidel" United States out of Saudi Arabia carried out the bombings. Three groups, including the Islamic Movement for Change, claimed responsibility. U.S. officials suspect that Osama bin Laden was involved. Bin Laden is opposed to U.S. presence in Saudi Arabia and U.S. support for Israel.

- November 15, 1995 — An explosive device was discovered on a power line to a U.S. military complex in Sagmihara, Japan. No group claimed responsibility. The incident was most likely related to opposition to U.S. military presence in Japan.

- February 15, 1996 — Unidentified assailants fired a rocket at the U.S. embassy compound in Athens, Greece, causing minor damage to three diplomatic vehicles and surrounding buildings. The State Department noted that the circumstances suggested it was an attack by the group November 17. November 17 attacked U.S. targets because of "American imperialism-nationalism."

- May 31, 1996 — A gang of former disgruntled Contra guerrillas kidnapped an employee of the U.S. Agency for International Development who was assisting in election preparations in Nicaragua. She was later released unharmed.

- June 25, 1996 — A truck bombing of the U.S. military apartment complex of Khobar Towers near Dhahran, Saudi Arabia, killed nineteen U.S. airmen, wounded 515 persons (including 240 U.S. citizens), and resulted in many other casualties. Muslim militants seeking to topple the Saudi monarchy and push the "infidel" United States out of Saudi Arabia carried out the bombings. U.S. officials have linked Osama bin Laden to the bombing. Some analysts also suspect Iranian complicity.
- February 23, 1997 — Ali Hassan Abu Kamal, a Palestinian, opened fire on the observation deck of the Empire State Building in New York City. After killing and wounding tourists, he committed suicide. He sought revenge for the treatment of Palestinians by the United States and Israel.
- July 31, 1997 — Police in Brooklyn arrested two Palestinian men who allegedly planned suicide bombings of the subway and a commuter bus. They had a portrait of Sheik Omar Abdul Rahman in their possession. This evidence indicates that — like Rahman — the Palestinians were probably motivated by opposition to U.S. policies in the Middle East.
- November 12, 1997 — Four employees of Union Texas Petroleum died in an attack on their vehicle one mile from the U.S. consulate in Karachi, Pakistan. Two groups — Islamic Revolutionary Council and the Aimal Secret Committee — claimed that the killings were revenge for the conviction of Mir Aimal Kansi. Kansi was the Pakistani who murdered CIA employees to protest the treatment of Muslims in Bosnia. (Kansi was angry about the treatment of Muslims in Bosnia and told his roommate that he would get even by shooting up the CIA, the White House, and the Israeli embassy.)
- December 23, 1997 — Assailants fired shots at the teachers' residential compound of the Karachi American School. The school and teachers' residence are in the same neighborhood as other consulate residences. One guard was shot at a guard post that had been established after the November 12, 1997, shooting of Union Texas Petroleum employees in Karachi. Because of the timing — about a month after the first incident — and location, this attack was probably also in retaliation for the conviction of Mir Aimal Kansi.
- April 3, 1998 — The Greek November 17 Movement claimed responsibility for a rash of attacks against U.S. targets. The movement's victims since 1975 include a CIA station chief and three other Americans.

The group issued a statement saying the campaign was "aimed against American imperialism-nationalism."

- August 7, 1998 — Simultaneous car bombings of the U.S. embassies in Kenya and Tanzania — allegedly linked to wealthy Saudi Osama bin Laden — led to over two hundred deaths. Prior to the bombings, bin Laden declared openly that he would kill Americans and would not discriminate between military personnel and civilians. Bin Laden objected to the U.S. presence in Saudi Arabia and American support for Israel. On August 20, 1998, the United States launched cruise missiles on bin Laden's training camp in Afghanistan and a chemical factory in Sudan. The Clinton administration claimed that the factory produced chemical weapons and was allegedly linked (at least tangentially) to bin Laden.
- August 25, 1998 — Bombing of a Planet Hollywood restaurant (an American chain) in South Africa in retaliation for U.S. cruise missile attacks on Afghanistan and Sudan. South African authorities said the likely culprits were local terrorists ("Muslims Against Global Oppression") taking aim at the United States. The authorities said that the attack should be seen against the backdrop of U.S. cruise missile attacks against Afghanistan and Sudan.
- August 26, 1998 — A U.S. government information center in Pristina, Kosovo, was firebombed by an unknown person. The incident was most likely aimed at U.S. and NATO policy on Kosovo.
- Early September 1998 — The Ugandan government and the FBI uncovered a plot by Osama bin Laden's terrorist organization to bomb the U.S. embassy in Kampala, Uganda. This effort was the second attempt to bomb the embassy; the first effort was an attempt on August 7 in conjunction with the bombings of the U.S. embassies in Kenya and Tanzania. U.S. and Ugandan officials agreed that the August 7 attempt failed because Ugandan society had more experience and was more prepared to deal with terrorism than were Kenyan and Tanzanian societies. Ugandan officials say that the U.S. cruise missile strike on Sudan in retaliation for the bombings in Kenya and Tanzania may have prompted the bombers to try a second time to attack the embassy in Kampala. Several arrests were made in this bombing.

Appendix 2:

Total Information Awareness Calculator

Example of 240 million adults and 5,000 terrorists:

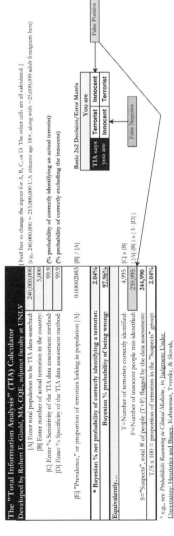

Example of 3.6 million U.S. male Muslims and 19 hijackers:

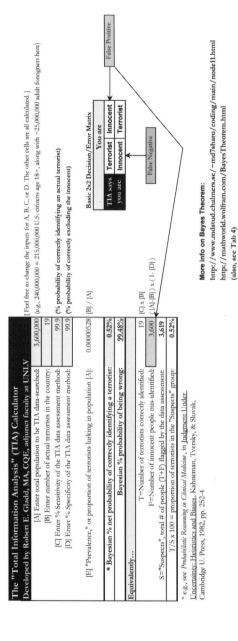

The "Total Information Analysis" (TIA) Calculator
Developed by Robert E. Gladd, MA, CQE, adjunct faculty at UNLV

[Feel free to change the inputs for A, B, C, or D. The other cells are all calculated.]

[A] Enter total population to be TIA data-searched:	3,600,000
[B] Enter number of actual terrorists in the country:	19
[C] Enter % Sensitivity of the TIA data assessment method:	99.9
[D] Enter % Specificity of the TIA data assessment method:	99.9

(e.g., 240,000,000 = 215,000,000 U.S. citizens age 18+, along with ~25,000,000 adult foreigners here)

(% probability of correctly identifying an actual terrorist)
(% probability of correctly excluding the innocent)

[E] "Prevalence," or proportion of terrorists lurking in population [A]:	0.00000528	[B] / [A]
Bayesian % net probability of correctly identifying a terrorist:	0.52%	
Bayesian % probability of being wrong:	99.48%	

Equivalently...

T=Number of terrorists correctly identified:	19	[C] x [B]
F=Number of innocent people mis-identified:	3,600	[A]-[B]) x (1- [D])
S="Suspects", total # of people (T+F) flagged by the data assessment:	3,619	
T/S x 100 = proportion of terrorists in the "Suspects" group:	0.52%	

* e.g., see *Probabilistic Reasoning in Clinical Medicine*, in Judgment Under
Uncertainty: Heuristics and Biases, Kahneman, Tversky, & Slovak,
Cambridge U. Press, 1982, pp. 252-4

Basic 2x2 Decision/Error Matrix

		You are	
		Terrorist	Innocent
TIA says you are	Terrorist	Terrorist	Innocent
	Innocent	Innocent	Terrorist

False Positive

False Negative

More info on Bayes Theorem:
http://www.mdstud.chalmers.se/~md7sharo/coding/main/node11.html
http://mathworld.wolfram.com/BayesTheorem.html
(also, see Tab 4)

Notes

Introduction: The Un-War

1 George W. Bush, "President Bush Discusses Progress in the War on Terror," July 12, 2004, http://www.whitehouse.gov/news/releases/2004/07/20040712-5.html.

2 Richard Morin and Dan Balz, "Bush Loses Advantage in War on Terrorism," *Washington Post*, June 22, 2004, A1.

3 Richard Morin and Claudia Deane, "Bush Better Suited to Deal With Terror Threat, Poll Finds," *Washington Post*, July 14, 2004, A9.

4 National Commission on Terrorist Attacks Upon the United States, *The 9/11 Commission Report* (New York: W. W. Norton, 2004), 66.

5 Tom Ridge, "Statement for Secretary Tom Ridge U.S. Department of Homeland Security," July 8, 2004, http://www.dhs.gov/dhspublic/display?content=3810.

6 George W. Bush, "President Addresses the Nation in Prime Time Press Conference," April 14, 2004, http://www.whitehouse.gov/news/releases/2004/04/20040413-20.html.

7 Donald H. Rumsfeld and Richard Myers, "Defense Department Operational Update Briefing," December 22, 2004, http://www.defenselink.mil/transcripts/2004/tr20041222-secdef1861.html.

8 Colin L. Powell, "U.S. Secretary of State Colin Powell Addresses the Security Council," February 5, 2003, http://www.whitehouse.gov/news/releases/2003/02/20030205-1.html.

9 Quoted in "Islamic Army in Iraq Threatens Attacks in U.S.: Website," Agence France Presse, January 3, 2005. Parentheses in original.

10 For example, "A state of open, armed, often prolonged conflict carried on between nations, states, or parties," *American Heritage Dictionary*, 4th ed. (Boston: Houghton Mifflin, 2000).

11 Carl Von Clausewitz, *On War*, indexed ed., ed. and trans. Michael Howard and Peter Paret (Princeton, NJ: Princeton University Press, 1984), 88.

12 Ibid., 75.

13 Ibid., 87.

14 "This will be a different kind of conflict against a different kind of enemy," George W. Bush, "Radio Address of the President to the Nation," September 15, 2001, http://www.whitehouse.gov/news/releases/2001/09/20010915.html.

15 Sun Tzu, *The Art of War*, Denma translation (Boston: Shambhala, 2002), 11.
16 Donald Rumsfeld, "Rumsfeld's War on Terror Memo," *USAToday.com*, October 22, 2003, http://www.usatoday.com/news/washington/executive/rumsfeld-memo.htm.
17 George W. Bush, "Remarks by the President in Photo Opportunity With the National Security Team," September 12, 2001, http://www.whitehouse.gov/news/releases/2001/09/20010912-4.html.
18 Bush, "Radio Address of the President to the Nation."
19 David Frum and Richard Perle, *An End to Evil: How to Win the War on Terrorism* (New York: Random House, 2003), 9.
20 Eliot A. Cohen, "From Colin to Condoleezza," *Wall Street Journal*, November 17, 2004, A16.
21 At best, authors such as Stephen Hayes, *The Connection: How Al Qaeda's Collaboration With Saddam Hussein Has Endangered America* (New York: Harper Collins, 2004), argue that some circumstantial evidence raises, but does not conclusively answer, questions about a possible connection between Saddam Hussein and al Qaeda. Ultimately, Hayes's allegations of such a connection rest on the inability to disprove that such a connection existed — but the inability to prove a negative does not incontrovertibly mean that the positive is true.
22 Department of State, *Patterns of Global Terrorism 1999* (Washington, DC: Department of State, 2000), 33.

Chapter 1: Enemy at the Gates

1 George W. Bush, "Remarks by the President and Secretary of Defense Donald Rumsfeld Swearing-in Ceremony," January 26, 2001, http://www.white house.gov/news/releases/20010126-6.html.
2 George W. Bush, "Remarks by the President to the Troops and Personnel," February 13, 2001, http://www.whitehouse.gov/news/releases/20010213-1.html.
3 George W. Bush and Tony Blair, "President Bush and Prime Minister Blair Hold Press Conference," February 23, 2001, http://www.whitehouse.gov/news/releases/2001/02/20010226-1.html.
4 George W. Bush and Kim Dae-jung, "Joint Statement Between the United States and the Republic of Korea," March 7, 2001, http://www.whitehouse.gov/news/releases/2001/03/20010307-2.html.
5 George W. Bush, "Remarks by the President to Students and Faculty at National Defense University," May 1, 2001, http://www.whitehouse.gov/news/releases/2001/05/20010501-10.html.
6 George W. Bush, "Remarks by the President in Roundtable Interview With Foreign Press," July 17, 2001, http://www.whitehouse.gov/news/releases/2001/07/20010718.html.
7 George W. Bush, "President Discusses Defense Priorities at American Legion," August 29, 2001, http://www.whitehouse.gov/news/releases/2001/08/20010829-2.html.
8 George W. Bush and John Howard, "Joint Statement Between the United States of America and Australia," September 10, 2001, http://www.whitehouse.gov/news/releases/2001/09/20010910-8.html.
9 Dick Morris, "Why Clinton Slept," *VOTE.com*, http://www.vote.com/magazine/columns/dickmorris/column40105429.phtml.

10 Bill Gertz, *Breakdown: How America's Intelligence Failures Led to September 11* (Washington, DC: Regnery, 2002).

11 In response to the embassy bombings, President Clinton ordered cruise missile strikes against al Qaeda training camps in Afghanistan and what was thought to be a chemical weapons facility in Sudan. However, bin Laden was not at any of the training camps and the attack did little to disrupt terrorist training there, and the purported chemical weapons facility was a pharmaceutical plant.

12 George W. Bush, "President Addresses the Nation in Prime Time Press Conference," April 13, 2004, http://www.whitehouse.gov/news/releases/2004/04/20040413-20.html.

13 Jeffrey Record, "Bounding the Global War on Terrorism," Strategic Studies Institute monograph, Army War College, December 2003, 13.

14 Ibid., 16.

15 Bob Woodward, *Bush at War* (New York: Simon & Schuster, 2002), 49. CBS News also reported that "barely five hours after American Airlines Flight 77 plowed into the Pentagon, Defense Secretary Donald H. Rumsfeld was telling his aides to come up with plans for striking Iraq—even though there was no evidence linking Saddam Hussein to the attacks." "Plans for Iraq Attack Began On 9/11," *CBSNews.com*, September 4, 2002, http://www.cbsnews.com/stories/2002/09/04/september11/main520830.shtml.

16 "Wolfowitz seized the opportunity. Attacking Afghanistan would be uncertain. He worried about 100,000 American troops bogged down in mountain fighting in Afghanistan six months from then. In contrast, Iraq was a brittle oppressive regime that might break easily. It was doable." Woodward, *Bush at War*, 83.

17 Ibid., 99.

18 "Bush Sought 'Way' to Invade Iraq?" *CBSNews.com*, January 11, 2004, http://www.cbsnews.com/stories/2004/01/09/60minutes/main592330.shtml; Dave Moniz and Peronet Despeignes, "Ex-aide Says Bush Targeted Iraq From Start," *USA Today*, January 12, 2004, A6; "O'Neill: Bush Planned Iraq Invasion Before 9/11," *CNN.com*, January 14, 2004, http://www.cnn.com/2004/ALLPOLITICS/01/10/oneill.bush/. According to Pulitzer Prize winner Ron Suskind, *The Price of Loyalty: George W. Bush, the White House, and the Education of Paul O'Neill* (New York: Simon & Schuster, 2004), 129: "Bush's campaign positions, that the U.S. would be noninterventionist—that we would hesitate to become embroiled in disputes; that we would be 'humble abroad' and not 'engage in nation-building'—were the very opposite of the policy that O'Neill and Powell saw unfolding. Actual plans, to O'Neill's astonishment, were already being discussed to take over Iraq and occupy it—complete with disposition of oil fields, peacekeeping forces, and war crimes tribunals—carrying forward an unspoken doctrine of preemptive war."

19 Richard A. Clarke, *Against All Enemies: Inside America's War on Terror* (New York: Free Press, 2004), 264.

20 Paul Wolfowitz, "Statement Before the House National Security Committee," in Gary Schmitt, "Wolfowitz Statement on U.S. Policy Toward Iraq" (memorandum to opinion leaders) Project for the New American Century, September 18, 1998, http://newamericancentury.org/iraqsep1898.htm.

21 Stephen J. Solarz and Paul Wolfowitz, "How to Overthrow Saddam," *Foreign Affairs* 78:2 (March/April 1999): 160.

22 Elliott Abrams, Richard L. Armitage, et al., "Letter to President Clinton," Project for the New American Century, January 26, 1998, http://www.new americancentury.org/iraqclintonletter.htm.

23 Elliot Abrams, William J. Bennett, et al., "Project Letter to Newt Gingrich and Trent Lott," Project for the New American Century, May 29, 1998, http://www.newamericancentury.org/iraqletter1998.htm.

24 George W. Bush, "Address to a Joint Session of Congress and the American People," September 20, 2001, http://www.whitehouse.gov/news/releases/2001/09/20010920-8.html.

25 George W. Bush, "Radio Address of the President to the Nation," October 6, 2001, http://www.whitehouse.gov/news/releases/2001/10/20011006.html.

26 George W. Bush, "President Welcomes Aid Workers Rescued From Afghanistan," November 26, 2001, http://www.whitehouse.gov/news/releases/2001/11/20011126-1.html.

27 Ibid. "Q: I'm just asking if you've expanded your definition to countries who don't just harbor terrorists, but also develop such weapons. THE PRESIDENT: Have I expanded the definition? I've always had that definition, as far as I'm concerned."

28 Ibid.

29 George W. Bush, "President Speaks on War Effort to Citadel Cadets," December 11, 2001, http://www.whitehouse.gov/news/releases/2001/12/20011211-6.html.

30 George W. Bush, "The President's State of the Union Address," January 29, 2002, http://www.whitehouse.gov/news/releases/2002/01/20020129-11.html.

31 Quoted in Walter Pincus, "Tenet Says Al Qaeda Still Poses Threat," *Washington Post*, February 7, 2002, A1.

32 Philip Shenon and James Risen, "Qaeda Deputy Reported to Plan New Attacks," *New York Times*, February 14, 2002, A1.

33 Quoted in John J. Lumpkin, "Al-Qaida E-mails Intercepted," Associated Press, March 7, 2002.

34 Quoted in Vernon Loeb and Bradley Graham, "American Troops Play Greater Role in Latest Offensive," *Washington Post*, March 4, 2002, A1.

35 Bush, "State of the Union," January 29, 2002.

36 *Authorization for Use of Military Force (Agreed to by the House)*, HJ Res. 64, 107th Cong., 1st sess. (September 14, 2001).

37 Quoted in David E. Sanger, "Bush Aides Say Tough Tone Put Foes on Notice," *New York Times*, January 31, 2002, A1.

38 According to *American Heritage Dictionary*, 4th ed., "axis" means "an alliance of powers, such as nations, to promote mutual interests and policies," 130.

39 "Iran-Iraq War (1980–1988)," *GlobalSecurity.org*, http://www.globalsecurity.org/military/world/war/iran-iraq.htm.

40 Defense Intelligence Agency, "North Korea: The Foundations for Military Strength," *Federation of American Scientists.com*, October 1991, http://www.fas.org/irp/dia/product/knfms/knfms_chp3a.html#HDR11.

41 Richard F. Grimmett, "Conventional Arms Transfers to Developing Nations,

1993–2000," Congressional Research Service Report for Congress, August 16, 2001, 46.
42 Ibid., 58.
43 Ibid. "Precise figures on North Korea's arms trade, economy, and foreign trade balance are not available. Rough estimates indicate North Korea earned over $4 billion from 1981 through 1989. Arms sales during the peak year 1982 represented nearly 37 percent of North Korea's total exports."
44 Thomas R. Wilson, "Global Threats and Challenges Through 2015," Statement for the Record, Senate Select Committee on Intelligence, 107th Cong., 1st sess. (February 7, 2001). For example: "Iran has a relatively large ballistic missile force—hundreds of Chinese CSS-8s" and "Aided by China, Iran has developed a potent anti-ship cruise missile capability to threaten sea traffic from shore, ship, and aircraft platforms."
45 Quoted in Sanger, "Bush Aides Say Tough Tone Put Foes on Notice."
46 Barbara Starr, "N. Korea, Iraq in Scud Pact?" *ABC News.com*, August 10, 2000, http://abcnews.go.com/sections/world/DailyNews/scuds081000.html.
47 Ibid. The report even raised the question of "whether one of the key foreign players is for some reason laying a false paper trail to implicate all three countries."
48 International Institute for Strategic Studies, *The Military Balance 2001–2002* (London: Oxford University Press, 2001), 19, 195, 132, 134.
49 Ibid., 299–301.
50 China's active-duty military force is actually larger than the U.S. active-duty force. And the combined active-duty and reserve forces of North Korea are larger than the U.S. combined active-duty and reserve forces.
51 Central Intelligence Agency, "Unclassified Report to Congress on the Acquisition of Technology Relating to Weapons of Mass Destruction and Advanced Conventional Munitions, 1 July Through 31 December 2001," January 2003, http://www.cia.gov/cia/reports/721_reports/july_dec2001.htm.
52 National Intelligence Council, *Foreign Missile Developments and the Ballistic Missile Threat Through 2015* (Washington, DC: National Intelligence Council, 2001).
53 Michael Dobbs, "How Politics Helped Redefine Threat," *Washington Post*, January 14, 2002, A16.
54 The No Dong program has reportedly been plagued by technical and financial problems. See Federation of American Scientists, "No Dong," http://www.fas.org/nuke/guide/dprk/missile/nd-1.htm (accessed on December 2, 2005).
55 Quoted in Dobbs, "How Politics Helped Redefine Threat."
56 Michael Dobbs, "A Story of Iran's Quest for Power," *Washington Post*, January 13, 2002, A1.
57 Quoted in ibid.
58 Quoted in ibid.
59 Wilson, "Global Threats and Challenges Through 2015."
60 NIC, *Foreign Missile Developments and the Ballistic Missile Threat Through 2015.*
61 Department of Defense, "Findings of the Nuclear Posture Review," January 9, 2002, http://www.defenselink.mil/news/Jan2002/020109-D-6570C-001.pdf. It should be noted that nations are not named.
62 Department of State, *Patterns of Global Terrorism 2000* (Washington, DC: Department of State, 2001), http://www.state.gov/s/ct/rls/pgtrpt/2000/2441.htm.

63 Ibid.
64 Ibid.
65 For example, the bombing of the U.S. embassy in Beirut in April 1983 and the suicide truck bomb attack on the U.S. embassy that destroyed the U.S. Marine barracks in Beirut in October 1983. For a more complete discussion and analysis, see Ivan Eland, "Does U.S. Intervention Overseas Breed Terrorism?" Cato Institute Foreign Policy Briefing No. 50, December 17, 1998.
66 Ibid.
67 Ibid.
68 "Atta Met Twice With Iraqi Intelligence," *CNN.com*, October 11, 2001, http://www.cnn.com/2001/US/10/11/inv.atta.meetings/.
69 Robertson is quoted in Robert Novak, "No Iraqi Connection," *TownHall.com*, October 15, 2001, http://www.townhall.com/columnists/robertnovak/rn20011015.shtml.
70 Quoted in "Israel Denies Iraqi Terror Attack Link," *BBCNews.com*, September 23, 2001, http://news.bbc.co.uk/hi/english/world/middle_east/newsid_1559000/1559353.stm.
71 Dana Priest and Glenn Kessler, "Iraq, 9/11 Still Linked by Cheney," *Washington Post*, September 29, 2003, A1.
72 Quoted in ibid.
73 Ibid.
74 *9/11 Commission Report*, 228–229.
75 George W. Bush, "President Discusses Ag Policy at Cattle Industry Convention," February 8, 2002, http://www.whitehouse.gov/news/releases/2002/02/20020208-1.html.
76 George W. Bush, "President Outlines War Effort," April 17, 2002, http://www.whitehouse.gov/news/releases/2002/04/20020417-1.html.
77 George W. Bush, "President Bush Delivers Graduation Speech at West Point," June 1, 2002, http://www.whitehouse.gov/news/releases/2002/06/20020601-3.html.
78 George W. Bush, "President Salutes Troops of the 10th Mountain Division," July 19, 2002, http://www.whitehouse.gov/news/releases/2002/07/20020719.html.
79 George W. Bush, "President Presses Congress for Action on Defense Appropriations Bill," September 27, 2002, http://www.whitehouse.gov/news/releases/2002/09/20020927-3.html.
80 George W. Bush, "President Discusses Iraq, Syria," April 13, 2003, http://www.whitehouse.gov/news/releases/2003/04/20030413-1.html.
81 John R. Bolton, "Testimony of John R. Bolton, Under Secretary for Arms Control and International Security, Before the House International Relations Committee, Subcommittee on the Middle East and Central Asia," 108th Cong., 1st sess. (September 16, 2003).
82 *Syria Accountability and Lebanese Sovereignty Restoration Act of 2003*, Public Law 108-175, 108th Cong., 1st sess. (December 12, 2003), 6.
83 White House, "Fact Sheet: Implementing the Syria Accountability and Lebanese Sovereignty Restoration Act of 2003," May 11, 2004, http://www.whitehouse.gov/news/releases/2004/05/20040511-7.html.
84 "Libya Letter: Full Text," BBC News Scotland, August 16, 2003, http://

news.bbc.co.uk/2/low/uk_news/scotland/3155825.stm.

85 Scott McClellan, "Statement by the Press Secretary," August 15, 2003, http://www.whitehouse.gov/news/releases/2003/08/20030815-10.html.

86 Quoted in "Bush, Blair: Libya to Dismantle WMD Programs," *CNN.com*, December 20, 2003, http://www.cnn.com/2003/WORLD/africa/12/19/bush.libya/.

87 Quoted in Jill Lawless, "Libya Weapons Breakthrough Vindicates Blair Foreign Policy, Ministers Say," Associated Press, December 21, 2003.

88 Quoted in "Bush Official: Libya's Nuclear Program a Surprise," *CNN.com*, December 19, 2003, http://www.cnn.com/2003/WORLD/africa/12/19/libya.nuclear/index.html.

89 Quoted in Andrea Koppel, "El Baradei: Libya Nuclear Program Dismantled," *CNN.com*, December 29, 2003, http://www.cnn.com/2003/WORLD/africa/12/29/libya.nuclear/.

90 George W. Bush and President Lagos, "President Bush Welcomes President Lagos of Chile," July 19, 2004, http://www.whitehouse.gov/news/releases/2004/07/20040719-2.html.

91 Caroline Glick, "Feith to 'Post': US Action Against Iran Can't Be Ruled Out," *Jerusalem Post*, December 12, 2005, 1.

92 Quoted in "Bush Raises Option of Using Force Against Iran," Reuters, August 13, 2005.

93 Record, "Bounding the Global War on Terrorism," 42.

94 "Bush: As Long as It Takes, Dead or Alive," *CNN.com*, December 28, 2001, http://archives.cnn.com/2001/US/12/28/gen.war.against.terror/.

95 The Honeynet Project, *Know Your Enemy: Revealing the Security Tools, Tactics, and Motives of the Blackhat Community* (Boston: Addison-Wesley, 2001), 1.

Chapter 2: A Dangerous Distraction

1 George W. Bush, "President Bush Announces Major Combat Operations in Iraq Have Ended," May 1, 2003, http://www.whitehouse.gov/news/releases/2003/05/iraq/20030501-15.html.

2 George W. Bush, "President Addresses the Nation," September 7, 2003, http://www.whitehouse.gov/news/releases/2003/09/20030907-1.html.

3 George W. Bush, "Remarks by the President at Bush-Cheney 2004 Luncheon," November 3, 2003, http://www.whitehouse.gov/news/releases/2003/11/20031103-8.html.

4 George W. Bush, "State of the Union Address," February 2, 2005, http://www.whitehouse.gov/news/releases/2005/02/20050202-11.html: "That country [Iraq] is a vital front in the war on terror, which is why the terrorists have chosen to make a stand there. Our men and women in uniform are fighting terrorists in Iraq, so we do not have to face them here at home."

5 George W. Bush, "President Holds Press Conference," October 28, 2003, http://www.whitehouse.gov/news/releases/2003/10/20031028-2.html. "THE PRESIDENT: David Kay's report said that Saddam Hussein was in material breach of 1441, which would have been casus belli. . . . But one of the things that he first found was that there is clear violation of the U.N. Security Council Resolution 1441. Material breach, they call it in the diplomatic circles. Casus belli, it means . . . that would have been a cause for a war."

6 "In Cheney's Words: The Administration Case for Removing Saddam Hussein," *New York Times,* August 27, 2002, A8.

7 George W. Bush, "President Bush Outlines Iraqi Threat," October 7, 2002, http://www.whitehouse.gov/news/releases/2002/10/20021007-8.html.

8 Quoted in Walter Pincus, "Bush Faced Dwindling Data on Iraq Nuclear Bid," *Washington Post,* July 16, 2003, A1. Cheney clarified his March 2003 statement six months later: "We never had any evidence that [Hussein] had acquired any nuclear weapons," quoted in Helen Thomas, "Hussein Link Was Sales Job," *Miami Herald,* September 27, 2003, A27.

9 Central Intelligence Agency, *Iraq's Weapons of Mass Destruction Programs* (Washington, DC: Central Intelligence Agency, 2002), 1.

10 Ibid., 10.

11 Ibid.

12 Ibid., 13.

13 Central Intelligence Agency, "Unclassified Report to Congress on the Acquisition of Technology Relating to Weapons of Mass Destruction and Advanced Conventional Munitions, 1 July Through 31 December 2000," September 2001, http://www.cia.gov.cia/publications/bian/bian_jan_2002.htm.

14 CIA, *Iraq's Weapons of Mass Destruction Programs,* 1.

15 Ibid., 5 and 6. The CIA's previous assessment about Iraq's ability to develop a nuclear weapon was largely the same: "Iraq has probably continued low-level theoretical R&D associated with its nuclear program. A sufficient source of fissile material remains Iraq's most significant obstacle to being able to produce a nuclear weapon," CIA, "Unclassified Report to Congress on the Acquisition of Technology, 1 July Through 31 December 2000."

16 CIA, *Iraq's Weapons of Mass Destruction Programs,* 6.

17 International Institute for Strategic Studies, *Iraq's Weapons of Mass Destruction: A Net Assessment* (London: International Institute for Strategic Studies, 2002), 27.

18 David Kay, "Statement by David Kay on the Interim Progress Report on the Activities of the Iraq Survey Group (ISG) Before the House Permanent Select Committee on Intelligence, the House Subcommittee on Appropriations, Subcommittee on Defense, and the Senate Select Committee on Intelligence," 108th Cong., 1st sess. (October 2, 2003).

19 Quoted in Dana Priest and Walter Pincus, "Search in Iraq Finds No Banned Weapons," *Washington Post,* October 3, 2003, A1.

20 Quoted in Dana Milbank and Walter Pincus, "Cheney Goes on Offensive Over Iraq," *Washington Post,* October 11, 2003, A1.

21 Quoted in "Transcript: David Kay at Senate Hearing," *CNN.com,* January 28, 2004, http://www.cnn.com/2004/US/01/28/kay.transcript/.

22 Charles Duelfer, transmittal message of "Comprehensive Report of the Special Advisor to the DCI on Iraq's WMD," September 23, 2004, http://www.cia.gov/cia/reports/iraq-_wmd_2004/transmittal.html.

23 Charles Duelfer, "Comprehensive Report of the Special Advisor to the DCI on Iraq's WMD," September 30, 2004, http://www.cia.gov/cia/reports/iraq-_wmd_2004/chap5.html.

24 Duelfer, "Comprehensive Report on Iraq's WMD," http://www.cia.gov/cia/reports/iraq-_wmd_2004/chap6.html.

25 George W. Bush, "President Delivers 'State of the Union,'" January 28, 2003,

http://www.whitehouse.gov/news/releases/2003/01/20030128-19.html.

26 "Fake Iraq Documents 'Embarassing' for U.S.," *CNN.com*, March 14, 2003, http://www.cnn.com/2003/US/03/14/sprj.irq.documents/index.html; "Ex-envoy: Uranium Claim Unfounded," *CNN.com*, July 8, 2003, http://www.cnn.com/2003/US/07/07/cnna.wilson/index.html; "Tenet Admits Error in Approving Bush Speech," *CNN.com*, July 12, 2003, http://www.cnn.com/2003/ALLPOLITICS/07/11/sprj.irq.wmdspeech/index.html.

27 Senate Select Committee on Intelligence, *Report on the U.S. Intelligence Community's Prewar Intelligence Assessments on Iraq*, 108th Cong., 2nd sess. (July 7, 2004), 75.

28 Before the war, there was open disagreement within the U.S. intelligence community over whether the aluminum tubes were for centrifuges or artillery rockets. State Department and Department of Energy analysts thought the tubes were too long and too thick for centrifuges. The CIA and Pentagon analysts thought the tubes could be cut down and reamed out. See Pincus, "Bush Faced Dwindling Data on Iraq Nuclear Bid." And the International Atomic Energy Agency concluded in January 2003 that the tubes were likely for artillery rockets and not suitable for uranium enrichment without significant modification. See Joby Warrick, "Doubts Remain About Purpose of Specialized Aluminum Tubes," *Washington Post*, February 6, 2003, A29.

29 *Report on the U.S. Intelligence Community's Prewar Intelligence Assesments on Iraq*, 131.

30 Quoted in ibid.

31 David Kay, "Statement by Dr. David Kay, Special Advisor to the Director of Central Intelligence," November 2, 2003, http://www.cia.gov/cia/public_affairs/press_release/2003/pr11032003.htm.

32 Quoted in Milbank and Pincus, "Cheney Goes on Offensive Over Iraq."

33 Duelfer, "Comprehensive Report on Iraq's WMD," http://www.cia.gov/cia/reports/iraq-_wmd_2004/chap4.html.

34 Katherine Pfleger Shrader, "White House Says Iraq Weapons Search Over," Associated Press, January 12, 2005; "Official: U.S. Calls off Search for Iraqi WMDs," *CNN.com*, January 12, 2005, http://www.cnn.com/2005/US/01/12/wmd.search/; Dafna Linzer, "Search for Banned Arms in Iraq Ended Last Month," *Washington Post*, January 12, 2005, A1; "Search for Illicit Weapons in Iraq Ends," *New York Times*, January 12, 2005, A10.

35 ABC *20/20* transcript, January 14, 2005.

36 IISS, *Iraq's Weapons of Mass Destruction*, 71.

37 CIA, *Iraq's Weapons of Mass Destruction Programs*, 17.

38 NIC, *Foreign Missile Developments and the Ballistic Missile Threat Through 2015*, 11.

39 Ibid., 11–12.

40 *Report on the U.S. Intelligence Community's Prewar Intelligence Assessments on Iraq*, 235–236.

41 Quoted in William B. Arkin, "U.S. Nukes in the Gulf," *The Nation*, December 31, 1990, 834.

42 Neil Livingstone, "Iraq's Intentional Omission," *Sea Power*, June 1991, 29–30.

43 Keith B. Payne, "Why We Must Sustain Nuclear Deterrence," National Institute for Public Policy, 1998, http://www.nipp.org/Adobe/Op%20Ed%203_20_98.pdf.

44 George Tenet, letter to Senator Bob Graham, October 7, 2002, http://

news.findlaw.com/hdocs/docs/cia/ciassci10702iraqltr.pdf.

45 Ibid.
46 Bush, "State of the Union," January 29, 2002.
47 George W. Bush, "President's Remarks at the United Nations General Assembly," September 12, 2002, http://www.whitehouse.gov/news/releases/2002/09/20020912-1.html.
48 George W. Bush, "President Bush Discusses Iraq with Congressional Leaders," September 26, 2002, http://www.whitehouse.gov/news/releases/2002/09/20020926-7.html.
49 Bush, "President Bush Outlines Iraqi Threat."
50 George W. Bush, "Iraq Must Disarm Says President in South Dakota Speech," November 3, 2002, http://www.whitehouse.gov/news/releases/2002/11/20021103-3.html.
51 Bush, "State of the Union," January 28, 2003.
52 Quoted in Walter Pincus, "CIA Finds No Evidence Hussein Sought to Arm Terrorists," *Washington Post*, November 16, 2003, A20.
53 Bush, "State of the Union," January 28, 2003.
54 George W. Bush, "President George Bush Discusses Iraq in National Press Conference," March 6, 2003, http://www.whitehouse.gov/news/releases/2003/03/20030306-8.html.
55 Bush, "President Bush Announces Major Combat Operations in Iraq Have Ended."
56 Bush, "President Addresses the Nation."
57 "Interview With Condoleezza Rice: The War on Terror and in Iraq," ABC *Good Morning America* transcript, September 8, 2003.
58 "Vice President Dick Cheney Discusses the War With Iraq, the Economy, and Other Topics," NBC *Meet the Press* transcript, September 14, 2003.
59 Dana Milbank and Claudia Deane, "Hussein Link to 9/11 Lingers in Many Minds," *Washington Post*, September 6, 2003, A1.
60 Quoted in Dana Milbank, "Bush Disavows Hussein–Sept. 11 Link," *Washington Post*, September 18, 2003, A18.
61 "Iraq, 9/11, Al Qaeda and Weapons of Mass Destruction," Harris Poll #79, October 21, 2004, http://www.harrisinteractive.com/harris_poll/index.asp?PID=508.
62 Colin Powell, "U.S. Secretary of State Colin Powell Addresses the U.N. Security Council," February 5, 2003, http://www.whitehouse.gov/news/releases/2003/02/20030205-1.html.
63 Jason Burke, *Al Qaeda: Casting a Shadow of Terror* (London: I. B. Tauris, 2003), 234.
64 Gordon Corera, "Unraveling Zarqawi's Al Qaeda Connection," *Terrorism Monitor* (Jamestown Foundation) 2:24 (December 16, 2004),http:www.jamestown.org/publications_details.php?volume_id=400&&issue_id=3179.
65 Department of State, *Patterns of Global Terrorism 2002* (Washington, DC: Department of State, 2003), 128.
66 Quoted in Spencer Ackerman, "The Weakest Link," *Washington Monthly*, November 2003, 18.
67 Quoted in Warren P. Strobel, Jonathan S. Landay, and John Walcott, "Doubts Cast on Efforts to Link Saddam, Al-Qaida," Knight Ridder, March 3, 2004.
68 *9/11 Commission Report*, 66.

69 Quoted in ibid.
70 "Bin Laden Tape: Text," *BBCNews.com*, February 12, 2003, http://news.bbc. co.uk/2/hi/middle_east/2751019.stm.
71 Quoted in Dana Priest and Walter Pincus, "Bin Laden-Hussein Link Hazy," *Washington Post*, February 13, 2003, A20.
72 Department of State, *Patterns of Global Terrorism 2002*, 79.
73 According to the State Department, the ANO "has not staged a major attack against Western targets since the late 1980s." The Abu Abbas faction of the PLF "was responsible for the attack in 1985 on the Italian cruise ship *Achille Lauro* and the murder of US citizen Leon Klinghoffer." Ibid., 101 and 117.
74 Department of State, "Overview of State Sponsored Terrorism," *Patterns of Global Terrorism 2000*.
75 This is how Peter Bergen, author of *Holy War, Inc.* and one of the few Western journalists to interview Osama bin Laden, described al Qaeda in an interview, "Terrorism's CEO," *TheAtlantic.com*, January 9, 2002, http://www.theatlantic. com/unbound/interviews/int2002-01-09.htm (subscription required).
76 "Bin Laden Tape: Text."
77 Quoted in "'Al Qaeda' Urges Fresh Attacks," *BBCNews.com*, May 21, 2003, http://news.bbc.co.uk/2/hi/middle_east/3047457.stm.
78 Quoted in "Al Qaeda Tape 'Authentic,'" *BBCNews.com*, September 11, 2003, http://news.bbc.co.uk/2/hi/middle_east/3101182.stm.
79 "Bin Laden Messages: Full Text," *BBCNews.com*, October 18, 2003, http://news. bbc.co.uk/2/hi/middle_east/3204230.stm.
80 "Full Text: 'Bin Laden' Tape," *BBCNews.com*, January 5, 2004, http://news. bbc.co.uk/1/hi/world/middle_east/3368957.stm.
81 Quoted in "'Bin Laden' Offers Gold for Killing of Bremer," *Guardian Unlimited.com*, May 7, 2004, http://www.guardian.co.uk/alqaida/story/ 0,12469,1211740,00.html.
82 See Michael Vlahos, "The Story of War," Tech Central Station, November 6, 2003, http://www.techcentralstation.com/110603A.html.
83 Quoted in Rajiv Chandrasekaran, "Unelected Mayor Rallies Supporters Against Marines," *Washington Post*, April 24, 2003, A1.
84 "Iraq Is Split on War and Its Aftermath," *USA Today*, April 28, 2004, 4A.
85 Thomas E. Ricks, "80% in Iraq Distrust Occupation Authority," *Washington Post*, May 13, 2004, A10.
86 "Survey Finds Deep Divisions in Iraq," Zogby International, January 28, 2005, http://www.zogby.com/news/ReadNews.dbm?ID=957.
87 Quoted in "15 Killed in Baghdad Shiite Mosque Blast After Zarqawi Vows Holy War," Agence France Presse, January 21, 2005.
88 Ibid.
89 "Iraq Is Split on War and Its Aftermath."
90 "Survey Finds Deep Divisions in Iraq."
91 See Douglas Jehl, "Iraq May Be Prime Place for Training of Militants, C.I.A. Report Concludes," *New York Times*, June 22, 2005, A10; Tom Regan, "Blowback in Iraq?" *Christian Science Monitor*, June 23, 2005, http://www.csmonitor.com/ 2005/0623/dailyUpdate.html; "'New Militant Threat' From Iraq," *BBCNews.com*, June 23, 2005, http://news.bbc.co.uk/2/hi/middle_east/ 4122040.stm.

92 The Ab Hafs el-Masri Bridgades, a group that links itself to al Qaeda, claimed responsibility for the bombing, but the attack has also been blamed on Baathists from the former Saddam Hussein regime. See "'Martyrs' Claim They Hit UN HQ," *News24.com* (South Africa), August 25, 2003, http://www.wheels24. co.za/News24/World/Iraq/0,,2-10-1460_1406766,00.html.

93 A would-be bomber who was caught was carrying a Syrian passport, and being a foreign fighter in Iraq is one piece of evidence that supports potential al Qaeda involvement. See "Baghdad Terror Blasts Kills Dozens," *BBCNews.com*, October 27, 2003, http://news.bbc.co.uk/1/hi/world/middle_east/3216539.stm.

94 According to Army Gen. John Abizaid, head of the U.S. Central Command and the top military commander in Iraq, the "clear and most dangerous enemy to us at the present time are the former regime loyalists." Quoted in Mike Allen, "Al Qaeda at Work in Iraq, Bush Tells BBC," *Washington Post*, November 6, 2003, A22.

95 "When Deadly Force Bumps Into Hearts and Minds," *The Economist*, January 1, 2005, 31.

96 Johanna McGeary, "Mission Still Not Accomplished," *Time*, September 20, 2004, 37.

97 Mark Mazzewtti, "Insurgents Are Mostly Iraqis, U.S. Military Says," *Los Angeles Times*, September 28, 2004, A10.

98 Barbara Starr, "Official: 13,000–17,000 Insurgents in Iraq," *CNN.com*, February 9, 2005, http://www.cnn.com/2005/WORLD/meast/02/08/iraq.main/ . BBC News had previously reported "the numerical strength of Tawhid and Jihad [Zarqawi's network in Iraq] running from 20 to 500," Gordon Corera, "Zarqawi and Bin Laden: Brothers in arms?" *BBCNews.com*, October 18, 2004, http://news.bbc.co.uk/1/hi/world/middle_east/3754618.stm.

99 Quoted in "Zarqawi 'Shows Bin Laden Loyalty'" *BBCNews.com*, October 18, 2004, http://news.bbc.co.uk/2/hi/middle_east/3752616.stm.

100 "'Bin Laden' Tape: Key Excerpts," *BBCNews.com*, December 27, 2004, http://news.bbc.co.uk/2/hi/middle_east/4129173.stm.

101 International Institute for Strategic Studies, *The Military Balance 2003–2004* (London: Oxford University Press, 2003), 354.

102 It is telling that the mid-November 2003 military operation was dubbed "Operation Iron Hammer," which carries a much harsher and darker tone than the original "Operation Iraqi Freedom."

103 Quoted in Slobodan Lekic, "U.S. Military Policeman Killed in Iraq," Associated Press, November 10, 2003.

104 Quoted in Andrew Gray, "Bremer Sees More Iraq Attacks, Oilman Shot," Reuters, November 10, 2003.

105 Quoted in Jackie Spinner, "In One Night, Iraqi Turns From Friend to Foe," *Washington Post*, January 23, 2005, A20.

106 John F. Burns, "The Mideast in Turmoil: The Attacker," *New York Times*, October 7, 2003, A13.

107 According to al Qaeda expert Rohan Gunaratna: "What Osama and his followers object to is not so much the American way of life, not so much Americans themselves, as what they perceive the American government, in the shape of its foreign policy, is doing to Muslim countries, including Saudi Arabia, the occupation of which is intolerable to Osama," Rohan Gunaratna, *Inside Al Qaeda*

(New York: Columbia University Press, 2002), 45. This is reinforced by Peter Bergen: "What he [bin Laden] condemns the United States for is simple: its policies in the Middle East. Those are, to recap briefly: the continued U.S. military presence in Arabia; U.S. support for Israel; its continued bombing of Iraq; and its support for regimes such as Egypt and Saudi Arabia that bin Laden regards as apostates from Islam," Peter L. Bergen, *Holy War, Inc.* (New York: Free Press, 2001), 223.

108 "Deputy Secretary Wolfowitz Interview With Sam Tannenhaus, *Vanity Fair*," May 9, 2003, http://www.defenselink.mil/transcripts/2003/tr20030509-depsecdef0223.html.

109 John R. Bradley, "US Troops Quit Saudi Arabia," *The Telegraph* (London) online, August 28, 2003, http://www.telegraph.co.uk/news/main.jhtml?xml=/news/2003/08/28/wsaud28.xml.

110 Bush, "State of the Union," February 2, 2005.

111 George W. Bush, "President Bush Discusses Freedom in Iraq and Middle East," November 6, 2003, http://www.whitehouse.gov/news/releases/2003/11/20031106-2.html.

112 Quoted in ibid.

113 After a meeting with Iraqi women at the White House, Bush said: "I assured these five women that America wasn't leaving. . . . When they hear me say we're staying, that means we're staying." George W. Bush, "President Bush Meets With Iraqi Women Leaders," November 17, 2003, http://www.whitehouse.gov/news/releases/2003/11/20031117-4.html.

114 Michael Hirsh and John Barry, "Drawing Down Iraq," *Newsweek*, August 8, 2005, http://www.msnbc.com/id/8770418/site/newsweek/.

115 Bradley Graham, "Army Plans to Keep Iraq Troop Level Through '06," *Washington Post*, January 25, 2005, A1.

116 "Army Preparing Four Years Ahead in Iraq War," Associated Press, August 21, 2005.

117 According to President Bush: "We will not set an artificial timetable for leaving Iraq, because that would embolden the terrorists and make them believe they can wait us out. We are in Iraq to achieve a result: A country that is democratic, representative of all its people, at peace with its neighbors, and able to defend itself. And when that result is achieved, our men and women serving in Iraq will return home with the honor they have earned," Bush, "State of the Union," February 2, 2005.

118 George W. Bush, "President Bush Addresses United Nations General Assembly," September 23, 2003, http://www.whitehouse.gov/news/releases/2003/09/20030923-4.html.

Chapter 3: Clearing the Decks for War

1 IISS, *Military Balance 2003–2004*, 16.

2 Calculated from International Institute for Strategic Studies, *The Military Balance 2004–2005* (London: Oxford University Press, 2004), 264 and 294.

3 Ibid., 353–354.

4 "Since the mid-1980s [until the end of the Cold War], the Soviet Union devoted between 15 and 17 percent of its annual gross national product to military spending, according to United States government sources," "Russian Mili-

tary Budget," *GlobalSecurity.org*, http://www.globalsecurity.org/military/world/russia/mo-budget.htm (accessed on March 15, 2005).

5 For example, U.S.-China Economic and Security Review Commission, *2004 Annual Report to Congress* (Washington, DC: Government Printing Office, 2004); Bill Gertz, *The China Threat: How the People's Republic Targets America* (Washington, DC: Regnery, 2000). John Mearsheimer also expresses concern about China becoming a threat. John J. Mearsheimer, *The Tragedy of Great Power Politics* (New York: W. W. Norton, 2001), 396–400.

6 Harold Brown, Joseph W. Prueher, and Adam Segal, *Chinese Military Power* (New York: Council on Foreign Relations, 2003), 2.

7 Calculated from IISS, *Military Balance 2004–2005*, 322.

8 Ibid., 355.

9 Ibid.

10 For further analysis of Russia and China as potential threats, see Ivan Eland, "Tilting at Windmills: Post–Cold War Military Threats to U.S. Security," Cato Institute Policy Analysis No. 332, February 8, 1999, 18–30; Eland, *Putting "Defense" Back Into U.S. Defense Policy: Rethinking U.S. Security in the Post–Cold War World* (Westport, CT: Praeger, 2001), 48–63; and Eland, "Is Chinese Military Modernization a Threat to the United States?" Cato Institute Policy Analysis No. 465, January 23, 2003.

11 The North Koreans could have as many as eight nuclear weapons. See David E. Sanger and William J. Broad, "Atomic Activity in North Korea Raises Concerns," *New York Times*, September 12, 2004, 1. And they have deployed new medium- and intermediate-range ballistic missiles with an estimated range of 2,500–4,000 kilometers based on the decommissioned Soviet R-27 SLBM (NATO designation SS-N-6) rather than cruder Scud missiles. See Joseph Bermudez, "North Korea Deploys New Missiles," *Jane's Defense Weekly*, August 4, 2004, 6.

12 Iran is thought to be on the verge of acquiring the capability to process uranium that could be used for nuclear weapons, whereas North Korea is no doubt capable of building nuclear weapons. See Joseph Cirincione and Jon B. Wolfsthal, "North Korea and Iran: Test Cases for an Improved Nonproliferation Regime?" *Arms Control Today* 33:10 (December 2003): 11–14. Similarly, North Korea's ballistic missile program is more advanced than Iran's. In fact, Iran's ballistic missile program has been supplied by North Korea. See Andrew Feickert, "Missile Survey: Ballistic and Cruise Missiles of Foreign Countries," Congressional Research Service Report for Congress RL30427, updated March 5, 2004.

13 For a prescient analysis of the terrorist threat to the United States, see Ivan Eland, "Protecting the Homeland: The Best Defense Is to Give No Offense," Cato Policy Analysis No. 306, May 5, 1998.

14 Ted Galen Carpenter, *Peace and Freedom* (Washington, DC: Cato Institute, 2002), 12.

15 Ibid., 1–2.

16 Ibid., 1.

17 "Vice President Gore and Governor Bush Participate in Second Presidential Debate Sponsored by the Presidential Debate Commission," FDCH Political Transcripts, October 11, 2000.

18 Quoted in Walter A. McDougall, *Promised Land, Crusader State: The American*

Encounter With the World Since 1776 (Boston: Mariner Books, 1997), 131.

19 William J. Clinton, "Confronting the Challenges of a Broader World" (address to the UN General Assembly, New York, September 27, 1993). And Anthony Lake, Clinton's national security adviser, said in a speech entitled "From Containment to Enlargement" that the "the second imperative for our strategy must be to help democracy and markets expand and survive in other places where we have the strongest security concerns and where we can make the greatest difference." Anthony Lake, "From Containment to Enlargement" (address at the School of Advanced International Studies, Johns Hopkins University, Washington, DC, September 21, 1993).

20 "Letter to Congress on Increasing U.S. Ground Forces," Project for the New American Century, January 28, 2005, http://www.newamericancentury.org/defense-20050128.htm.

21 George W. Bush, *The National Security Strategy of the United States of America* (Washington, DC: White House, 2002), 3.

22 George W. Bush, "President Discusses the Future of Iraq," February 26, 2003, http://www.whitehouse.gov/news/releases/2003/02/20030226-11.html.

23 George W. Bush, "President Sworn-In to Second Term," January 20, 2005, http://www.whitehouse.gov/news/releases/2005/01/20050120-1.html.

24 Bush, "State of the Union," February 2, 2005.

25 See Central Intelligence Agency, *The World Factbook,* "Field Listing—Government Type," http://www.cia.gov/cia/publications/factbook/fields/2128.html (accessed on March 15, 2005).

26 *American Heritage Dictionary,* 4th ed.

27 In February 2005 Mubarak ordered the Egyptian constitution changed to allow for opposition candidates. How far democratic reform in Egypt will go remains to be seen. For example, Mubarak did not call for recognizing more political parties; this means one of his strongest rivals—the Muslim Brotherhood—might not be able to field a candidate because it is an outlawed group. And whether opposition candidates will have equal access to the state-run media is not clear. See Megan K. Stack and Sonni Efron, "President of Egypt Calls for Open Election," *Los Angeles Times,* February 27, 2005, A1; and Associated Press, "Election Reform Announced in Egypt," *CNN.com,* February 26, 2005, http://www.cnn.com/2005/WORLD/meast/02/26/egypt.ap/index.htm.

28 CIA, *World Factbook 2004,* "Zimbabwe," http://www.cia.gov/cia/publications/factbook/geos/zi.html.

29 Department of State, introduction to *Country Reports on Human Rights Practices 2004,* February 28, 2005, http://www.state.gov/g/drl/rls/hrrpt/2004/41586.htm.

30 Bush, *National Security Strategy,* 5.

31 Ibid., 14.

32 Bush, "State of the Union," January 28, 2003.

33 See for example, Michael B. Oren, *Six Days of War: June 1967 and the Making of the Modern Middle East* (New York: Ballantine Books, 2002).

34 Bush, *National Security Strategy,* iv.

35 Bush, "State of the Union," January 28, 2003.

36 Richard K. Betts, "The New Threat of Mass Destruction," *Foreign Affairs* 77:1 (January/February 1998): 41.

37 Office of Homeland Security, *National Strategy for Homeland Security* (Washington, DC: Office of Homeland Security, 2002), 5.

38 The democratic peace theory was first put forward by Immanuel Kant in his essay "Perpetual Peace" (1775). A modern proponent of democratic peace theory is professor R. J. Rummel at the University of Hawaii. Rummel distinguishes between a "war" version of democratic peace, i.e., democracies do not make war against each other, and a "general" version of democratic peace, i.e., democracy is a general method of nonviolence. See R. J. Rummel, "What Is the Democratic Peace?" http://www.hawaii.edu/powerkills/DP.IS_WHAT.HTM (accessed on March 11, 2005). According to Rummel, (1) democracies do not make war on each other, (2) the more democratic two nations are, the less severe the violence between them, (3) the more democratic a nation, the less severe its foreign violence, (4) the more democratic a nation, the less its collective domestic violence, and (5) the more democratic a nation, the less its domestic democide, i.e., mass murder or genocide. See R. J. Rummel, "The Democratic Peace," http://www.hawaii.edu/powerkills/MIRACLE.HTM (accessed on March 11, 2005).

39 R. J. Rummel, *Death by Government* (New Brunswick, NJ: Transaction Publishers, 1994), 2. It can be argued, however, that democratic nations have waged war against each other. The German Imperial Reichtag during World War I was democratically elected. Although Adolf Hitler would not have risen to power in democratic elections along the lines of those held in the United States, he was nonetheless elected as chancellor of Germany (albeit not by a majority vote). The first Indo-Pak War (1948–49) was between two fledgling democracies (India and Pakistan). The Croatian War of Independence (1991–92) was between two nations (Croatia and Yugoslavia) whose governments were put in place through free elections. See also Christopher Lane, "Kant or Cant: The Myth of the Democratic Peace," *International Security* 19:2 (Fall 1994): 5–49.

40 Bush, "State of the Union," January 28, 2003.

41 Pew Research Center, *Trends 2005* (Washington, DC: Pew Research Center, 2005), 107.

42 Zogby International, "Impressions of America 2004: How Arabs View America, How Arabs Learn About America" (New York: Zogby International, 2004), 3.

43 Pew Research Center, *Trends 2005*, 107. Jordan's favorable rating of the United States was 15 percent according to Zogby, "Impressions of America 2004," 3.

44 Reuel Marc Gerecht, *The Islamic Paradox: Shiite Clerics, Sunni Fundamentalists, and the Coming of Arab Democracy* (Washington, DC: AEI Press, 2004), 54.

45 Bush, "Address to a Joint Session of Congress and the American People."

46 Department of Defense, *Report of the Defense Science Board Task Force on Strategic Communication* (Washington, DC: Office of the Under Secretary of Defense for Acquisition, Technology, and Logistics, 2004), 40.

47 Pew Research Center, "A Year After Iraq War: Mistrust of America in Europe Ever Higher, Muslim Anger Persists," Pew Global Attitudes Project, March 16, 2004, 1.

48 Zogby, "Impressions of America 2004," 2.

49 Associated Press, "Europe Polled on Why 9/11 Happened," *CBSNews.com*, September 4, 2002, http://www.cbsnews.com/stories/2002/08/28/september11/main520058.shtml.

50 "Global Survey Results Give a Thumbs Down to U.S. Foreign Policy," Gallup International, Voice of the People, September 7, 2002, http://www.voice-of-the-people.net/ContentFiles/docs/Terrorism_and_US_foreign_policy.pdf.

51 Pew Research Center, *Trends 2005*, 106.

52 *9/11 Commission Report*, 375.

53 Department of Defense, *The Defense Science Board 1997 Summer Study Task Force on DOD Responses to Transnational Threats*, vol. 1, Final Report (Washington, DC: Office of the Undersecretary of Defense for Acquisition and Technology, 1997), 15.

54 Department of Defense, "Active Duty Military Personnel Strengths by Regional Area and by Country (309A)," September 30, 2004, http://web1.whs.osd.mil/mmid/M05/hst0409.pdf.

55 Carpenter, *Peace and Freedom*, 34.

56 George W. Bush, "President Speaks at VFW Convention," August 16, 2004, http://www.whitehouse.gov/news/releases/2004/08/20040816-12.html.

57 Calculated from IISS, *Military Balance 2004–2005*.

58 Article 5 states: "The Parties agree that an armed attack against one or more of them in Europe or North America shall be considered an attack against them all and consequently they agree that, if such an armed attack occurs, each of them, in exercise of the right of individual or collective self-defence recognised by Article 51 of the Charter of the United Nations, will assist the Party or Parties so attacked by taking forthwith, individually and in concert with the other Parties, such action as it deems necessary, including the use of armed force, to restore and maintain the security of the North Atlantic area." *The North Atlantic Treaty*, April 4, 1949, http://www.nato.int/docu/basictxt/treaty.htm.

59 DOD, "Active Duty Military Personnel Strengths."

60 CIA, *World Factbook 2004*, "Korea, North," December 16, 2004, http://www.cia.gov/cia/publications/factbook/geos/kn.html.

61 IISS, *Military Balance 2004–2005*, 323.

62 Ibid.

63 Ibid., 322. According to IISS, China's defense budget was $22.4 billion but total military spending was $56 billion. There is a wide range of estimates for Chinese military spending. For example, the RAND Corporation estimates the full Chinese military budget at $31–$38 billion, Keith Crane, Roger Cliff, Evan Medeiros, James Mulvenon, and William Overholt, "Modernizing China's Military: Opportunities and Constraints," RAND Project Air Force, MG260-1-AF, 2005, 133. The Council on Foreign Relations estimates Chinese defense spending at $44–$67 billion, Brown, Prueher, and Segal, *Chinese Military Power*. And the Defense Department suggests that the defense sector in China could receive up to $90 billion in 2005, Office of the Secretary of Defense, *Annual Report to Congress: The Military Power of the People's Republic of China* (Washington, DC: Office of the Secretary of Defense, 2005), 22.

64 Bush, "President Speaks at VFW Convention."

65 David Isenberg, "The U.S. Global Posture Review: Reshaping America's Global Military Footprint," *BASIC Notes (Occasional Papers on International Security Policy)*, November 19, 2004, http://www.basicint.org/pubs/Notes/BN041119.htm.

66 Department of Defense, "Defense Department Background Briefing on Global Posture Review," news transcript, August 16, 2004, http://www.defenselink.mil/transcripts/2004/tr20040816-1153.html.

67 Ibid.

68 Jeanne Meserve, "Officials: Bin Laden Message to Al-Zarqawi Intercepted," *CNN.com*, March 1, 2005, http://www.cnn.com/2005/US/02/28/threat.info/ ; Associated Press, "Bin Laden Enlisting Al-Zarqawi for Attacks," *USA Today.com*, March 1, 2005, http://www.usatoday.com/news/washington/2005-02-28-terror-iraq_x.htm.

69 Walter Pincus, "Analysts See Bin Laden, Zarqawi as Independent Operators," *Washington Post*, March 2, 2005, A15.

70 Emerson Vermaat, "Bin Laden's Terror Networks in Europe," Mackenzie Institute Occasional Paper, http://www.mackenzieinstitute.com/2002/2002_Bin_Ladens_Networks.html (accessed on June 16, 2005).

71 Tom Post, "Help From the Holy Warriors," with Joel Brand, *Newsweek*, October 5, 1992, 52.

72 Middle East Media Research Institute, "Al-Qaeda in Iraq: The Drafters of the Iraqi Constitution and Those Who Support Them Are Infidels," special dispatch, August 19, 2005, http://memri.org/binarticles.cgi?Page=archives&Area=sd&ID=SP96205.

73 Bush, "President Discusses the Future of Iraq."

74 Bob Davis, "Bush Economic Aide Says the Cost of Iraq War May Top $100 Billion," *Wall Street Journal*, September 16, 2002, 1.

75 Quoted in Matt Kelley, "Analysts Made Accurate Iraq War Estimates," Associated Press, October 31, 2003.

76 Elisabeth Bumiller, "Estimated Cost of Iraq War Reduced," *New York Times*, December 31, 2002, A1.

77 According to White House spokesman Trent Duffy, "He [Daniels] said it could, could be $60 billion. It is impossible to know what any military campaign would ultimately cost," quoted in Dana Bash, "Cost of Second War in Iraq 'Impossible to Know,'" *CNN.com*, December 31, 2002, http://archives.cnn.com/2002/US/12/31/sproject.irq.war.cost/.

78 "DOD News Briefing—Secretary Rumsfeld and Gen. Myers," news transcript, October 2, 2003, http://www.defenselink.mil/transcripts/2003/tr20031002-secdef0726.html.

79 Sharon Otterman, "Iraq: The War's Price Tag," Council on Foreign Relations, updated June 7, 2004, http://www.cfr.org/publication/7663/iraq.html.

80 Steven M. Kosiak, "One Year Later: The Cost of U.S. Military Operations in Iraq," Center for Strategic and Budgetary Assessments, March 18, 2004, http://www.csbaonline.org/4Publications/Archive/U.20040318.OIFSpending/U.20040318.OIFSpending.pdf.

81 Lael Brainard and Michael E. O'Hanlon, "The Heavy Price of America's Going It Alone," *Financial Times*, August 6, 2003, 17.

82 Quoted in Otterman, "Iraq: The War's Price Tag."

83 Council on Foreign Relations, *Iraq: The Day After* (New York: Council on Foreign Relations, 2003), 1–2.

84 Kosiak, "One Year Later."

85 Jonathan Weisman, "President Requests More War Funding," *Washington Post*,

February 15, 2005, A4.

86 *Department of Defense Appropriations Act, 2005,* HR 4613, 108th Cong., 2nd sess. (June 18, 2004). See also Terence Hunt, "Bush Signs Bill With $25B More for Wars," Associated Press, August 5, 2004.

87 Bradley Graham, "Army Plans to Keep Iraq Troop Level Through '06," *Washington Post,* January 25, 2005, A1.

88 "Iraq War Topping $5.8 Billion a Month," United Press International, November 18, 2004. Some previous estimates were $3.9 billion a month (Steve Bowman, "Iraq: U.S. Military Operations," Congressional Research Service Report for Congress RL31701, updated October 2, 2003, 8) and $4.4 billion a month (Otterman, "Iraq: The War's Price Tag.").

89 "Gulf War Facts," *CNN.com,* http://www.cnn.com/SPECIALS/2001/gulf.war/facts/gulfwar/ (accessed on December 2, 2005).

90 Quoted in Guy Dinmore, "Just One More Miscalculation: Bush's Pipe Dreams for Reconstructing Iraq," *Financial Times,* January 16, 2004, 9.

91 "DOD News Briefing—Secretary Rumsfeld and Gen. Myers."

92 See Howard LaFranchi, "Why Iraq Oil Money Hasn't Fueled Rebuilding," *Christian Science Monitor,* July 14, 2005, 2; Associated Press, "Iraq Tallies $11.4 Billion in Lost Oil Revenue," *MSNBC.com,* July 3, 2005, http://www.msnbc.msn.com/id/8454087/; David Isenberg, "Iraqi Oil Revenues Not Materializing," *Asia Times,* August 12, 2003, http://www.atimes.com/atimes/Middle_East/EH12Ak02.html; David R. Baker, "Iraqi Oil Facing Long Slog," *San Francisco Chronicle,* June 30, 2004, C1.

93 Dave Moniz and Steven Komarow, "Shifts From Bin Laden Hunt Evoke Questions," *USA Today,* March 28, 2004, A4.

94 Barton Gellman and Dafna Linzer, "Afghanistan, Iraq: Two Wars Collide," *Washington Post,* October 22, 2004, A1.

95 Quoted in ibid.

96 Ann Scott Tyson, "Military Offers Special Perks in Bid to Retain Special Forces," *Christian Science Monitor,* January 21, 2005, 3.

97 Lee Hockstader, "Army Stops Many Soldiers From Quitting," *Washington Post,* December 29, 2003, A1.

98 Tom Squitieri, "Army Expanding 'Stop Loss' Order to Keep Soldiers From Leaving," *USA Today,* January 5, 2005, http://www.usatoday.com/news/nation/2004-01-05-army-troops_x.htm.

99 "Iraq: U.S. Forces Order of Battle," *Global Security.com,* March 4, 2005, http://www.globalsecurity.org/military/ops/iraq_orbat.htm.

100 "General: Army to Miss Recruiting Goals in '05," *FoxNews.com,* August 23, 2005, http://www.foxnews.com/story/0,2933,166490,00.html.

101 Reuters, "Army Raises Enlistment Age for Reservists to 30," *Houston Chronicle,* March 22, 2005, http://www.chron.com/disp/story.mpl/nation/3095522.html.

102 Department of Defense, "DOD Announces OEF/OIF Rotational Units," December 14, 2004, http://www.defenselink.mil/releases/2004/nr20041214-1823.html

103 "Iraq: U.S. Forces Order of Battle."

104 Douglas Holtz-Eakin, "The Ability of the U.S. Military to Sustain an Occupation in Iraq," Congressional Budget Office testimony, November 5, 2003, Appendix C: Deployment Tempo and Rotation Ratios, 34–39.

105 Jack Reed, "Reed, Hagel Will Introduce Bill to Increase the Size of the Army," February 17, 2005, http://reed.senate.gov/sasc/FY06EndStrengthIntro2-17-05.htm.

106 Center for American Progress, "Neglecting the National Guard and Reserves," *Daily Talking Points*, July 19, 2004, http://www.americanprogress.org/site/pp.asp?c=biJRJ8OVF&b=124344.

107 Douglas Holtz-Eakin, "The Ability of the U.S. Military to Sustain an Occupation in Iraq."

108 See James T. Quinlivan, "Burden of Victory: The Painful Arithmetic of Stability Operations," *RAND Review*, Summer 2003, 28.

109 Department of Defense, *Defense Science Board 2004 Summer Study on Transition to and from Hostilities* (Washington, DC: Office of the Under Secretary of Defense for Acquisition, Technology, and Logistics, 2004), 42.

110 Quoted in "Top U.S. General Sees Lasting Iraq Insurgency," Reuters, February 25, 2005.

111 Speaking about Guard and reserve forces, GAO's director of defense capabilities and management told the House Subcommittee on Military Personnel: "DOD could eventually run out of forces," Derek B. Stewart, "A Strategic Approach Is Needed to Address Long-term Guard and Reserve Force Availability," testimony before the House Subcommittee on Military Personnel, Committee on Armed Services, 109th Cong., 1st sess. (February 2, 2005).

112 "The Second Bush-Kerry Presidential Debate," Commission on Presidential Debates, October 8, 2004, http://www.debates.org/pages/trans2004c.html.

113 *Universal National Service Act of 2003*, HR 163, 108th Cong., 1st sess. (January 7, 2003).

Chapter 4: A War Not Won by the Military

1 Steven M. Kosiak, "Final Action on the FY 2005 Defense Appropriations Act," Center for Strategic and Budgetary Assessments, August 4, 2005.

2 Department of Defense, "Fiscal 2005 Department of Defense Budget Release," February 2, 2004, http://www.defenselink.mil/releases/2004/nr20040202-0301.html.

3 Ibid.

4 "Weapons," Campaign 2004: Ad Archive, George W. Bush-Dick Cheney, April–May '04, Standford University, Political Communication Lab, http://pcl.stanford.edu/campaigns/campaign2004/archive.html. MPEG file of ad: http://pcl.stanford.edu/common/media/campaign/2004/general/bush/b40423weapons.mpg.

5 Department of Defense, *National Defense Budget Estimates for FY 2006* (Washington, DC: Office of the Under Secretary of Defense [Comptroller], April 2005), 67.

6 Data compiled from IISS, *Military Balance 2004–2005*, 353–358. Note that IISS uses the term "defense expenditures" to mean actual defense budget outlays plus any other defense related outlays that may not be part of a country's defense budget. For NATO countries, defense expenditures are calculated using NATO's definition: "the cash outlays of central or federal government to meet the costs of national armed forces. The term 'armed forces' includes strategic, land, naval, air, command, administration, and support forces. It also includes paramilitary forces such as the *gendarmerie*, the customs service, and the bor-

der guard if these forces are trained in military tactics, equipped as a military force, and operate under military authority in the event of war," 12.

7 Data compiled from ibid., 353–358. Inflation factors to convert to constant FY 2005 dollars derived from "Table 6-1: Department of Defense TOA by Title," in Department of Defense, *National Defense Budget Estimates for FY 2005* (Washington, DC: Office of the Undersecretary of Defense [Comptroller], March 2004), 66–67.

8 Data for 1997 compiled from International Institute for Strategic Studies, *The Military Balance 1998–1999* (London: Oxford University Press, 1998), 295–300.

9 Steven M. Kosiak, "FY 2005 Defense Budget Request: DOD Stays the Course on Spending Plans," Center for Strategic and Budgetary Assessments, January 30, 2004.

10 Carpenter, *Peace and Freedom*, 3.

11 Steven M. Kosiak, "Analysis of the FY 2005 Defense Budget Request," Center for Strategic and Budgetary Assessments, January 2004, 3.

12 Department of Defense, "Active Duty Military Personnel Strengths by Regional Area and by Country," December 31, 2002, http://web1.whs.osd.mil/mmid/M05/hst1202.pdf.

13 Eland, *Putting "Defense" Back into U.S. Defense Policy*, 85.

14 For a more detailed bottom-up analysis of changing U.S. force structure for a balancer-of-last-resort strategy see ibid., 104–116. Eland recommends reducing U.S. Army active-duty divisions by 50 percent; U.S. Air Force active-duty air wings by 30 percent and heavy bombers by 10 percent; U.S. Navy total ships by 37 percent, aircraft carriers by 50 percent, air carrier wings by 45 percent, and attack submarines by 55 percent; and U.S. Marine Corps active-duty divisions by 67 percent. Although Eland's book is now nearly three years old, the military threat environment that was the basis for determining the U.S. force structure then is essentially the same as today.

15 This figure represents the discretionary budget authority requested by the Defense Department. Note, however, the *National Defense Budget Estimates for FY 2006* lists different budget figures: $419.9 billion for total obligational authority (TOA), which is the value of direct defense programs for a fiscal year; $421.1 billion for budget authority, which is the authority to incur legally binding obligations that will result in immediate or future outlays; and $447.4 for total national defense outlays, which represent actual expenditures, p. 4. The latter two categories include Department of Energy and other defense-related expenditures. For analytic purposes, the $419.9 TOA figure — which is just Department of Defense expenditures — is used as the FY 2005 baseline budget.

16 DOD, "Military Personnel Programs (M-1)," *Department of Defense Budget Fiscal Year 2006* (Washington, DC: Office of the Under Secretary of Defense [Comptroller], 2005), 16 and 18.

17 Data derived from ibid., 1–14.

18 For analytic purposes, the assumption here is that a 40 percent reduction in military personnel would directly result in a 40 percent cost savings. Depending on the type of personnel reduced, the actual cost savings might be marginally more or less.

19 DOD, "Operations Programs (O-1)," *Department of Defense Budget Fiscal Year 2006*, 1.

20 Kenneth L. Adelman and Norman R. Augustine, *The Defense Revolution: Intelligent Downsizing of America's Military* (Oakland, CA: ICS Press, 1992), 55.

21 J. Douglas Beason, "Technology Update in Directed Energy Weapons and Laser Development" (presentation, Directed Energy Weapons and Laser Development Conference, Arlington, VA, January 19, 2005).

22 Associated Press, "Army Ends 20-Year Helicopter Program," *CNN.com*, February 23, 2004, http://www.cnn.com/2004/US/02/23/helicopter.cancel.ap/.

23 "F-15 Eagle Specifications," *GlobalSecurity.org*, http://www.globalsecurity.org/military/systems/aircraft/f-15-specs.htm (accessed December 2, 2005).

24 Department of Defense, "SAR [Selected Acquisition Report] Program Acquisition Cost Summary" (Washington, DC: Department of Defense, June 30, 2005).

25 DOD, "Program Acquisition Costs by Weapon System," *Department of Defense Budget Fiscal Year 2006*, 16.

26 According to the Congressional Budget Office, "the average procurement costs of the 179 F/A-22s not yet purchased is about $120 million," or $21.5 billion total. Congressional Budget Office, *Budget Options* (Washington, DC: Congressional Budget Office, 2005), 32.

27 Office of Naval Intelligence, *Worldwide Challenges to Naval Strike Warfare*, 34–35, cited in Michael O'Hanlon, *How to Be a Cheap Hawk: The 1999 and 2000 Defense Budgets* (Washington, DC: Brookings Institution, 1998), 120.

28 IISS, *Military Balance 2004–2005*, 26, 172.

29 On July 7, 2004, the General Accounting Office (GAO) became the Government Accountability Office.

30 General Accounting Office, "Progress of the F/A-18E/F Engineering and Manufacturing Development Program," Report to Congressional Committees, GAO-NSIAD-99-127, June 1999, 3.

31 General Accounting Office, "F/A-18 Will Provide Marginal Operational Improvement at High Cost," Report to Congressional Committees, GAO-NSIAD-96-98, June 1996, 5.

32 DOD, "SAR Program Acquisition Cost Summary."

33 DOD, "Program Acquisition Costs by Weapon System," 7.

34 Center for Defense Information, "U.S. Military Transformation: Not Just More Spending, But Better Spending," January 31, 2002, http://www.cdi.org/mrp/transformation.cfm (accessed on July 29, 2004).

35 DOD, "SAR Program Acquisition Cost Summary."

36 DOD, "Program Acquisition Costs by Weapon System," 21.

37 For more detailed analysis of the V-22, see Charles V. Peña, "V-22: Osprey or Albatross?" Cato Institute Foreign Policy Briefing No. 72, January 8, 2003.

38 For a more detailed analysis of nuclear attack submarines, see Ivan Eland, "Subtract Unneeded Nuclear Attack Submarines From the Fleet," Cato Institute Foreign Policy Briefing No. 47, April 1, 1998.

39 *Military Balance 2003–2004*, 153 and 19. "China has stated that it has built two Xia-class SSBNs, each of which can carry 12 JL-1 SLBMs [submarine launched ballistic missiles]. However, reports conflict as to whether China has actually deployed two SSBNs. Most analysts estimate only one is operational (the 09-2)." Nuclear Threat Initiative, "China's Nuclear Submarine Program," *NTI.org*, http://www.nti.org/db/china/wsubdat.htm (accessed on August 31, 2005).

40 DOD, "SAR Program Acquisition Cost Summary."

41 DOD, "Program Acquisition Costs by Weapon System," 42.

42 CBO, *Budget Options*, 19.

43 Congressional Budget Office, *Transforming the Navy's Surface Combatant Force* (Washington, DC: Congressional Budget Office, 2003), 59.

44 The Navy's FY 2006 budget proposes to retire the USS *John F. Kennedy* (CV-76); this would reduce the carrier fleet to eleven ships. See Ronald O'Rourke, "Navy Aircraft Carriers: Proposed Retirement of USS *John F. Kennedy*—Issues and Options for Congress," Congressional Research Service Report for Congress RL32732, updated May 25, 2005.

45 Obviously, the United States is faced with a serious terrorist threat. However, asymmetric threats posed by men wielding box cutters or bombers using TNT as in the Madrid attacks will not be deterred or defeated by any of the military systems advocated to be cut in this study.

46 Eland, *Putting "Defense" Back into U.S. Defense Policy*, 105.

47 Ibid., 203–220.

48 Inflation factor from DOD, *National Defense Budget Estimates for FY 2006*, 47.

49 For a more detailed analysis of intelligence capabilities needed for the war on terrorism, see James W. Harris, "Building Leverage in the Long War: Ensuring Intelligence Community Creativity in the Fight Against Terrorism," Cato Institute Policy Analysis No. 439, May 16, 2002.

50 *9/11 Commission Report*, 410.

51 Air Force Intelligence, Army Intelligence, Central Intelligence Agency, Defense Intelligence Agency, Department of Energy (Office of Intelligence), Department of Homeland Security (Information Analysis and Infrastructure Protection), Department of State (Bureau of Intelligence and Research), Department of Treasury (Office of Intelligence Support), Federal Bureau of Investigation, Marine Corps Intelligence, National Geospatial-Intelligence Agency, National Reconnaissance Office, National Security Agency, and Navy Intelligence. U.S. Intelligence Community, "Members of the Intelligence Community," June 24, 2005, http://www.intelligence.gov/1-members.shtml. See David E. Kaplan, "Mission Impossible," *U.S. News & World Report*, August 2, 2004, 38–39.

52 Douglas Jehl, "Disclosing Intelligence Budgets Might Be Easiest of 9/11 Panel's Recommendations," *New York Times*, July 29, 2004, A16. See also Center for Defense Information, "Intelligence Funding and the War on Terror," February 26, 2002, http://www.cdi.org/terrorism/intel-funding.cfm.

53 Lisa Myers, Doug Pasternak, and the NBC News Investigative Unit, "'Eyes in the Sky' Flying Blind?" *MSNBC.com*, updated January 2, 2004, http://msnbc.msn.com/id/3660554/.

54 Quoted in "Profile: John Walker Lindh," *BBCNews.com*, January 24, 2002, http://news.bbc.co.uk/1/hi/world/americas/1779455.stm.

55 Reported in Gail Kaufman, "UAVs Shifted Role in Iraq Operations," *Defense News*, December 8, 2003, 24.

56 "U.S. Missile Hits Suspected Al Qaeda Leader," *CNN.com*, February 7, 2002, http://www.cnn.com/2002/WORLD/asiapcf/central/02/07/ret.hellfire.alqaeda/.

57 Walter Pincus, "U.S. Strike Kills Six in Al Qaeda," *Washington Post*, November 5, 2002, A1. See also Associated Press, "U.S. Kills Al-Qaeda Suspects in Yemen,"

USA Today, November 5, 2002, http://www.usatoday.com/news/world/2002-11-04-yemen-explosion_x.htm.

58 Office of the Secretary of Defense, *Unmanned Aerial Vehicles Roadmap: 2002–2027*, (Washington, DC: Office of the Secretary of Defense, 2002), iv.

59 Quoted in Jim Garamone, "Unmanned Aerial Vehicles Fly High After Afghanistan," *DefendAmerica.mil*, April 2002, http://www.defendamerica.mil/articles/apr2002/a041602b.html.

60 Quoted in Lisa Myers, "Osama Bin Laden: Missed Opportunities," *MSNBC.com*, March 17, 2004, http://www.msnbc.com/id/4540958/.

61 Office of the Secretary of Defense, *Unmanned Aerial Vehicles Roadmap*, 59.

62 DOD, "Program Acquisition Cost by Weapon System," 20.

63 Office of the Secretary of Defense, *Unmanned Aerial Vehicles Roadmap*, 59–60.

64 Obviously, an added benefit of UAVs is that pilots' lives are not at risk with every sortie. Though hard to quantify in budgetary terms, that benefit is real and should be acknowledged.

65 Quoted in Associated Press, "Bush: Al Qaeda Capture Shows War on Terror Is Succeeding," *FoxNews.com*, March 4, 2003, http://www.foxnews.com/story/0,2933,80149,00.html.

66 Department of Defense, "United States Special Operations Forces: Posture Statement 2003–2004" (Washington, DC: U.S. Special Operations Command, n.d.), 36.

67 Barbara Starr, "Sources: Rumsfeld Calls for Special Ops Covert Action," *CNN.com*, August 2, 2002, http://www.cnn.com/2002/US/08/02/rumsfeld.memo/.

68 Doug Sample, "DOD Official Updates Congress on Special Ops Transformation," Armed Forces Press Service, March 30, 2004, http://www.soc.mil/News/releases/04MAR/040330-01.htm.

69 Donald H. Rumsfeld, "Statement of Secretary of Defense Donald H. Rumsfeld, FY 2006 Department of Defense Budget," Senate Armed Services Committee, 109th Cong., 1st sess. (February 17, 2005), 9. Senate Committee on Appropriations, *Defense Subcommittee Hearing on FY 2006 Budget for the Department of Defense: Testimony of the Honorable Tina W. Jonas, Under Secretary of Defense (Comptroller)*, 109th Cong., 1st sess. (March 2, 2005).

70 Andrew Feickert, "U.S. Special Operations Forces (SOF): Background and Issues for Congress," Congressional Research Service Report RS21048, September 28, 2004, 1.

71 Tzu, *Art of War*, 14–15.

72 Government Accounting Office, "Foreign Languages: Workforce Planning Could Help Address Staffing and Proficiency Shortfalls," GAO-02-514T, testimony of Susan S. Westin before the Subcommittee on International Security, Proliferation, and Federal Services, Senate Committee on Governmental Affairs, 107th Cong., 2nd sess., March 12, 2002, 6.

73 Quoted in "Pentagon People Person," *GovExec.com*, February 9, 2004, http://www.govexec.com/dailyfed/0204/020904ff.htm.

74 Federal Document Clearing House, transcript of "U.S. Representative Frank R. Wolf (R-VA) Holds Hearing on FBI Appropriations," March 17, 2004, http:/web.lexis-nexis.com/universe/.

75 Niraj Warikoo, "CIA Steps Up Recruitment of Arab-American Agents," *Detroit Free Press*, July 23, 2004, A1.

76 GAO, "Foreign Languages," 1.
77 "Reforming Law Enforcement, Counterterrorism, and Intelligence Collection in the United States," Staff Statement No. 12 of the National Commission on Terrorist Attacks Upon the United States, http://www.9-11commission.gov/hearings/hearing10/staff_statement_12.pdf.
78 Quoted in Katherine McIntire Peters, "Lost in Translation," *GovExec.com*, May 1, 2002, http://www.govexec.com/features/0502/0502s4.htm.
79 Anne Hull, "How 'Don't Tell' Translates," *Washington Post*, December 3, 2003, A1.

Chapter 5: Yin and Yang of al Qaeda

1 Bush, "Address to a Joint Session of Congress and the American People."
2 Bush, "President Discusses Ag Policy at Cattle Industry Convention."
3 Bush, "Remarks by the President in Photo Opportunity with the National Security Team."
4 Bush, "President Bush Delivers Graduation Speech at West Point."
5 Bush, "State of the Union," January 28, 2003.
6 George W. Bush, "President's Radio Address," September 11, 2004, http://www.whitehouse.gov/news/releases/2004/09/20040911-3.html.
7 Quoted in "Iraq Mosque Blasts Kills 85," *CBSNews.com*, August 29, 2003, http://www.cbsnews.com/stories/2003/08/29/iraq/main570897.shtml.
8 George W. Bush, "President Condemns Terrorism in Russia," September 12, 2004, http://www.whitehouse.gov/news/releases/2004/09/20040912-1.html.
9 *9/11 Commission Report*, 362.
10 *9/11 Commission Report*, 363.
11 Danish physicist Niels Bohr understood that there was a connection between quantum physics and Eastern and Chinese philosophy. According to Bohr, "Here we are faced with complementary phenomena related to the human situation which, in an unforgettable way, is expressed in ancient Chinese philosophy which reminds us that in the great drama of life we are both actors and audience." Ministry of Foreign Affairs of Denmark, "Niels Bohr," Embassy of Denmark, Washington, DC, http://www.ambwashington.um.dk/en/menu/InformationaboutDenmark/EducationandTraining/FamousDanishScientists/NielsBohr.htm (accessed on September 4, 2005).
12 Young's experiment was simple. He placed a screen with two slits—each of which could be covered—in front of a light source. On the other side of the screen was a wall that the light coming through the slits could illuminate. First, he turned the light source on with only one of the slits open. Then he repeated the experiment with both slits uncovered. If light was a particle, then the image on the wall with both slits uncovered should have been simply twice as much light as with one slit. Instead, the result was alternating bands of light and darkness; this demonstrated that the light was behaving like a wave. The dark bands represented two waves of light canceling each other out—in the same way that the crest of one wave of water cancels out the trough of another wave to create an area of calm water.
13 Gary Zukav, *The Dancing Wu Li Masters: An Overview of the New Physics* (New York: Bantam Books, 1980), 65.
14 Bush, "Address to a Joint Session of Congress and the American People."

15 Peter L. Bergen, "Illusions of the War on Terrorism," *Foreign Affairs.org*, July 2003, http://www.foreignaffairs.org/20020301faupdate8054/peter-l-bergen/illusions-of-the-war-on-terrorism.html.

16 Bush, "President Addresses the Nation."

17 Bush, "State of the Union," February 2, 2005.

18 Bergen, "Illusions of the War on Terrorism."

19 "Who's Who in Al Qaeda," *BBCNews.com*, updated September 29, 2004, http://news.bbc.co.uk/2/hi/middle_east/2780525.stm.

20 "Who's Who in Al Qaeda." There is some dispute as to al-Libbi's place in the al Qaeda hierarchy. When he was first captured, President Bush described him as a "top general for bin Laden," "Pakistan Seizes 'Al Qaeda No. 3,'" *CNN.com*, May 5, 2005, http://www.cnn.com/2005/WORLD/asiapcf/05/04/pakistan.arrest/. But some experts believe al-Libbi may have only been a mid-level al Qaeda operative and not a member of the top leadership, Christina Lamb and Mohammad Shezad Islamabad, "Captured Al-Qaeda Kingpin Is Case of 'Mistaken Identity,'" *Times* (London), May 8, 2005, http://www.timesonline.co.uk/article/0,,2089-1602568,00.html.

21 In April 2003 coalition forces were issued a deck of cards that identified the most wanted members of Saddam Hussein's regime, who were to be pursued, killed, or captured. See Linda D. Kozaryn, "Deck of Cards Help Troops Identify Regime's Most Wanted," American Forces Information Service, April 12, 2003, http://www.defenselink.mil/news/Apr2003/n04122003_200304124.html. The deck of cards is depicted at "Personality Identification Playing Cards," http://www.defenselink.mil/news/Apr2003/pipc10042003.html (accessed on September 4, 2005). See also, Headquarters United States Central Command, "Iraqi Top 55," news release number 03-04-112, April 12, 2003, http://www.centcom.mil/CENTCOMNews/news_release.asp?NewsRelease=200304112.txt.

22 Quoted in Susan Schmidt and Douglas Farah, "Al Qaeda's New Leaders," *Washington Post*, October 29, 2002, A1.

23 Quoted in ibid.

24 See Paul Baran, "On Distributed Communications," RAND Memorandum RM-3420-PR, August 1964, http://www.rand.org/publications/RM/RM3420/.

25 Baran, "On Distributed Communications," http://www.rand.org/publications/RM/RM3420/RM3420.chapter4.html.

26 Faye Bowers, "Al Qaeda's Profile: Slimmer but Menacing," *Christian Science Monitor*, September 9, 2003, http://www.csmonitor.com/2003/0909/p03s01-usfp.html.

27 Scott McClellan, "Press Gaggle by Scott McClellan," August 4, 2003, http://www.whitehouse.gov/news/releases/2003/08/20030804-4.html.

28 Baran, "On Distributed Communications," http://www.rand.org/publications/RM/RM3420/RM3420.chapter4.html.

29 Thomas E. Ricks and Vernon Loeb, "Afghan War Faltering, Military Leader Says," *Washington Post*, November 8, 2002, A1.

30 Some speculated that Abu Zubaydah may have taken on the role of No. 3 in between Atef and Khalid Sheikh Mohammed. See Bowers, "Al Qaeda's Profile."

31 Although Al-Adel is still on the FBI's most wanted terrorists list and is con-

sidered at large, one report says he was put under house arrest in Iran. See Bowers, "Al Qaeda's Profile."

32 Figures 5.6, 5.7, and 5.8 originally appeared in a briefing by Marc Sageman entitled "Understanding Al Qaeda Networks," http://www.bfrl.nist.gov/ PSSIWG/presentations/Understanding_al_Qaeda_Networks.pdf. The graphics were created by the Artificial Intelligence Lab at the University of Arizona by Dr. Hsinchun Chen, Ms. Jennifer Xu, and Mr. Jualun Qin.

33 See "Al Qaeda May Use Internet to Regroup," *BBCNews.com*, March 6, 2002, http://news.bbc.co.uk/1/hi/world/south_asia/1857538.stm; "How Al Qaeda Uses the Internet," *ABC News.com* (Australia), March 19, 2004, http:// www.abc.net.au/news/newsitems/s1069629.htm; Gordon Corera, "A Web Wise Terror Network," *BBCNews.com*, October 6, 2004, http://news.bbc.co.uk/ 2/hi/in_depth/3716908.stm; "Al Qaeda Flourishing on the Internet, Intelligence Officials Warn," *CBC.com* (Canada), March 8, 2005, http://www.cbc.ca/ story/world/national/2005/03/08/terrorist-internet050308.html; and Marc Sageman, *Understanding Terror Networks* (Philadelphia: University of Pennsylvania Press, 2004), 160–163.

34 For example, "Today, with our help, the people of Iraq are working to create a free, functioning and prosperous society. The terrorists know that if these efforts are successful, their ideology of hate will suffer a grave defeat," George W. Bush, "President's Radio Address," September 13, 2003, http:// www.whitehouse.gov/news/releases/2003/09/20030913.html. "My record is one of reforming education, of lowering taxes, of providing prescription drug coverage for our seniors, for improving homeland security, and for waging an aggressive war against the ideologues of hate," George W. Bush, "Remarks by the President at Sunrise, Florida, Victory 2004 Rally," October 16, 2004, http://www.whitehouse.gov/news/releases/2004/10/20041016-3.html. "We will find them, we will bring them to justice, and at the same time, we will spread an ideology of hope and compassion that will overwhelm their ideology of hate," George W. Bush, "President Offers Condolences to People of London, Will Not Yield to Terrorists," July 7, 2005, http:// www.whitehouse.gov/news/releases/2005/07/20050707-2.html.

35 For example, "And we're helping to build a free Iraq, because free nations do not threaten others or breed the ideologies of murder," George W. Bush, "Remarks by the President to the Philippine Congress," October 18, 2003, http:// www.whitehouse.gov/news/releases/2003/10/20031018-12.html. "Terrorists rejoice in the killing of the innocent, and have promised similar violence against Americans, against all free peoples, and against any Muslims who reject their ideology of murder," George W. Bush, "Embargoed Until Delivery: Radio Address of the President to the Nation," May 15, 2004, http:// www.whitehouse.gov/news/releases/2004/05/20040515.html. "Only the fire of liberty can purge the ideologies of murder by offering hope to those who yearn to live free," George W. Bush, "President's Radio Address," March 19, 2005, http://www.whitehouse.gov/news/releases/2005/03/20050319.html.

36 Reuel Marc Gerecht, "The Gospel According to Osama Bin Laden," *Atlantic Monthly*, January 2002, 47.

37 "The Coming War," PBS Online NewsHour, *PBS.org*, August 25, 1998, http://www.pbs.org/newshour/bb/military/july-dec98/war_8-25.html.

38 Anonymous, *Imperial Hubris: Why the West Is Losing the War on Terror* (Washington, DC: Brassey's, Inc., 2004), xiii.

39 "Bin Laden's Fatwa," PBS Online NewsHour, *PBS.org*, http://www.pbs.org/newshour/terrorism/international/fatwa_1996.html (accessed on April 15, 2005).

40 "Al Qaeda's Fatwa," PBS Online NewsHour, *PBS.org*, http://www.pbs.org/newshour/terrorism/international/fatwa_1998.html (accessed on April 15, 2005).

41 "Bin Laden: 'Your Security Is in Your Own Hands,'" *CNN.com*, October 29, 2004, http://www.cnn.com/2004/WORLD/meast/10/29/bin.laden.transcript/.

42 Gunaratna, *Inside Al Qaeda*, 45.

43 Bergen, *Holy War, Inc.*, 223.

44 Anonymous, *Imperial Hubris*, 9–10.

45 Quoted in Bergen, *Holy War, Inc.*, 98.

46 "Al Qaeda's Fatwa."

47 In his 1996 fatwa, bin Laden claimed, "The latest and greatest of these aggressions . . . is the occupation of the land of the two Holy Places—the foundation of the house of Islam, the place of the revelation, the source of the message, and the place of the noble Ka'ba, the Qublah of all Muslims—by the armies of the American Crusaders and their allies," "Bin Laden's Fatwa."

48 Quoted in Bergen, *Holy War, Inc.*, 98.

49 Quoted in Hamid Mir, "Osama Bin Laden Interview," *Dawn* (Pakistan), November 9, 2001.

50 Gunaratna, *Inside Al Qaeda*, 85.

51 According to Gunaratna, "defensive *jihad* is a compulsory duty" (*Inside Al Qaeda*, 85). According to Middle East historian Bernard Lewis, "Jihad is thus a religious obligation. In discussing the obligation of the holy war, the classical Muslim jurists distinguish between offensive and defensive warfare. . . . In a defensive war, it becomes an obligation of every able-bodied individual. It is this principle that Osama bin Laden invoked in his declaration of war against the United States." Bernard Lewis, *The Crisis of Islam: Holy War and Unholy Terror* (New York: Modern Library, 2003), 31.

52 Quoted in Gunaratna, *Inside Al Qaeda*, 87.

53 "Transcript of Bin Laden's October Interview," *CNN.com*, February 5, 2002, http://archives.cnn.com/2002/WORLD/asiapcf/south/02/05/binladen.transcript/.

54 Middle East Research Institute, "'Why We Fight America': Al-Qa'ida Spokesman Explains September 11 and Declares Intentions to Kill 4 Million Americans With Weapons of Mass Destruction," Special Dispatch Series No. 388, June 12, 2002. http://www.memri.org/bin/articles.cgi?Page=archives&Area=sd&ID=SP38802.

55 Jason Burke, *Al Qaeda: Casting a Shadow of Terror* (London: I. B. Tauris, 2003), 34–35.

56 "Bin Laden Tape: Text," *BBCNews.com*, February 12, 2003, http://news.bbc.co.uk/1/hi/world/middle_east/2751019.stm.

57 "Transcript of Osama Bin Laden Tape Broadcast on Aljazeera," Associated Press, February 11, 2003.

58 *Al Qaeda Training Manual*, translated text, released by the U.S. Department of

Justice, December 6, 2001, 10, http://www.fas.org/irp/world/para/aqmanual.pdf.

59 Quoted in "Wrath of God," *Time Asia* 153:1 (January 11, 1999), http://www.time.com/time/asia/asia/magazine/1999/990111/osama1.html.

60 "Transcript of Osama Bin Laden Tape Broadcast on Aljazeera."

61 Gunaratna, *Inside Al Qaeda*, 90.

62 Middle East Media Research Institute, "A New Bin Laden Speech," Special Dispatch Series No. 539, July 18, 2003.

63 Lewis, *Crisis of Islam*, 79–80.

64 Sayyid Qutb, *Milestones* (Cedar Rapids, IA: Mother Mosque Foundation, 1981), 82.

65 Ibid., 83–84.

66 Ibid., 61.

67 Ibid., 76.

68 Also, an alleged al Qaeda plot to attack the U.S. embassy in Jordan was thwarted in April 2004. See "Jordan Says Major al Qaeda Plot Disrupted," *CNN.com*, April 26, 2004, http://www.cnn.com/2004/WORLD/meast/04/26/jordan.terror/.

69 Quoted in "Spain Blasts Are Retaliation: Bakri," *The Age* (Australia), March 13, 2004, http://www.theage.com.au/articles/2004/03/13/1078594593471.html.

70 Bergen, "Illusions of the War on Terrorism."

71 Burke, *Al Qaeda*, 17.

72 Fritjof Capra, *The Tao of Physics: An Exploration of the Parallels Between Modern Physics and Eastern Mysticism*, 4th ed. (Boston: Shambala, 2000), 114.

73 Thomas Cleary, trans., *The Essential Tao* (Edison, NJ: Castle Books, 1998), 54.

Chapter 6: Tao of Strategy

1 Lau Tzu, "Tao Te Ching," in Cleary, *Essential Tao*, 48.

2 IISS, *Military Balance 2004–2005*, 378.

3 *9/11 Commission Report*, 366–367.

4 Quoted in "Profile: Abu Zubayda," *BBCNews.com*, April 2, 2002, http://news.bbc.co.uk/1/hi/world/south_asia/1907462.stm.

5 Quoted in "Profile: Al Qaeda 'Kingpin,'" *BBCNews.com*, March 5, 2003, http://news.bbc.co.uk/2/hi/south_asia/2811855.stm.

6 At least one senior FBI official believes al-Libbi's "influence and position have been overstated," quoted in Lamb and Shezad, "Captured Al Qaeda Kingpin Is Case of 'Mistaken Identity.'"

7 Quoted in "Pakistani Sources: Al-Zawahiri Surrounded," *CNN.com*, March 18, 2004, http://www.cnn.com/2004/WORLD/asiapcf/03/18/pakistan.alqaeda/.

8 In a similar episode, in September 2004 Israeli Radio reported that al-Zawahiri had been arrested in Pakistan. Pakistani officials claimed the report to be incorrect, but some intelligence sources said they would not be surprised if the reports of al-Zawahiri's arrest turned out to be true. See "Pakistan Denies Catching Zawahiri," United Press International, September 27, 2004.

9 Associated Press, "Pakistani Troops Ambushed in Terror Sweep," *FoxNews.com*, March 23, 2004, http://www.foxnews.com/story/0,2933,114916,00.html.

10 Michael Hirsh, "A Troubled Hunt," Newsweek World News, *MSNBC.com*,

May 22, 2005, http://msnbc.msn.com/id/7937013/site/newsweek/.

11 "Pakistan 'Ends Al Qaeda Search,'" *BBCNews.com*, April 22, 2004, http://news.bbc.co.uk/2/hi/south_asia/3649421.stm.

12 "Pakistan Pulls Troops From Afghan Border Area," *CNN.com*, November 27, 2004, http://www.cnn.com/2004/WORLD/asiapcf/11/27/pakistan.al.qaeda/.

13 "Text of Report by Pakistan's PTV World Television on 1 December," BBC Worldwide Monitoring, December 1, 2004.

14 Quoted in "U.S. Military Claim Angers Pakistan," *BBCNews.com*, April 20, 2005, http://news.bbc.co.uk/2/hi/south_asia/4464559.stm.

15 Quoted in Amir Mir, "War and Peace in Waziristan," *AsiaTimes.com*, May 4, 2005, http://www.atimes.com/atimes/South_Asia/GE04Df03.html.

16 "Bin Laden's Fatwa."

17 Craig Whitlock, "Al Qaeda Shifts Its Strategy in Saudi Arabia," *Washington Post*, December 19, 2004, A28.

18 Quoted in Whitlock, "Al Qaeda Shifts Its Strategy in Saudi Arabia."

19 Brian Murphy, "Muslim Brotherhood Feels Homeland Pressure," Associated Press, May 14, 2005.

20 Murphy, "Muslim Brotherhood Feels Homeland Pressure."

21 According to Albert del Rosario, Philippine Ambassador to the United States: "Although the numbers of the group [Abu Sayyaf] have been reduced from an estimated 1,200 to what is now purportedly at less than 100, we're talking about the core group now," quoted in "Widening the War," PBS Online NewsHour, *PBS.org*, January 16, 2002, http://www.pbs.org/newshour/bb/asia/jan-june02/rosario_1-16.html. According to the State Department, the Abu Sayyaf are estimated to have two hundred to five hundred members, Department of State, *Patterns of Global Terrorism 2003* (Washington, DC: Department of State, 2004), 115.

22 Even Philippine president Gloria Macapagal Arroyo admits that evidence of al Qaeda in the Philippines is only up until 1995, Lally Weymouth, "We Will Do the Fighting," *Washington Post*, February 3, 2002, B1.

23 Maria A. Ressa, *Seeds of Terror: An Eyewitness Account of Al-Qaeda's Newest Center of Operations in Southeast Asia* (New York: Free Press, 2003), 104.

24 Ressa, *Seeds of Terror*, 124.

25 Quoted in Simon Elegant, "Still Going Strong," *Time Asia*, December 15, 2003, http://www.time.com/time/asia/magazine/article/0,13673,501031222-561532,00.html.

26 Quoted in Orlando de Guzman, "The Philippines' MILF Rebels," *BBCNews.com*, May 6, 2003, http://news.bbc.co.uk/2/hi/asia-pacific/3003809.stm.

27 Jim Gomez, "Philippines: Keep Group off Terror List," Associated Press, March 30, 2005, http://www.sanluisobispo.com/mld/sanluisobispo/news/world/11267996.htm.

28 CIA, *World Factbook*, "Indonesia," http://www.cia.gov/cia/publications/factbook/geos/id.html (accessed on May 17, 2005).

29 Tim Palmer, "Abu Bakar Bashir Jailed," transcript of *PM*, ABC (Australia), March 5, 2005, http://www.abc.net.au/pm/content/2005/s1315511.htm.

30 J. T. Caruso, "Al Qaeda International," testimony before the Subcommittee on International Operations and Terrorism, Senate Committee on Foreign Rela-

tions, 107th Cong., 1st sess. (December 18, 2001), http://www.fbi.gov/congress/congress01/caruso121801.htm.

31 James Phillips, "Somalia and Al Qaeda: Implications for the War on Terrorism," Heritage Foundation Backgrounder #1526, April 5, 2002, http://www.heritage.org/Research/HomelandDefense/BG1526.cfm.

32 Gunaratna, *Inside Al Qaeda*, 60.

33 Data from "Muslim Population Worldwide," http://www.islamic population.com/europe_general.html (accessed on May 31, 2005).

34 "Schroeder: We Won't Strike Iraq," *CNN.com*, August 9, 2002, http://www.cnn.com/2002/WORLD/europe/08/09/iraq.britain/.

35 "Against America? Moi?" *The Economist*, March 15, 2003, http://www.economist.com/world/europe/displayStory.cfm?Story_ID=1633583.

36 "Rumsfeld: France, Germany Are 'Problems' in Iraqi Conflict," *CNN.com*, January 23, 2003, http://www.cnn.com/2003/WORLD/meast/01/22/sprj.irq.wrap/.

37 R. C. Longworth, "When Rumsfeld Speaks, Europe Bristles," *Chicago Tribune*, February 16, 2003, 17.

38 Robert Nolan, "'Wild Cowboys' and the 'Axis of Weasel': Western Alliance on the Rocks," Foreign Policy Association, February 13, 2003, http://www.fpa.org/newsletter_info_sub_list.htm?section=%93Wild%20Cowboys%94%20and%20the%20%93Axis%20of%20Weasel%94%3A%20%20Western%20Alliance%20on%20the%20Rocks.

39 Multiple sources have reported this telephone conversation, including: "War on Iraq Could Start March 13: British Report," Agence France Presse, March 2, 2003; Andrew Neil, "Bush Tells Chirac: 'We Will Not Forget or Forgive," *The Business* (UK), March 2, 2003, 1; Fraser Nelson, "How Schroeder Could Find His Saviour in Blair," *The Scotsman*, March 13, 2002, 14; Brian Brady, "Split Deepens as Blair Faces Dreaded Choice," *Scotland on Sunday*, March 2, 2003, 16.

40 "House Restaurants Change Name of 'French Fries' and 'French Toast,'" *CNN.com*, March 11, 2003, http://www.cnn.com/2003/ALLPOLITICS/03/11/freedom.fries/index.html.

41 Ted Galen Carpenter, "Time to Disagree Without Being Disagreeable," *Financial Times*, March 10, 2003.

42 Kenneth R. Timmerman, "France Uncovers Al Qaeda Bombers," *Insight*, January 8, 2003, http://www.insightmag.com/main.cfm?include=detail&storyid=342932.

43 "France Arrests Al Qaeda Suspects," BBC News (UK Edition), June 6, 2003 http://news.bbc.co.uk/1/hi/world/europe/2967202.stm.

44 Zachary K. Johnson, "Chronology: The Plots," *PBS.org*, January 25, 2005, http://www.pbs.org/wgbh/pages/frontline/shows/front/special/cron.html.

45 Department of State, "Appendix H: Statistical Review," in *Patterns of Global Terrorism 2002*.

46 "Muslim Population Worldwide."

47 "Muslim Population Worldwide."

48 Donald H. Rumsfeld, "World Affairs Council of Philadelphia," May 25, 2005, http://www.defenselink.mil/speeches/2005/sp20050525-secdef1461.html.

49 Rumsfeld, "World Affairs Council of Philadelphia."

50 Clausewitz, *On War*, 595–596.

51 Anonymous, *Imperial Hubris*, 263.
52 "Bin Laden's Warning: Full Text," *BBCNews.com*, October 7, 2001, http://news.bbc.co.uk/2/hi/south_asia/1585636.stm.
53 Clyde R. Mark, "Israel: U.S. Foreign Assistance," Congressional Research Service Issue Brief for Congress, July 10, 2003, 1.
54 Ibid., 11–12.
55 Glenn Kessler, "U.S. Plans to Provide Direct Aid to Palestinians," *Washington Post*, July 9, 2003, A1.
56 According to Mark: "There were reports in February 2001 and again in the summer of 2002 that the U.S. Government was investigating if Israel misused U.S. Military equipment, including Apache helicopters, in assassinating Palestinian leaders, and later reports that Members of Congress inquired if Israel misused Apache and Cobra helicopters and F-16 fighter-bombers in attacking Palestinian facilities," Mark, "Israel: U.S. Foreign Assistance," 7. See also Molly Moore, "Israelis Kill Four Hamas Militants," *Washington Post*, August 25, 2003, A1, which makes explicit the use of AH-64 Apache helicopters and that they are U.S.-built.
57 "The Millennium Challenge Account," http://www.whitehouse.gov/infocus/developingnations/millennium.html (accessed on May 31, 2005).
58 Tzu, "Tao Te Ching," 48.
59 According to Secretary of Defense Rumsfeld: "Iraq was a threat in the region, and because that threat will be gone, we also will be able to rearrange our forces," Associated Press, "U.S. Moves Air Center From Saudi Arabia," *ABCNews.com*, April 29, 2003, http://abcnews.go.com/wire/World/ap20030429_598.html.
60 Ibid.
61 Department of Energy, "Saudi Arabia," Country Analysis Brief, June 2003, http://www.eia.doe.gov/cabs/saudi.html.
62 Data from Department of Energy, "Top Suppliers of Crude Oil and Petroleum, 2004," http://www.eia.doe.gov/neic/rankings/totimportsby_country.htm (accessed on December 2, 2005).
63 M. A. Adelman, *The Economics of Petroleum Supply* (Cambridge: MIT Press, 1993), 545. For more analysis about the economics of oil, see also M. A. Adelman, *The Genie out of the Bottle* (Cambridge: MIT Press, 1996).
64 Adelman, *Economics of Petroleum Supply*, 545.
65 Ibid., 492.
66 Doug Bandow, "Befriending Saudi Princes: A High Price for a Dubious Alliance," Cato Institute Policy Analysis No. 428, March 20, 2002, 3.
67 Bush, *National Security Strategy*, 3.
68 Bandow, "Befriending Saudi Princes," 9.
69 Senate Select Committee on Intelligence and House Permanent Select Committee on Intelligence, *Joint Inquiry Into Intelligence Community Activities Before and After the Terrorist Attacks of September 11, 2001*, S. Rep. 107-351, H. Rep. 107-792, 107th Cong., 2nd sess. (December 2002), 173.
70 Ibid., 173.
71 Ibid., 174.
72 Ibid., 174.
73 James Risen and David Johnston, "Report on 9/11 Suggests a Role by Saudi

Spies," *New York Times*, August 2, 2003, A1. See also "Classified Section of 9/11 Report Draws Connections Between High-Level Saudi Princes and Associates of the Hijackers," *Newsweek* news release, July 27, 2003, http://www.prnewswire.com/cgi-bin/micro_stories.pl?ACCT=138744&TICK=NEWS&STORY=/www/story/07-27-2003/0001989701&EDATE=Jul+27,+2003; and Michael Isikoff and Daniel Klaidman, "Failure to Communicate," *Newsweek*, August 4, 2003, 34–36.

74 Mike Allen, "Bush Won't Release Classified 9/11 Report," *Washington Post*, July 30, 2003, A1.

75 "Graham Calls on Bush to Permit Declassifying More of 9/11 Report," *CNN.com*, July 28, 2003, http://www.cnn.com/2003/ALLPOLITICS/07/28/graham.bush/index.html.

76 "Shelby: More of 9/11 Report Should Be Public," *CNN.com*, July 24, 2003, http://www.cnn.com/2003/ALLPOLITICS/07/24/cnna.shelby/index.html.

77 Ibid.

78 Matthew Clark, "Diplomatic Hand-Holding," *Christian Science Monitor*, April 26, 2005, http://www.csmonitor.com/2005/0426/dailyUpdate.html.

79 U.S. Agency for International Development, "About USAID/Egypt: Overview," http://www.usaid-eg.org/detail.asp?id=5 (accessed on December 2, 2005).

80 Department of State, *Country Reports on Human Rights Practices 2002*, March 31, 2003, http://www.state.gov/g/drl/rls/hrrpt/2002/18274.htm.

81 Ibid.

82 Michael Stackman, "Egypt Sees U.S. Going Cairo's Way," *Los Angeles Times*, July 10, 2002, A4.

83 Quoted in ibid.

84 Bush, *National Security Strategy*, 1–2.

85 Ruth M. Beitler and Cindy R. Jebb, "Egypt as a Failing State: Implications for US National Security," Institute for National Security Studies Occasional Paper 51, U.S. Air Force Academy, July 2003, 36.

86 Jackson Diehl, "Don't Rock the Boat Diplomacy," *Washington Post*, June 24, 2002, A19.

87 Beitler and Jebb, "Egypt as a Failing State," 39.

88 Paul Anderson, "Pakistan Takes Step to Civilian Rule," *BBCNews.com*, February 24, 2003, http://www.bbcnews.co.uk/2/hi/south_asia/2792837.stm.

89 Zaffar Abbas, "Analysis: Musharraf Sidelines Parliament," *BBCNews.com*, August 21, 2002, http://www.bbcnews.co.uk/2/hi/south_asia/2207859.stm.

90 Department of State, "Appendix B: Background Information on Designated Foreign Terrorist Organizations," *Patterns of Global Terrorism 2002*.

91 "Intelligence Inputs Indicate Al Qaeda-ISI Nexus," *IndiaExpress.com*, December 3, 2002, http://www.indiaexpress.net/news/national/20021203-1.html. "ISI Escort for Al Qaeda Men," *The Tribune* (Chandigarh, India), news clipping on the Ministry of External Affairs India website, http://meadev.nic.in/news/clippings/20020708/trib1.htm (accessed on August 26, 2003).

92 Subodh Atal, "Extremist, Nuclear Pakistan: An Emerging Threat?" Cato Institute Policy Analysis No. 472, March 5, 2003, 10.

93 Department of State, *Country Reports on Human Rights Practices 2002*, March 31, 2003, http://www.state.gov/g/drl/rls/hrrpt/2002/18400.htm.

94 Andrea Koppell and Elise Labott, "U.S.-Uzbek Ties Grow Despite Rights Concerns," *CNN.com*, March 12, 2002, http://www.cnn.com/2002/US/03/12/ret.uzbek.us/index.html.
95 Quoted in "Uzbek Officials Put Toll at 169," *BBCNews.com*, May 17, 2005, http://news.bbc.co.uk/1/hi/world/asia-pacific/4555621.stm.
96 Rumsfeld, "World Affairs Council of Philadelphia."

Chapter 7: The Last Line of Defense

1 Center for Strategic and International Studies, *Transnational Threats Update* 1:10 (July 2003), 2.
2 CSIS, *Transnational Threats Update* 2:4 (January 2004), 1. According to James Bevan at the Small Arms Survey (an independent research project at the Graduate Institute of International Studies in Geneva, Switzerland), seventy-three countries have first-generation MANPADS and ninety-three countries have second-generation MANPADS, James Bevan, "Man-portable Air Defence Systems" (presentation to the Geneva Process on Small Arms, Geneva, September 8, 2004).
3 James Chow, James Chiesa, Paul Dreyer, Mel Eisman, Theodore W. Karasik, Joel Kvitky, Sherrill Lingerl, David Ochmanek, and Chad Shirley, "Protecting Commercial Aviation Against the Shoulder-Fired Missile Threat," RAND Corporation Occasional Paper, 2005, 4.
4 Douglas Jehl and David E. Sanger, "U.S. Expands List of Lost Missiles," *New York Times*, November 6, 2004, A1.
5 Loren B. Thompson, "MANPADS: Scale and Nature of the Threat," November 12, 2003, http://www.lexingtoninstitute.org/defense/pdf/111203MANPADS.pdf.
6 Thomas B. Hunter, "The Proliferation of MANPADS," *Jane's Intelligence Review*, November 28, 2002, http://www.janes.com/security/international_security/news/jir021128_1_n.shtml. According to the RAND study, "Al Qaeda and many other groups hostile to the United States have MANPADS and the ability to use them. . . . Al Qaeda in particular has at least first-generation MANPADS, has the ability to move them around internationally, and has decided to employ MANPADS attacks as part of its terror campaign," Chow et al., "Protecting Commercial Aviation," 4. In May 2002 the FBI issued a warning that "given al Qaeda's demonstrated objective to target the U.S. airline industry, its access to U.S. and Russian-made MANPAD systems, and recent apparent targeting of U.S.-led military forces in Saudi Arabia, law enforcement agencies in the United States should remain alert to potential use of MANPADs against U.S. aircraft," "FBI Warns of Shoulder-Fired Missiles Threat," *CNN.com*, May 31, 2002, http://archives.cnn.com/2002/US/05/30/missile.threat/.
7 Pablo Wangerman, "Economic Impact of 9/11 on the Airline Industry" (presentation to the Joint University Program for Air Transportation Research, Princeton, NJ, January 11, 2002), http://acy.tc.faa.gov/jup/jupq_011002/special_guest/wangerman/presentation.pdf.
8 Peter Navarro and Aron Spencer, "September 11, 2001: Assessing the Costs of Terrorism," *The Milken Institute Review*, Fourth Quarter 2001, 21.
9 Mark J. Warshawsky, testimony before the House Financial Services Subcom-

mittee on Oversight and Investigation, 107th Cong., 2nd sess. (February 27, 2002), 1.

10 Bureau of Labor Statistics, "Extended Mass Layoffs in 2002," U.S. Department of Labor, August 2003, 2.

11 Joint Economic Committee, U.S. Congress, "The Economic Costs of Terrorism," May 2002, 11, http://www.house.gov/jec/terrorism/costs.pdf.

12 Chow et al., "Protecting Commercial Aviation," 9.

13 Ibid., 14.

14 "City of Los Angeles," *LosAngelesAlmanac.com*, http://www.losangele salmanac.com/LA/index.htm; and "City of Los Angeles Housing Demographics," *LosAngelesAlmanac.com*, http://www.losangelesalmanac.com/LA/la50.htm.

15 Chow et al., "Protecting Commercial Aviation," 14.

16 Ibid., 5.

17 More than three thousand direct infrared countermeasure (DIRCM) systems are deployed worldwide. The Northrop Grumman Nemesis DIRCM system has been installed on more than three hundred military aircraft, including U.S. Air Force C-17s and C-130s.

18 Chow et al., "Protecting Commercial Aviation," 23–28.

19 Office of Management and Budget, "FY06 Budget Priorities," Table S-1: Budget Totals, http://www.whitehouse.gov/omb/budget/fy2006/tables.html (accessed on December 2, 2005).

20 Citizens Against Government Waste, *2004 Pig Book*, 1, http://www.cagw.org/site/PageServer?pagename=reports_pigbook2004 (accessed on March 2, 2005).

21 Ibid., 12, 37.

22 Citizens Against Government Waste, *Prime Cuts 2004* (database), http://www.cagw.org/site/PageServer?pagename=reports_primecuts and http://www.cagw.org/site/FrameSet?style=User&url=http://publications.cagw.org/publications/prime/primecuts.php3 (accessed on March 2, 2005).

23 BENS Tail-to-Tooth Commission, *The Revolution in Military Business Affairs* (briefing book, October 1997), 2.

24 Tom Ridge, "Prepared Remarks by Secretary Tom Ridge at the US-VISIT Announcement at the Atlanta Hartsfield-Jackson Airport," January 5, 2004, http://www.gahomelandsecurity.com/news/USDHS/010504b.htm.

25 *Michelle D. Green; John F. Shaw; David C. Fathi; Sarosh Syed; Mohamed Ibrahim; David Nelson; Alexandra Hay, on behalf of themselves and all other similarly situated, Plaintiffs, v. Transportation Security Administration; David M. Stone; Department of Homeland Security; Tom Ridge, Defendants*, U.S. District Court for the Western District of Washington at Seattle, April 6, 2004, http://news.findlaw.com/cnn/docs/aclu/greenvtsa40604cmp.pdf.

26 Sara Kehaulani Goo, "Sen. Kennedy Flagged by No-Fly List," *Washington Post*, August 20, 2004, A1; "Ted Kennedy's Airport Adventure," *CBSNews.com*, August 19, 2004, http://www.cbsnews.com/stories/2004/04/06/terror/main610466.shtml.

27 Associated Press, "'No-Fly List' Keeps Infants off Planes," *CNN.com*, August 16, 2005, http://www.cnn.com/2005/TRAVEL/08/15/no.fly.babies.apindex.html.

28 "Air France Flight to U.S. Diverted Over Suspect Passenger," Agence France Presse, May 12, 2005.

29 "Alitalia Flight Diverted, Passenger Removed," Reuters, May 17, 2005.
30 Sally B. Donnelly, "You Say Yusuf, I say Youssouf . . . ," *Time.com*, September 25, 2004, http://www.time.com/time/nation/article/0,8599,702062,00.html. The name "Yusuf Islam" is not actually on the no-fly list, but "Youssouf Islam" is.
31 Stephen E. Flynn, "The Neglected Home Front," *Foreign Affairs* 83:5 (September/October 2002): 22–23.
32 "Jordan Says Major Al Qaeda Plot Disrupted," *CNN.com*, April 26, 2004, http://www.cnn.com/2004/WORLD/meast/04/26/jordan.terror/; "Jordan 'Was Chemical Bomb Target,'" *BBCNews.com*, April 17, 2004, http://news.bbc.co.uk/2/hi/middle_east/3635381.stm.
33 Bureau of Transportation Statistics, "U.S.-Canada Trade by All Surface Modes and Top Ten Commodities, 2002," Department of Transportation, http://products.bts.gov/transborder/reports/annual02/us_can_val_wt_2002_ten.html (accessed on June 3, 2005).
34 U.S. Army Corps of Engineers, "National Inventory of Dams," http://crunch.tec.army.mil/nid/webpages/nid.cfm (accessed on June 3, 2005).
35 "Man Allegedly in Al Qaeda Plot to Bomb Ohio Shopping Mall," *MSNBC.com*, June 15, 2004, http://www.msnbc.msn.com/id/5209103/; "Psych Exam for Accused Terrorist," *CBSNews.com*, June 16, 2004, http://www.cbsnews.com/stories/2004/06/14/terror/main622950.shtml.
36 Maria Kalkias, "Threatening Shoppers, Profits," *Dallas Morning News*, June 27, 2004, D1.
37 Ibid.; and Anita Chang, "Malls Nationwide Setting Curfews for Teens," Associated Press, September 17, 2004.
38 For a comprehensive list of terror alerts in 2002, see "The Year of Fear," *CTV.ca*, December 30, 2002, http://www.ctv.ca/servlet/ArticleNews/story/CTVNews/1041294767854_221/?hub=TopStories.
39 "Cheney: Future Attack on U.S. 'Almost Certain,'" *CNN.com*, May 20, 2002, http://archives.cnn.com/2002/ALLPOLITICS/05/20/cheney.terrorism/; "Officials: Terrorists May Target Tall Apt. Bldgs.," *CNN.com*, May 20, 2002, http://archives.cnn.com/2002/US/05/20/gen.war.on.terror/; Kwame Holman, "Background: Terror Warnings," *PBS.org*, May 21, 2002, http://www.pbs.org/newshour/bb/terrorism/jan-june02/bkgdwarnings_5-21.html; Donald H. Rumsfeld, "Transcript of Testimony by Secretary of Defense Donald H. Rumsfeld at Defense Subcommittee of Senate Appropriations Committee," 107th Cong., 2nd sess. (May 21, 2002), http://www.defenselink.mil/speeches/2002/s20020521-secdef.html
40 "Coast Guard Warns of Waterfront Threat," *CNN.com*, June 11, 2002, http://archives.cnn.com/2002/US/06/09/coastguard.terror/
41 "Securing Small Airports, Flight Schools," *CBSNews.com*, July 5, 2002, http://www.cbsnews.com/stories/2002/07/05/national/main514356.shtml.
42 Bill Gertz, "Al Qaeda Remains a Silent Menace in U.S., Senators Say," *Washington Times*, July 12, 2002, A10.
43 Associated Press, "FBI Tracking Terrorists on U.S. Soil," *CBSNews.com*, July 12, 2002, http://www.cbsnews.com/stories/2002/07/09/attack/main514572.shtml.
44 "Al Qaeda May Be Planning Attacks," *CNN.com*, July 2, 2002, http://archives.cnn.com/2002/US/07/01/july4.threat/.

45 "Osama 'Alive and Well,'" Reuters, July 10, 2002.

46 Quoted in "U.S. at 'High Alert' on Eve of 9/11," *CNN.com*, September 11, 2002, http://archives.cnn.com/2002/US/09/10/ar911.threat.level.wrap/.

47 Quoted in "Director Ridge, Attorney General Ashcroft Discuss Threat Level," September 10, 2002, http://www.whitehouse.gov/news/releases/2002/09/20020910-5.html.

48 Quoted in "Bush Scales Back Threat Alert," *CNN.com*, September 24, 2002, http://archives.cnn.com/2002/US/09/24/threat.level/.

49 George W. Bush, "Homeland Security Presidential Directive–3," March 2002, http://www.whitehouse.gov/news/releases/2002/03/20020312-5.html.

50 Quoted in "FBI Warns of Possible Terrorist Attack on Transport Systems," Associated Press, October 24, 2002.

51 John Mintz and Sari Horwitz, "'Orange' Alert Is Dropped in D.C. and N.Y.," *Washington Post*, November 11, 2004, A1.

52 Quoted in Mimi Hall, "Ridge Reveals Clashes on Alerts," *USA Today*, May 11, 2005, A1.

53 Quoted in Jeanne Meserve, "Terror Alert Level Raised to 'Orange,'" *CNN.com*, March 17, 2003, http://www.cnn.com/2003/US/03/17/terror.alert/.

54 Independence Hall Association, "The Quotable Franklin," http://www.ushistory.org/franklin/quotable/quote04.htm (accessed on September 12, 2005).

55 *USA PATRIOT Act*, HR 3162, 107th Cong., 1st sess. (October 24, 2001), 33–34.

56 For a more detailed analysis of delayed notification of warrants see American Civil Liberties Union, "How the Anti-Terrorism Bill Expands Law Enforcement 'Sneak and Peak' Warrants," October 23, 2001, http://www.aclu.org/NationalSecurity/NationalSecurity.cfm?ID=9151&c=111.

57 *USA PATRIOT Act*, 37–39. For a more detailed analysis of Section 215 of the PATRIOT Act see ACLU, "Section 215 FAQ," October 24, 2002, http://www.aclu.org/Privacy/Privacy.cfm?ID=11054&c=130; and ACLU, "Surveillance Under the USA PATRIOT Act," http://www.aclu.org/SafeandFree/SafeandFree.cfm?ID=12263&c=206 (accessed on June 7, 2005).

58 *USA PATRIOT Act*, 246–250.

59 Quoted in Toni Locy, "Court Strikes Down Patriot Act Provision," *USA Today*, September 30, 2004, A3.

60 Quoted in ACLU, "In ACLU Case, Federal Court Strikes Down Patriot Act Surveillance Power as Unconsitutional," September 29, 2004, http://www.aclu.org/SafeandFree/SafeandFree.cfm?ID=16603&c=282.

61 Quoted in "A Mixed Verdict on the Terror War," *CNN.com*, July 6, 2004, http://www.cnn.com/2004/LAW/06/28/scotus.terror.cases/.

62 Quoted in Robert Block, "In Terrorism Fight, Government Finds Surprising Ally: FedEx," *Wall Street Journal*, May 26, 2005, A1.

63 ACLU, "ACLU Hails Victories in New Homeland Security Bill," November 13, 2002, http://www.aclu.org/SafeandFree/SafeandFree.cfm?ID=11295&c=206.

64 Quoted in Associated Press, "Pentagon Promises Safeguards on Surveillance System," *USAToday.com*, May 20, 2003, http://www.usatoday.com/tech/news/2003-05-20-tia-report_x.htm.

65 The statistical model to calculate these results was developed by Robert E.

Gladd, MA, CQP, adjunct faculty at the University of Las Vegas Nevada, and is based on Bayes Theorem for calculating conditional probabilities. See Appendix 2.

66 Robert S. Mueller, "Testimony of Robert S. Mueller, III, Director Federal Bureau of Investigation, Before the Senate Committee on Intelligence of the United States Senate," 109th Cong., 1st sess. (February 16, 2005).

67 Quoted in CBS/AP, "Man Charged in Plot to Kill Bush," *CBSNews.com*, February 22, 2005, http://www.cbsnews.com/stories/2005/02/23/terror/main675934.shtml.

68 Quoted in "U.S. Court Dismisses Landmark Terror Convictions," Reuters, September 3, 2004.

69 Quoted in "Judge Throws Out Terror Convictions," Associated Press, September 1, 2004.

70 Transactional Records Clearinghouse, "Criminal Terrorism Enforcement Since the 9/11/01 Attacks," December 8, 2003, http://trac.syr.edu/tracreports/terrorism/report031208.html. The *Washington Post* has reported that even fewer people have been convicted. Based on 361 cases defined as terrorism investigations by the Department of Justice from September 11, 2001, through late September 2004, "Of the 142 individuals on the list linked to terrorist groups, 39 were convicted of crimes related to terrorism or national security," Dan Eggen and Julie Tate, "U.S. Campaign Produces Few Convictions on Terrorism Charges," *Washington Post*, June 12, 2005, A1.

71 Quoted in "1984: Memories of the Brighton Bomb," *BBCNews.com*, http://news.bbc.co.uk/onthisday/hi/witness/october/12/newsid_3665000/3665388.stm (accessed on September 12, 2005).

Afterword

1 Bush, "State of the Union," February 2, 2005.

2 Dana Priest and Spencer Hsu, "U.S. Sees Drop in Terrorist Threats," *Washington Post*, May 1, 2005, A1.

3 Jonathan S. Landay, "Bush Administration Eliminating 19-Year-Old International Terrorism Report," Knight Ridder, April 15, 2005.

4 "Police Follow Camera Lead in NYC Blasts," *CNN.com*, May 5, 2005, http://www.cnn.com/2005/US/05/05/uk.consulate/.

5 George W. Bush, "President's Remarks to the General Conference of the National Guard Association of the United States," September 14, 2004, http://www.whitehouse.gov/news/releases/2004/09/20040914-23.html.

6 *9/11 Commission Report*, 376.

7 Quoted in Robin Wright, "U.S. Struggles to Win Hearts, Minds in the Muslim World," *Washington Post*, August 20, 2004, A1.

Suggested Reading

This is by no means an exhaustive list, and I am not in agreement with the views, analyses, or policy prescriptions of all the authors listed. In fact, I strongly disagree with some of them. Nonetheless, I consider all these books and articles worth reading because they help provide a broad perspective on the war on terrorism.

Anonymous. *Imperial Hubris: Why the West Is Losing the War on Terror*. Washington, DC: Brassey's, Inc., 2004.
>   The former head of the CIA's Bin Laden Unit, Michael Scheuer, makes the case that the greatest danger we face is continuing to wrongly believe that Muslims attack us for what we are and what we think rather than what we do, i.e., specific U.S. policies and their attendant military, political, and economic implications.

———. *Through Our Enemies' Eyes: Osama bin Laden, Radical Islam, and the Future of America*. Washington, DC: Brassey's, Inc., 2002.
>   Scheuer's analysis of bin Laden and al Qaeda that describes the motives of radical Muslims for declaring war against America and the West. He argues that militants throughout the Islamic world are enraged by what they believe is Western aggression against their people, religion, and culture and that even if bin Laden is brought to justice, the dangers posed by radical Islamic militants will not disappear.

Baer, Robert. *Sleeping With the Devil: How Washington Sold Our Soul for Saudi Crude*. New York: Crown Publishers, 2003.
>   Former CIA officer argues that U.S. addiction to cheap oil and Saudi petrodollars has resulted in a hypocritical and corrupt relationship between the United States and Saudi Arabia, where the ruling family funnels millions of dollars to militant Islamic groups—including al Qaeda—to dissuade them from overthrowing the monarchy.

Benjamin, Daniel, and Steven Simon. *The Age of Sacred Terror*. New York: Random House, 2002.
>   Two former members of the National Security Council during the

Clinton administration offer an inside view of U.S. policy and policy processes in response to the al Qaeda threat.

Bergen, Peter. *Holy War, Inc.: Inside the Secret World of Osama bin Laden*. New York: Free Press, 2001.
Considered by many to be the "definitive" book on bin Laden and al Qaeda by a CNN terrorism analyst and one of the few Western journalists to have interviewed bin Laden, and rushed into publication after 9/11. A description of bin Laden's background; a summary of how the al Qaeda terrorist network developed in the Middle East, Europe, and America; and a narrative of terrorist events through 9/11. Bergen catalogs the motives for bin Laden's hostility to America: his religious opposition to an American military presence in Saudi Arabia, American policy toward Israel, and the "un-Islamic" behavior of Egypt and Saudi Arabia.

Bovard, James. *Terrorism and Tyranny: Trampling Freedom, Justice, and Peace to Rid the World of Evil*. New York: Palgrave MacMillan, 2003.
A scathing analysis and indictment of how government power has been expanded in the name of fighting terrorism but at the expense of civil liberties, personal freedom, and judicial process.

Burke, Jason. *Al-Qaeda: Casting a Shadow of Terror*. London: I. B. Tauris, 2003.
Chief reporter for the London Observer argues that "al Qaeda" is a convenient label applied misleadingly to a broad and diverse global movement with roots in the politics, societies, and history of the Islamic world, and that eradicating any single terrorist or terrorist group will not end the threat.

Carpenter, Ted Galen. *Peace and Freedom: Foreign Policy for a Constitutional Republic*. Washington, DC: Cato Institute, 2002.
A blueprint for a new U.S. foreign policy based on "strategic independence" that emphasizes a vigorous defense of America's vital interests and rigorous adherence to America's fundamental values by cutting back obsolete U.S. security commitments and eschewing promiscuous military interventions.

Carr, Caleb. *The Lessons of Terror: A History of Warfare Against Civilians*. New York: Random House, 2002.
A historical examination of terrorism that concludes: the practice of targeting enemy civilians is as old as war itself, it has always failed as a military and political tactic, and despite the dramatic increase in the lethality of weapons that can be used by terrorists, it will continue to fail in the future.

Coolsaet, Rik. *Al-Qaeda the Myth: The Root Causes of International Terrorism and How to Tackle Them*. Translated by Erika Peeters. Gent, Belgium: Academia Press, 2005.

Argues that international terrorism is not born out of religion or pov-
erty but bred by marginalization within society and that such exclusion constitutes the breeding ground for extremist splinter groups
searching for a way to justify their acts of terror.

Doran, Michael Scott. "Somebody Else's Civil War." *Foreign Affairs* 81:1 (Janu-
ary/February 2002): 22–42.
Argues that Osama bin Laden's attacks on the United States were aimed
at another audience: the entire Muslim world. Also asserts that war with
America was never his end; it was just a means to promote radical Islam.

Eland, Ivan. "Does U.S. Intervention Overseas Breed Terrorism? The Historical Record." Cato Institute Foreign Policy Briefing No. 50, December 17, 1998.
An empirical analysis that examines the historical record and catalogs
more than sixty terrorist attacks against U.S. targets that can be attributed to American foreign policy.

———. *Putting "Defense" Back Into U.S. Defense Policy: Rethinking U.S. Security in the Post-Cold War World*. Westport, CT: Praeger, 2001.
Questions the core assumptions of American foreign policy and details the military force structure more appropriate for a restrained
military policy in the post–Cold War era.

Frum, David, and Richard Perle. *An End to Evil: How to Win the War on Terror*.
New York: Random House, 2003.
A former Bush speechwriter and a former assistant secretary of defense in
the Reagan administration characterize the threat to America as evil itself and sug-
gest that the war on terrorism should be expanded to include Iran, Syria, and North
Korea, and even China and France.

Gerecht, Reuel Marc. *The Islamic Paradox: Shiite Clerics, Sunni Fundamentalists, and the Coming of Arab Democracy*. Washington, DC: AEI Press, 2004.
A former Middle Eastern specialist at the CIA argues that moderate
Muslims are not the likely solution to bin Ladenism. Rather, those
who have hated the United States the most—Shiite clerics and Sunni
fundamentalists—will probably liberate the Muslim Middle East from
its age-old reflexive hostility to the West.

Gunaratna, Rohan. *Inside Al Qaeda: Global Network of Terror*. New York: Columbia University Press, 2002.
Based on five years of extensive research, including field research and
interviews with al Qaeda members. Considered one of the "definitive" works on al Qaeda, it examines the leadership, ideology, structure, strategies, and tactics of the organization.

Hoffman, Bruce. *Inside Terrorism*. New York: Columbia University Press, 1998.
A pre-9/11 summary of some of the major historical trends in interna-

tional terrorism that explains the differences between the motivations that drive political (or ethno-nationalist) terrorism and religious terrorism.

Kepel, Gilles. *The War for Muslim Minds: Islam and the West.* Cambridge, MA: Belknap Press, 2004.
   An examination of the war on terrorism that concludes that the most important battle in the war for Muslim minds will be in the Muslim immigrant communities in London, Paris, and other European cities, where Islam is already a growing part of the West. May offer Muslim immigrants a new vision and way out of the dead-end politics that has paralyzed their countries of origin.

Leone, Richard C., and Gret Anrig Jr., eds. *The War on Our Freedoms: Civil Liberties in an Age of Terrorism.* New York: Public Affairs, 2003.
   A collection of essays that warn about the dangers of limiting civil liberties in the name of national security and that address why such actions are ultimately destructive of American values and ideals.

Lewis, Bernard. *The Crisis of Islam: Holy War and Unholy Terror.* New York: Modern Library, 2003.
   One of the most recognized historians of the Middle East maps the history of Muslim anxiety toward the West from the time of the Crusades through European imperialism and explains how America's increased presence in the region since the Cold War has been construed as a renewed cry of imperialism. Making the argument that "they hate us for who we are," Lewis notes that the American way of life is a direct threat to Islamic values and that basic Western democracy especially threatens Islamic extremism.

Lynch, Timothy. "Breaking the Vicious Cycle: Preserving Our Liberties While Fighting Terrorism." Cato Institute Policy Analysis No. 443, June 26, 2002.
   An analysis of antiterrorism legislation that argues that Americans must accept the reality that the U.S. government is not capable of preventing every possible terrorist attack from occurring and that policymakers should focus their attention on combating terrorism within the framework of a free society—otherwise our society will eventually lose the key attribute that has made it great: freedom.

Manji, Irshad. *The Trouble With Islam: A Muslim's Call for Reform in Her Faith.* New York: St. Martin's Press, 2003.
   A blunt, provocative, and deeply personal critique of Islam by a Canadian journalist and television personality, who is a Muslim by birth and faith (born in Uganda and of Pakistani origin).

McInerney, Thomas, and Paul Vallely. *Endgame: The Blueprint for Victory in the War on Terror.* Washington, DC: Regnery, 2004.
   Two former generals and Fox News military analysts perpetuate the

state-sponsored terrorism paradigm and argue from an almost purely
military perspective for regime change in Iran, Syria, and North Korea.

National Commission on Terrorist Attacks Upon the United States. *The 9/11
Commission Report: Final Report of the National Commission on Terrorist Attacks Upon
the United States.* New York: W. W. Norton, 2004.
A comprehensive historical document that traces the roots of al Qaeda's
strategies along with the emergence of the nineteen hijackers and how
they entered the United States and boarded airplanes and that details
the missed opportunities of law enforcement officials to avert disaster.

Olsen, Edward. *U.S. National Defense for the Twenty-First Century: The Grand
Exit Strategy.* London: Frank Cass, 2002.
A critique of the United States as the world's policeman that calls for
"exit strategy" as the central organizing principle of a U.S. national
strategy designed to extract the United States from unnecessary, costly,
and sometimes dangerous security obligations rather than a means to
rectify marginal mistakes.

Pape, Robert A. *Dying to Win: The Strategic Logic of Suicide Terrorism.* New
York: Random House, 2005.
A comprehensive database and analysis of every suicide terrorist attack in the world from 1980 through 2003, which concludes that suicide terrorism is not primarily a product of Islamic fundamentalism
and that every suicide terrorist attack has had a clear goal: to compel
a modern democracy to withdraw military forces from the territory
that the terrorists view as their homeland.

Phares, Walid. *Future Jihad: Terrorist Strategies Against America.* New York:
Palgrave MacMillan, 2005.
Argues that jihad is not a peaceful phenomenon and that Islamic fundamentalists are not freedom fighters; rather they are deadly adversaries of Western civilization who must be defeated at all costs.

Preble, Christopher, et al. *Exiting Iraq: Why the U.S. Must End the Military Oc-
cupation and Renew the War Against Al Qaeda.* Washington, DC: Cato Institute, 2004.
A special task force report that argues that the presence of U.S. troops in
Iraq emboldens a new class of terrorists to take up arms against the United
States and that U.S. strategic interests demand a military withdrawal.

Qutb, Sayyid. *Milestones.* Cedar Rapids, IA: Mother Mosque Foundation, 1981.
Considered by many as the basis for modern political Islam and a major
influence on Islamic extremism. Provides a religious justification for
fighting against Muslim rulers and for considering Muslims who didn't
share the radical goals of the Islamists as not being true Muslims.

Record, Jeffrey. "Bounding the Global War on Terrorism." Strategic Studies

Institute monograph, U.S. Army War College, December 2003.
Argues that the war on terrorism lacks strategic clarity, embraces unrealistic objectives, and may not be sustainable over the long haul, and calls for down-sizing the scope of the war on terrorism to reflect concrete U.S. security interests and the limits of American military power.

Ressa, Maria. *Seeds of Terror: An Eyewitness Account of Al-Qaeda's Newest Center of Operations in Southeast Asia.* New York: Free Press, 2003.
CNN's Jakarta bureau chief argues that the Philippines, Indonesia, Thailand, and Malaysia were crucial nodes in the al Qaeda network long before 9/11 and that since Operation Enduring Freedom in Afghanistan new camps in Southeast Asia have become the key training grounds for the future.

Sageman, Marc. *Understanding Terror Networks.* Philadelphia: University of Pennsylvania Press, 2004.
Combines network theory, modeling, and forensic psychology to understand the social bonds that inspire alienated young Muslims to join the Islamic jihadist movement.

Schanzer, Jonathan. *Al-Qaeda's Armies: Middle East Affiliate Groups and the Next Generation of Terror.* Washington, DC: Washington Institute for Near East Policy, 2004.
An examination of more than two dozen "affiliate groups" in Egypt, Lebanon, Algeria, Yemen, and Iraq that are local and autonomous but fight in the name of al Qaeda's global jihad.

Vlahos, Michael. "Culture's Mask: War and Change After Iraq." National Security Analysis Department monograph, Applied Physics Laboratory, Johns Hopkins University, September 2004.
A series of essays that deal with change or transformation to the very order of things, as in the Greek understanding of the word "metamorphosis," and that address: American empire, the U.S. military, Islamic revival, Europe's relationship with Islam, and America's relationship with Islam.

———. "Terror's Mask: Insurgency Within Islam." Occasional paper for the Joint Warfare Analysis Department, Applied Physics Laboratory, Johns Hopkins University, May 2002.
Argues that the war on terrorism is not about terrorism, but an insurgency within Islam, and that Islamic law and tradition legitimate the insurgency.

Walt, Stephen M. *Taming American Power: The Global Response to U.S. Primacy.* New York: W. W. Norton, 2005.
Argues that the best way for the United States to achieve its foreign policy goals and remain a dominant power is to adopt a policy of offshore balancing based on international relations realist principles.

Index

9/11 Commission Report
    on Atta and Czech Republic, 18
    on intelligence spending, 89
    on Iraq and al Qaeda, xxiii, 39
    on places al Qaeda dispersed to, 120
    on twofold threat to U.S., 98
    on U.S. foreign policy, 173

A

ABC 20/20, 30
Abdi, Nuradin, 161
Abizaid, Gen. John, 45
Abu Ali, Ahmed Omar, 168
Abu Hafez al-Masri Brigades, 117
Abu Nidal Organization (ANO), 17, 40
Abu Sayyaf, 125
Achille Lauro, 17
active-duty force reduction. *See* U.S.
    military
Adel, Saif al-, 100, 107
Adelman, Kenneth, 81
Adelman, Morris, 137
Afghanistan
    effect of military operations in, 46
    resources diverted to Iraq, 67–68
*Against All Enemies: Inside America's War
    on Terror* (Clarke), 6–7
airlines, security efforts and, 150–156
Akef, Mohammed Mahdi, 125
al Qaeda
    adaptability of, 106–107
    as clear and present danger to U.S.,
        49
    decentralized structure of, 101–110

    dual nature of, 97–101
    as ideology, xxvii–xxix, 110–117
    as independent of any nation-state,
        41
    Jemaah Islamiya and, 126–127
    leadership of, 100–101
    in *National Security Strategy* of U.S.,
        55
    need for cooperative effort to locate,
        120–131
    reaction to U.S. attack on Iraq, 44–48
    ties to Iraq as justification for war, 35–
        40
    U.S. foreign policy as motivator of,
        59–61, 132–147, 172–173, 175–186
    U.S. resources to fight diverted to
        Iraq, 67–68
American Muslims, treatment of, 167–
    169
Ani, Ahmad Khalil Ibrahim Samir al-,
    17–18
Ansar al-Islam, 37–39
antiaircraft missiles. *See* MANPADS
Arab Liberation Front (ALF), 17, 40
Aref, Yassin Muhiddin, 167
Armey, Dick, 164
Art of War, The (Sun Tzu), xxvii, 94
Ashcroft, John, 162–163
Atal, Subodh, 143–144
Atef, Mohammed, 100–101, 107
Atta, Mohammed, 17–18, 145
Augustine, Norman, 81
Australia, 75
axis of evil. *See also* evil, terrorism and

military threats to U.S., 12
relationships between countries named as, 10–12
as terrorism sponsor, 16–18
WMD and delivery of, 13–16
Azzam, Abdullah, 113–114

B

balancer-of-last-resort strategy, 78–81, 86–88
Balkans, 131
Bandow, Doug, 138–139
Baradei, Mohamed El, 22
Baran, Paul, 103–106
Barno, Lt. Gen. David, 122
Bashir, Abu Bakar, 117, 127
Bassnan, Osama, 140
Bayoumi, Omar al-, 139–141
Beason, J. Douglas, 81
Beitler, Ruth M., 142
Ben-Ahmed, Marwan, 131
Bergen, Peter, 100, 112, 117
Bermudez, Joseph S., 15
Betts, Richard K., 56
bin Laden, Osama
    as al Qaeda leader, 23, 100
    ideology of and hatred of U.S., 111–115
    on Iraq, 40, 41–42
    Saudi Arabia and, 48, 123
    Somalia and, 127
    Zarqawi and, xxv, 37–38, 44, 45–46
Binalshibh, Ramzi, 101, 120
Blix, Hans, 21
Bolton, John, 20
Bosnia, 64
Boykin, Gen. William, 43, 43n
Bremer, Paul, 98, 111
Brookings Institution, 66
Brown, Harold, 50–51
Burke, Jason, 38, 114
Burns, John, 47
Bush, George W.
    administration's shift of focus from al Qaeda to Iraq after 9/11, 5–10, 18–23
    on al Qaeda, 99–100, 110
    on democracy, 53–54, 58
    on evil as root of terrorism, xxvii, 97–98
    on fighting terrorism in Iraq, not U.S., 25, 44–48, 172
    on France, 130
    Global Posture Review and, 63
    on Iraq and al Qaeda, 35–36, 39n, 40
    on Iraq and WMD threat, 25, 30–31
    on Iraq as central front, xxiii–xxv , 25, 41–44
    on Iraq commitment, 65
    on Iraq giving WMD to terrorists, 34–35
    on Iraq violence, xxiv
    on military draft, 70
    on military size and design, 61, 63
    on threats to U.S., 162
    on U.S. safety, xxiii, 25, 41, 171
    on war on terrorism, 97
    on why U.S. is hated, 59
    on WMD and terrorism, prior to 9/11, 1–5
Bush at War (Woodward), 6

C

Capra, Fritjof, 118
cargo shipments, security efforts and, 159–160
Carpenter, Ted Galen, 52, 61, 77–78, 130
Casey, Gen. George W., 45
Central Intelligence Agency (CIA)
    assessment of Iraq's chemical weapons and missile programs, 27–29, 32
    publications of, 12, 13, 14
CG-47 Ticonderoga-class Aegis cruisers, 84
Chechnya, 132
Cheney, Richard
    on al Qaeda and Iraq, 39n
    on terrorists and Iraq, 37
    on WMD threat from Iraq, 26–27, 33
Chicago Council on Foreign Relations poll, 60
China, 14, 50–51, 62, 74, 75, 84
Chirac, Jacques, 129
Chu, David, 94
Citizens Against Government Waste

(CAGW), 155
civil liberties, 164–167
Clarke, Richard, 6–7
Clausewitz, Karl von, 132
Clifford, Ray, 95
Clinton, Bill, 4–5, 7, 52–53
Cohen, Eliot, xxviii
color-coded homeland security alert system, 161–164
Container Security Initiative (CSI), 159
Cordesman, Anthony, 35
Council on Foreign Relations, 50–51, 66
Country Reports on Human Rights Practices (State Department), 141, 144
Cuba, 51
Czech Republic, 17–18

D

dams, need to protect, 160–161
Daniels, Mitch, 66
Davis, Bart, 167
DD(X) destroyers, 84, 86
DDG-51 Arleigh Burke-class Aegis destroyers, 84
Defense Language Institute (DLI), 95
Defense Science Board, 59, 61, 70
democracy, U.S. attempts to spread, 52–61
    assumptions about peaceful nature of democracies, 58–59
    assumptions about why U.S. is hated, 59–61
Diehl, Jackson, 142
Downing, Gen. Wayne, 67–68, 92
Duelfer, Charles, 29

E

East Asia, proposed withdrawal of U.S. troops from, 62–63
Egypt
    as democracy, 54
    Muslim Brotherhood in, 124–125
    U.S. foreign policy and, 141–142, 145
    view of U.S. in, 58
Eland, Ivan, 78, 87–88
electronic eavesdropping, 89–90
Emerson, Steven, 167
Endgame: The Blueprint for Victory in the
War on Terror (McInerney and Vallely), xxix
Europe, proposed withdrawal of U.S. troops from, 61–62
evil, terrorism and, xxvii–xxviii, 97–98. *See also* axis of evil

F

F-22 Raptor fighter/bomber, 81–82, 86
F / A-18E / F Super Hornet, 82–83, 86
Fagih, Saad al-, 113
Faris, Iyman, 161
Feith, Douglas, 22–23
15 May Organization, 17
Fleischer, Ari, 10
Flynn, Stephen, 159
Foreign Missile Developments and the Ballistic Missile Threat Through 2015 (CIA), 12, 14
France
    Iraq war and, 128–131
    military expenditures of, 74, 75
    Muslim population in, 128
Franklin, Benjamin, 164
Frum, David, xxviii, xxix

G

Gadhafi, Moammar, 21
Gallup International poll, 60
Gamble, Alastari, 95
Gerecht, Reuel Marc, 58, 111
German Marshall Fund poll, 60
Germany
    Iraq war and, 129
    military expenditures of, 74, 75
    Muslim population in, 128
    U.S. troops and, 63
Gertz, Bill, 4
Ghaith, Sulaiman Abu, 100, 114
Ghamdi, Abd Al-Rahman al-Faqasi al-, 124
Gingrich, Newt, 7
Glen Canyon Dam, 160–161
Global Posture Review, 63
Glover, Cathleen, 95
Golez, Riolo, 126
Graham, Bob, 140
Graham, Maj. Gen. Andrew, 45
Granoien, Neil, 95

Gunaratna, Rohan, 39, 112, 113, 115, 120, 128

H

Hagel, Chuck, 69
Hamas, 124
Hambali, 127
Hamdi, Yaser, 165
Havel, Vaclav, 18
Hezbollah, 17
Hirsch, Michael, 121–122
Hollings, Fritz, 71
Holy War on the Home Front (Kushner and Davis), 167
homeland security efforts, 149–170
    aircraft and passengers, 150–156
    cargo shipments, 159–160
    civil liberties and, 164–167
    color-coded alert system, 161–164
    immigration and borders, 156–159
    paradox of, 169–170
    potential attack targets, 160–161
    treatment of Muslim Americans and, 167–169
homosexuality, linguists and, 95
Honeynet Project, 23
Hoover Dam, 160–161
Hussain, Gen. Safdar, 122
Hussein, Saddam. *See* Iraq

I

ideology of al Qaeda, xxvii–xxix, 110–117
immigration, security efforts and, 156–159
Imperial Hubris (Scheuer), 111
India, 75
Indonesia, 126–127
intelligence gathering, need for, 88–91
International Institute for Strategic Studies (IISS)
    on Afghanistan, 46
    on Iraq and WMD, 29, 31
    on Russia, 50
    on U.S. defense expenditures, 74
Iran
    Bush administration's tone toward, 22–23
    economy and military resources of,

12, 51
    Iraq and, 11
    North Korea and, 11–12
    Russia and, 11
    as terrorism sponsor, 16–18
    WMD and, 13–16
Iraq
    9/11 attacks and, 17–18, 35–37, 40
    as central front of war on terrorism, xxiii–xxv, 25, 41–48
    costs to U.S. of war in, 65–71
    economy and military spending of, 12
    Iran and, 11
    non-Iraqis in insurgency, 45
    proposed military withdrawal from, 63–71
    as terrorism sponsor, 16–18
    ties to al Qaeda, 35–40
    view of U.S. in, 41–47
    WMD and, 13–16, 25–36
Iraq Survey Group (ISG), 29–30
Irish Republican Army, 169
Isenberg, David, 63
Islam, Yusuf, 157
Islam/Islamists
    American Muslims and, 167–169
    European population and, 128
    reactions to U.S. invasion of Iraq, 41–47
    U.S. foreign policy and, 59–61, 132–147, 172–173, 175–186
Israel
    Egypt and, 142
    on Iraq and 9/11 attacks, 18
    military expenditures of, 75
    Palestine and, 133–135
    terrorist creation and, 47
Italy
    military expenditures of, 74, 75
    Muslim population in, 128

J

Jamali, Zafarullah Khan, 142–143
Japan, 62, 74, 75
Japanese Communist League-Red Army Faction, 16
Jaradat, Hanadi, 47

Jebb, Cindy R., 142
Jemaah Islamiya, 116–117, 125–127
jihad, declared to reestablish Islamic rule, 113–115
Joint Inquiry Into Intelligence Community Activities Before and After the Terrorist Attacks of September 11, 2001, 139–140. See also *9/11 Commission Report*
Jones, Walter, 130
Jordan, 58

K

Kadyrov, Rashid, 145
Karimov, Islam, 144, 145
Kay, David, 29–30, 35
Keleher, Robert, 151
Kennedy, Ted, 157
Khalil, Farooz Kashmiri, 143
Khidoyatova, Nigara, 145
Klinghoffer, Leon, 17
Korb, Lawrence, 66
Kosiak, Steven, 66, 77, 78
Kushner, Harvey, 167

L

Lackawanna Six, 168
Latvia, 62
Lau Tzu, 119
Lewis, Bernard, 116
Libbi, Abu Faraj al-, 101, 107, 120
Libya, 21–22
Lindh, John Walker, 90–91
Lindsey, Lawrence, 65–66, 67
linguists, need for, 94–95
Lott, Trent, 7
Lovelace, Lt. Gen. James, 68–69
Loy, James M., 163

M

Malaysia, 126
MANPADS (man portable air defense systems), 150–156
    attacks on civil aircraft, 151
    cost of protecting against, 155–156
    non-state use of, 152–153
Marrero, Victor, 165
Masri, Abu Mohammed al-, 100

McInerney, Thomas, xxix
Meekin, Brig. Gen. Stephen, 30
Milken Institute, 151
Mohammed, Khalid Sheikh, 101, 107, 120
Mohammed, Omar Bakri, 117
Moro Islamic Liberation Front (MILF), 116, 125–126
Morris, Dick, 4
Mubarak, Hosni, 124–125
Mueller, Robert, 9, 18, 94, 167
Mugabe, Robert, 54
Mujahedin-e Khalq, 17, 40
Murad, Al Haj, 126
Musharraf, Pervez, 120–123, 142–143
Muslim Brotherhood, 124–125
Myers, Gen. Richard, xxiv, 70, 106–107

N

National Intelligence Council, 16
National Security Strategy of the United States (2002)
    as Cold War carryover, 56–57
    on defense of liberty, 138
    rogue states and, 51, 55–56
    spread of democracy and, 52–61
    world reaction to interventionist nature of, 59–61, 175–186
New York Times, 9, 139–140
Newsweek, 64
Ney, Bob, 130
no-fly list, homeland security and, 157–158
Nogaidan, Mansour, 124
North Atlantic Treaty Organization (NATO), 50, 61–62
North Korea
    Iran and, 11–12
    military resources of, 12, 13–16, 51, 62–63
    as terrorism sponsor, 16–18
nuclear reactors, need to protect, 160

O

O'Connor, Sandra Day, 165
O'Hanlon, Michael, 66
O'Neill, Paul, 6
O'Neill, Tip, 133
oil supplies, U.S. foreign policy and, 136–137

P

Pakistan
    cooperation of, 120–123
    U.S. foreign policy and, 142–144
    view of U.S. in, 58
Palestine, 133–135
Palestine Liberation Front (PLF), 17, 40
PATRIOT ACT, 164–165
Patterns of Global Terrorism report (State
    Department), 16, 40, 172
Payne, Keith, 33
Perle, Richard, xxviii, xxix
Pew Global Attitudes Project, 59
Pew Research Center, 60
Philippines, 125–126
Phillips, James, 128
Powell, Colin, xxv, 29n, 37, 38
Predator UAVs, 91–93
Project for the New American Century,
    53
*Putting "Defense" Back Into U.S. Defense
    Policy* (Eland), 78

Q

Qutb, Sayyid, 115–116

R

RAND Corporation study on MAN-
    PADS, 150–155
Rangel, Charles, 71
Rashwin, Diaa, 125
Record, Jeffrey, 5, 23
Reed, Jack, 69
regional war, force structure for fighting,
    87–88
Ressa, Maria, 125
Rice, Condoleezza, 36–37
Ridge, Tom, xxiii, 156–157, 163–164
Robertson, Lord George, 17–18
rogue states, national security policy
    and, 51, 55–56
Rosen, Gerald, 168
Rummel, R. J., 58
Rumsfeld, Donald
    on al Qaeda, 132
    on France and Germany, 129
    on Iraq and WMD, 29n
    on Iraq as principle target, 6–8
    on Iraq war costs, 66, 67
    on need for better communication of
        foreign policy, 146–147
    on needed troop strength, 48
    on numbers of terrorists, xxvii
    on Saudi Arabia, 136
    special operations forces and, 93
Russia
    arms agreements and, 11
    Chechnya and, 132
    Latvia and, 62
    military resources of, 14, 50, 74, 75

S

Sadar, Moqtada al-, 44
Sageman, Marc, 107–110
Said, Sheikh, 100
Samore, Gary, 15
satellites, intelligence gathering and, 89
Saudi Arabia
    9/11 attacks and, 139–140
    bin Laden and U.S. presence in, 48,
        111–114
    cooperation of, 123–124
    military expenditures of, 75
    U.S. foreign policy and, 135–140, 144
    view of U.S. in, 58
Scheuer, Michael, 111, 112–113, 132–133
Schlesinger, James R., 66
Schoomaker, Gen. Peter, 48
Schroeder, Gerhard, 129
Schroen, Gary, 121
Senate Select Committee on Intelligence,
    30, 32
September 11 terrorist attacks. See also
    9/11 Commission Report
    al Qaeda on axis of evil's lack of con-
        nection to, 17–18
    economic losses from, 151
    Iraq's lack of involvement in, 17–18,
        35–37, 40–41
    Saudi Arabia and, 139–140
Shelby, Richard, 140
Shirhata, Thirwat Salah, 100
shopping malls, need to protect, 161
shoulder-fired antiaircraft missiles. *See*
    MANPADS
Slahi, Mohamedou Ould, 101

Somalia, 127–128
South Korea, 62–63, 75
special operations forces (SOFs), 74, 93–94
Spitzner, Lance, 23
stop-loss orders, in military, 68
Straw, Jack, 21
Strickland, Lee, 166
submarines, proposed reductions of, 84, 86
Sukarnoputri, Megawati, 127
Sun Tzu, xxvii, 94
Syria, 20–21, 51
Syria Accountability and Lebanese Sovereignty Restoration Act of 2003 (HR 2003), 20

T

Taepo Dong missiles, 14–15
Tao Te Ching, 118, 119
Telhami, Shibley, 173
Tenet, George, 9
Terrorism Information and Prevention System (TIPS), 165–166
terrorists. *See also* al Qaeda; war on terrorism
    Iraq and WMDs, 33–35
    U.S. foreign policy, 59–61, 132–147, 172–173, 175–186
Thompson, Loren, 90
Timini, Mohammed Ali al-, 167
Total Information Awareness (TIA), 166–167, 187–188
Transactional Records Access Clearinghouse, 169
Turkey, 75, 129

U

UAVs, 91–93
Unclassified Report to Congress on the Acquisition of Technology Relating to Weapons of Mass Destruction and Advanced Conventional Munitions, 1 July Through 31 December 2001 (CIA), 13
United Kingdom
    military expenditures of, 74, 75
    Muslim population in, 128
United Nations

Security Council Resolution 598, 11
Security Council Resolution 1441, 25, 26n
U.S. foreign policy
    Israel-Palestine conflict and, 133–135
    support of repressive regimes and, 135–147
    terrorists' motivation and, 59–61, 132–133, 172–173, 175–186
U.S. military
    costs of Iraq war to, 65–71
    lack of conventional military threats and, 50–51
    need for advanced technology, 91–93
    need for human intelligence gathering, 88–91
    need for linguists, 94–95
    need for special operations forces, 74, 93–94
    reducing of active-duty forces, 78–81
    reducing unneeded weapons systems, 81–88
    reducing with balancer-of-last-resort strategy, 78–81, 86–88
    size of, 12–13, 73–78
U.S. National Guard, 68–70
USS *Cole*, 127
U.S.-VISIT, 156–158
Uzbekistan, 144–146

V

V-22 Osprey, 83, 84–85, 86
Vallely, Paul, xxix
Venezuela, 54
Vermaat, Emerson, 64
Virginia-class submarines, proposed reduction of, 84, 86
Visitor and Immigrant Status Indicator Technology (U.S.-VISIT), 156–158

W

Walker, Clyde, 15
Walters, Barbara, 31
war on terrorism. *See also* U.S. foreign policy; U.S. military
    al Qaeda as proper focus of, xxix–xxx
    cooperation needed in, 120–131
    military's role in, 73–74

as "un-war," xxvi–xxvii
Washington Post, 68, 171
weapon systems, unneeded by U.S., 81–89
weapons of mass destruction (WMD)
  axis of evil and, 13–16
  Bush on, after 9/11, 5–10, 18–27
  Bush on, before 9/11, 1–5
  cargo shipments and, 159–160
  Iraq's threat to U.S. and, 25–35
Weatherington, Duke, 91–92
Wilson, Vice Adm. Thomas R., 11–12, 16
Wolfowitz, Paul D.
  on Iraq as principle target, 6–8
  on paying for Iraq war, 67
  on Saudi Arabia, 48
Woodward, Bob, 6

Y

Yemen, 127–128
Young, Thomas, 98

Z

Zahabi, Mohamad Kamal El-, 167
Zammar, Mohammed Haydar, 101
Zarei, Mohammed, 141–142
Zarqawi, Abu Musab al-
  bin Laden and, xxv, 37–38, 44, 45–46
  U.S. withdrawal from Iraq and, 63–65
Zawahiri, Ayman al-, 42, 100, 124
Zimbabwe, 54
Zogby International poll, 60
Zubaydah, Abu, 9, 101, 120
Zukav, Gary, 99

About the Author

Charles Peña is a senior fellow with the Coalition for a Realistic Foreign Policy and George Washington University's Homeland Security Policy Institute, an adviser to the Straus Military Reform Project, the former director of defense policy studies at the Cato Institute, and a terrorism analyst for MSNBC. His opinions have been cited by numerous publications including *USA Today*, *Washington Post*, *New York Times*, *Wall Street Journal*, and *Financial Times*. In addition to numerous network and cable television appearances, he has been on *The Radio Factor* with Bill O'Reilly and NPR's *Morning Edition*, and has also been a guest on *The McLaughlin Group*, television's original political talk show. A graduate of Claremont Men's College with a master of arts in security policy studies from the George Washington University, he lives in Arlington, Virginia.